WASH
Highest Mountains

FROM THE BOOK...

Inspiration Glacier Traverse *(Route 8)*

Intense alpine glaciation has resulted in many cols between pinnacles in the plateau, where constantly active ice and weather sculpt the landscape into otherworldly forms. It is a realm of staggering brilliance, of stark contrast between the blackness of the protruding, serrated rock crests and the seemingly endless and blinding expanse of white glacier and snow.

Cathedral Peak and Amphitheater Mountain *(Route 20)*

Blocky peaks jut above the green, rolling terrain, creating high artistic contrast and stirring visual drama. Cathedral Lakes, tucked away in the belly of the surrounding peaks, are a pretty an alpine milieu as any in the monster-crag region of the Cascade Crest.

Dark Peak *(Route 23)*

So why climb Dark Peak? Many climbers choose to forgo the headache…. Although this trip requires focus and energy, in return you'll get the unmitigated feeling of exploration and adventure, as if you were the first person on earth to be here.

Flora Mountain *(Route 27)*

The nearby trails are drainages away, requiring a cross-country odyssey to get to the summit. Consequently, Flora is little known and seldom attempted, yet it is the epitome of a tucked-away spot whose open country gives you the exhilaration of supremely solitary high-country roaming.

Sinister Peak and Dome Peak *(Route 28)*

The cross-country portion covers steep, complex, and treacherous terrain, demanding great energy, fortitude, and judgment. There are brutal losses and gains in elevation. But the reward for your sweat is an archetypal North Cascades expedition through old-growth forest and flowery parklands, along an isolated mountain massif, over ridgecrests near great, beckoning glaciers. If you crave alpine quests, you will find this awesome and lonesome trek irresistible.

WASHINGTON'S
Highest Mountains

Basic Alpine
& Glacier Routes

Peggy Goldman

 WILDERNESS PRESS · BERKELEY, CA

Washington's Highest Mountains

1st EDITION, March 2004

Copyright © 2004 by Peggy Goldman

Front cover photo © 2004 by Cliff Leight
Back cover photo © 2004 by Keith Wilson
Interior photos as noted
Maps: Peggy Goldman and Bart Wright, Fineline Maps
Cover design: Larry B. Van Dyke
Book design: Margaret Copeland, Terragrafix
Book composition: Margaret Copeland, Terragrafix; Jaan Hitt; Larry B. Van Dyke
Copy Editors: Kris Kaiyala, Thomas Winnett, Roslyn Bullas

ISBN 0-89997-290-X
UPC 7-19609-97290-7

Manufactured in the United States of America

Published by: **Wilderness Press**
1200 5th Street
Berkeley, CA 94710
(800) 443-7227; FAX (510) 558-1696
info@wildernesspress.com
www.wildernesspress.com

Visit our website for a complete listing of our books and for ordering information.

Cover photos: Redoubt Glacier, North Cascades National Park *(front);*
Dome Peak Summit *(back)*
Frontispiece: *Panorama of North Cascades with Fernow, Bonanza in center*
(photo by Steve Fry)

SAFETY NOTICE: Although Wilderness Press and the author have made every attempt to ensure that the information in this book is accurate at press time, they are not responsible for any loss, damage, injury, or inconvenience that may occur to anyone while using this book. You are responsible for your own safety and health while in the wilderness. The fact that a route is described in this book does not mean that it will be safe for you. Be aware that route conditions can change from day to day. Always check local conditions and know your own limitations.

Dedication

I dedicate this book to my parents, Doris and Mel,
who always inspired me with their love of life.

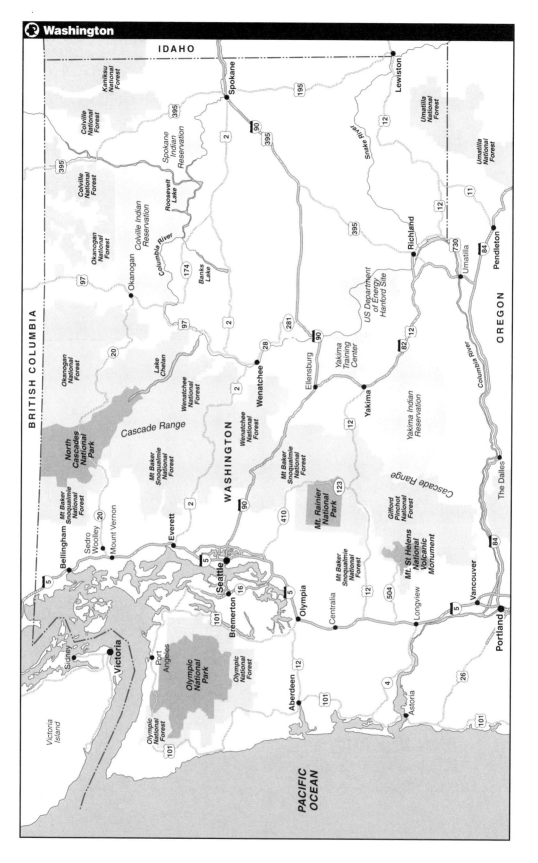

Contents

PREFACE xi

INTRODUCTION 1

CHAPTER 1: THE VOLCANOES 13
ROUTE 1   Mt. Rainier 17
ROUTE 2   Little Tahoma Peak 23
ROUTE 3   Mt. Baker 27
ROUTE 4   Glacier Peak 31

CHAPTER 2: NORTHERN CASCADES 36
ROUTE 5   Mt. Shuksan 39
ROUTE 6   Chilliwack Group 43
            Mt. Redoubt 46
            Mox Peaks, Southeast Twin Spire 47
            Mox Peaks, Northwest Twin Spire 48
            Mt. Spickard 49
            Mt. Rahm 50
            Mt. Custer 50
ROUTE 7   Snowfield Peak 53
ROUTE 8   Inspiration Glacier Traverse 58
            Primus Peak 60
            Austera Peak 60
            Klawatti Peak 61
            Dorado Needle 61
            Eldorado Peak 62

CHAPTER 3: CASCADE PASS 65
ROUTE 9   Forbidden Peak 69
ROUTE 10 Sahale Mountain and Boston Peak 75
ROUTE 11 Buckner Mountain and Horseshoe Peak 79
ROUTE 12 Mt. Formidable 85

CHAPTER 4: WASHINGTON PASS 88
ROUTE 13 Ragged Ridge 91
            Cosho Peak 92
            Kimtah Peak 92
            Mesahchie Peak 93
            Katsuk Peak 94
ROUTE 14 Black Peak 97

ROUTE 15 Harts Pass 101
    Tower Mountain 102
    Golden Horn 102
    Azurite Peak 102
ROUTE 16 Silver Star Mountain 107
ROUTE 17 Big Snagtooth 111
ROUTE 18 Reynolds Peak 115

CHAPTER 5: PASAYTEN WILDERNESS **118**
ROUTE 19 Jack Mountain 121
ROUTE 20 Cathedral Peak and Amphitheater Mountain 126
ROUTE 21 Blackcap Mountain 132

CHAPTER 6: LAKE CHELAN **135**
ROUTE 22 Stehekin Group 139
    Goode Mountain 141
    Storm King 142
    Mt. Logan 144
ROUTE 23 Dark Peak 147
ROUTE 24 Tupshin Peak and Devore Peak 151
ROUTE 25 Bonanza Peak and Martin Peak 157
ROUTE 26 Mt. Fernow and Copper Peak 163
ROUTE 27 Flora Mountain 167

CHAPTER 7: GLACIER PEAK WILDERNESS **170**
ROUTE 28 Sinister Peak and Dome Peak 174
ROUTE 29 Dumbell Mountain and Greenwood Mountain 183
ROUTE 30 South Spectacle Butte 187
ROUTE 31 Clark Mountain 191
ROUTE 32 Luahna Peak 195

CHAPTER 8: ALPINE LAKES WILDERNESS **198**
ROUTE 33 Cannon Mountain and McClellan Peak 201
ROUTE 34 Sherpa Peak and Mt. Stuart 207
ROUTE 35 Argonaut Peak 213

Appendix A—Contact Information 217
Appendix B—Trip Statistics 220
Appendix C—Bulger Top 100 List 222
Appendix D—Difficulty Ratings 224
Index 226

Acknowledgments

I want to thank everyone who contributed information, photographs, reviews, suggestions, or advice to this project. The original Bulgers, the people who first sought to climb Washington's highest peaks, deserve special mention for inspiring many people to follow in their footsteps, including myself. I am especially indebted to Dale Flynn for his expert review of the manuscript and attention to detail, as well as to Don Duncan, Keith Wilson, Jerry Baille, and Roy McMurtrey for their great input. I appreciate the comments and advice of Kelly Bush, District Ranger, North Cascades National Park. I thank Cliff Leight, Ed Cooper, Steve Fry, Chris Weidner, Dave LeBlanc, Susan Alford, Keith Wilson, Dale Flynn, Ronnie Parker, and others for their wonderful photographs. I also acknowledge the folks at Wilderness Press for bringing this book into existence, and for their suggestions and editing skills that make it presentable to you.

But most of all, I thank my husband, Jim Quade. His patience, support, expertise, and companionship in the mountains are more than I ever could have hoped for.

Read This

Mountaineering in the backcountry entails unavoidable risk that every climber assumes and must be aware of and respect. The fact that a trip is described in this book is not a representation that it will be safe for you. Trips vary greatly in difficulty and in the degree of conditioning and agility you need to enjoy them safely. On some routes, the access roads may have changed or conditions may have deteriorated since the descriptions were written. Also weather conditions can change dramatically. A route that is safe on a dry day or for a highly conditioned, agile, properly equipped climber may be completely unsafe for someone else or unsafe under adverse weather conditions. Mountaineering in Washington is particularly notorious for dense brush and rotten rock increasing the challenge of route finding and risk of rockfall.

You can minimize your risks on the climb by being knowledgeable, prepared and alert. There is not space in this book for a general treatise on safety in the mountains, but there are a number of good books and public courses on the subject and you should take advantage of them to increase your knowledge. Just as important, you should always be aware of your own limitations and of conditions existing when and where you are traveling. If conditions are dangerous, or if you're not prepared to deal with them safely, choose a different place or go on a different day. It's better to have wasted some time than to be the subject of a mountain rescue.

These warnings are not intended to scare you. Many people have safe and enjoyable climbs every year. However, one element of the beauty, freedom and excitement of the wilderness is the presence of risks that do not confront us at home. When you climb you assume those risks. They can be met safely, but only if you exercise your own independent judgment and common sense.

TELL US WHAT YOU REALLY THINK Something unclear, outdated, or just plain wrong in this book? Have a good suggestion for making it better? We welcome reader feedback on all of our publications. If we use your suggestion, we'll send you a free book. Please email comments to: *update@wildernesspress.com*

Preface

Why write a book about the alpine and glacier climbs on the highest mountains in Washington? Many of these peaks are considered dangerous due to the notoriously loose rock of the Cascade Range. Hence the Bulger Top 100 List does not appeal to many climbers. Still the pursuit of the "Top 100" highlights a story of exploration, effort, determination, and single-mindedness. Washington has always had a strong tradition of mountaineering due to its rich and diverse alpine environment. The weather is harsh and much of the terrain—consisting of the most heavily glaciated peaks in the lower 48 states—is forbidding. Many of the mountains are famous and classic, attracting climbers from near and far, but some of the remote areas of the state are little known. This is due, in part, to their distance from population centers, but also to the rigor required to approach and scale them. In climbing these peaks, you will enter parts of the state that are wild, rugged, and well off the beaten track.

The most difficult mountaineering in Washington consists of highly technical and demanding climbs over glaciers surrounded by vertical rock and ice, or over complex rock in remote alpine settings that only elite climbers will attempt. But for some, what makes the highest peaks attractive is that they have routes suited for the average mountaineer. With proper training and effort, even an ordinary athlete can develop the expertise, courage, and experience needed to complete the harder trips. *Washington's Highest Mountains* was designed for the climber who, with some forethought, can become proficient in competence and self-reliance.

Keith Wilson

Climber on Big Snagtooth summit with Silver Star Mountain behind

This book is not for beginners. To attempt the trips you must have adequate training in addition to desire and motivation, all tempered with good judgment. This book is intended to help you make an informed decision about where to climb, but you must pick the trips that are within your ability and commitment levels. To be among the few that finish all the trips, you will need extraordinary drive, determination, and valor. To complete them in only a few years, you will also need an iron will and a fierce focus.

Why should I write this book? As a physician I believe that mountaineering promotes fitness, ameliorates the aging process, and revitalizes energy. It also releases the endorphins that create the satisfying sensation of well being after strenuous exercise. Alpinism provides a sense of adventure and camaraderie, a freedom from the usual restrictions of the civilized world, and a sense of accomplishment. It fulfills some of the most basic human needs: contact with nature, an appreciation for all creatures, and spiritual renewal. More than mere asceticism, climbing is an avenue for creativity. Yet it is also an inherently dangerous sport. Many, if not all, of the peaks on the list are especially treacherous, due to the crumbling nature of Cascade rock. Mountaineering, therefore, is an intensely personal decision, for an individual is solely responsible for his or her safety in the perilous alpine environment.

I wanted to write this book for people like me—less than elite climbers, average athletes, with some strengths offset by some weaknesses. I came to mountaineering later in life; I always will struggle to catch other climbers with more talent, speed, or courage. I have worked hard and long, rearranging my priorities and redefining my identity in pursuit of mastering the alpine environment. People like me are no longer a rarity among the macho members of the climbing community. I believe that my perspective as a female has made this book particularly friendly to women and beginner climbers. My intention is to equip even a middle-aged woman who is new to the climbing scene with a challenging set of goals and objectives that, with patience and determination, are achievable over time. For my cohort of older female friends and myself, working diligently on our mountaineering pursuits has provided an enduring sense of self-esteem and accomplishment that carries into every aspect of our lives.

Adventure nurtures our spirits and imaginations. The trips in this book will expand your horizons, both literally and figuratively as you face the challenges and demands of doing them. Follow your heart, but use common sense: recognize when to back off and to let the universe take its course.

Happy climbing and have a great journey.

Introduction

As late as the early 1970s, much of the state of Washington's mountainous terrain was little known or traveled. In that decade, as U.S. Geological Survey (USGS) maps of adequate scale were published, it finally became possible to pinpoint all of Washington's major peaks. As the topographic information became available, a diverse group of young Seattle engineers at The Boeing Company began to meet to discuss their common love of the mountains. This loose association of mountaineers called themselves the Bulgers, a name derived from their whimsical interpretation of a popular rock song of the times. Using the latest USGS data, two of the members generated a list of the hundred highest mountains in Washington, now called the Bulger Top 100 List. A peak was included on the list if it met a set of rules based primarily on its prominence relative to neighboring peaks. From the list a challenge emerged that had never before been possible. In a time when first ascents of the greatest mountains in the world were their childhood memories, the Bulgers sought to create a new, local yardstick for accomplishment—to summit all Washington's "Top 100."

Sometimes with friendly rivalry, but most often with camaraderie, each Bulger set out to summit all the mountains on the list, an arduous

Chris Weidner

Near summit of Sahale Mountain

and demanding commitment. From 1980 to 1988 only eight men and one woman from the original group completed the list. Since then only a handful of others have finished. Even today, completing the Bulger Top 100 List remains a local standard of achievement for alpinists in the state of Washington.

Crevasse on Mt. Baker

The trips in this book are alpine or glacier climbs and are rated using the Yosemite Decimal System—a set of numeric ratings that rate the difficulty of travel. It is not the only rating system used by climbers, but it is the one preferred by most American climbing organizations. Class 1 is a hike on a trail or off-trail where the ground is level, and hands are not needed for balance. Class 2 involves the use of hands but not the use of a rope. Class 3 involves some exposure (steep terrain), requires the frequent use of hands, and may need a rope. Class 4 has significant vertical exposure; most climbers will use a rope because a fall could be serious or fatal. Class 5 involves intermediate climbing skills and the placement

Summit on Sahale Mountain

Dave LeBlanc

Summit of Sinister Peak

of protection to prevent injury should a fall occur. Class 5 is further subdivided into decimals depending on the difficulty.

Scrambles are categorized as class 1 or 2 with only an occasional class 3 move. In contrast, alpine climbs may have sustained portions of rocky class 3 or 4 terrain, and may involve traversing a crevassed glacier. They may also require class 5 climbing skills of belayed leading while placing rock protection. Alpine climbs can be classified in other categories that overlap: they can be glacier climbs with sections of rock scrambling, rock climbs with an approach on steep snow, or any combination. But the consistent themes of an alpine climb are that at least basic-level climbing skills are required to complete the route safely, and that a rope should be taken along even if it is not actually used. A basic-level climber must be proficient in the following skills: routefinding, navigation, steep snow travel, ice ax self-arrest, glacier travel, crevasse rescue, rope management, belaying, rappelling, and placing rock protection for class 4 or low class 5 rock routes. An intermediate-level climber must have all the basic-level skills, and in addition be proficient in the placement of protection for mid to high class 5 rock routes, and be able to climb ice. An advanced-level climber is skilled in all aspects of mountaineering including aid climbing.

This book covers the highest mountains in Washington, all above 8320 feet, as found on the Bulger list, except for the scrambles (hence Mt. Adams and Mt. Saint Helens, with scramble routes, and Mt. Olympus, 7965 feet, are omitted). *Washington's Highest Mountains* focuses only on class 3 to class 5 trips — the alpine and glacier climbs. At a minimum, alpine climbs require the ability to handle a rope for exposed class 3 moves, an understanding of rappel anchors, and the proper use of a hand line for safety. Because many alpine climbs consist of long sections of unroped class 3 climbing, they have a misleading reputation for being easier than roped climbs. But do not assume this; many have loose rock that is dangerous. Glacier climbs require certain skills: navigating through crevasses, crevasse rescue, and routefinding during a whiteout. All are

Cliff Leight

Climber on Inspiration Glacier heads to south face of Eldorado Peak

needed for the volcanoes and other glacier routes described in this book. For the handful of even more advanced alpine climbs here, even the easiest route to the summit requires the ability to place protection for class 5 rock climbing.

Washington's Highest Mountains includes 61 peaks in 35 trips that are technically easy to moderate and fall within the ability of the basic-level climber — the nontechnical trips are left out. Each trip describes the easiest route up one peak or the most energy-efficient combination of climbing for two or more adjacent peaks. Although the routes are the easiest ways up, each calls for greatly different degrees of effort, logistical planning, and time and energy spent. Most necessitate a long approach to base camp from the closest road. Most require long hikes along abandoned or unmaintained climbers' trails. Some of the peaks are not

Silver Star Glacier

considered glamorous or aesthetic. But if you avoid loose rock, you will do very little mountaineering in Washington. Nonetheless, every journey to the top of these "Big Boys"—all above treeline in a state known for abundant forests and rugged, high-alpine terrain—has in common spacious views and the unparalleled beauty of the mountain environment. These alpine and glacier climbs also share a satisfying sense of accomplishment you get when you reach their wild and scenic summits.

NOTES ABOUT THE BULGER TOP 100 LIST

John Lixvar and John Plimpton, two original members of the Bulgers, made up the Top 100 List. Three major rules governed whether a peak was included.

First, a summit must stand at least 400 feet above the surrounding terrain (called its "prominence"). Second, if a peak has an official USGS-approved name, it is on the list even if it does not conform to the 400-foot prominence requirement. Third, for a peak on a major volcano to be included, it must have at least 800 feet of prominence. For example, Liberty Cap and Columbia Crest on Mt. Rainier have official USGS names but do not conform to the 800-foot prominence requirement for volcanoes, and therefore are not on the list. But because Little Tahoma has greater than 800 feet of prominence over the surrounding portions of Mt. Rainier, it is on the Top 100 List. Note that seven of the peaks on the original Bulger Top 100 List (it has since been updated) do not conform to the 400-foot prominence rule; nevertheless, the original list is still the one that most climbers pursue (and is the one included in Appendix D).

A NOTE ABOUT CLIMBING IN WASHINGTON

While the Bulgers have inspired a new generation of climbers, another person has figured significantly in the history and the documentation of climbing in the Pacific Northwest. Fred Beckey is a life-long pioneer of new routes in the Cascades, many of them daring and cutting-edge for their time. His encyclopedia of nearly every peak in Washington—*Cascade Alpine Guide: Climbing and High Routes*—has been an inspiration to every climber in Washington seeking all-encompassing information.

HOW TO USE THIS BOOK

Washington's Highest Mountains includes 61 peaks in 35 trips that are basic alpine or glacier climbs. Compared to guidebooks that describe every route or favorite difficult routes to a summit, this book describes the easiest standard route up a peak or the most energy-efficient combination of climbing two or more adjacent peaks.

Celebrating the summit of Eldorado Peak

For each trip an information block, containing the following information, is inserted before the text that details the route's essential features.

Elevation of the peak is given in feet and in meters as shown on the USGS map, or from the Bulger List (see Appendix D) if no elevation is on the map. For trips containing multiple peaks, the elevation of each is listed in corresponding order. Elevations followed by a "+" have not yet been determined to the exact foot by the USGS.

Climbing Route is a description of the general location of the climb(s).

Distance is the route's total length in miles, rounded to the nearest mile. The distance was calculated using the following sources: the mileage of trail segments shown on Green Trails maps; estimation of off-trail segments using map scales; and a computerized topographic profile. The distance takes into account vertical gain, which adds to the horizontal length.

Elevation Gain is the total gain in feet for the trip, including elevation gains after partial descents along the way.

Days are the number of days a trip takes for a party moving at average speed (approximately 1000 feet of elevation gain per hour, or 2.5 miles per hour on level terrain) each day, without rest days. If the trip is

West Ridge on Forbidden Peak

long, its duration for groups traveling at different speeds will vary substantially, and therefore the minimum number of days for it is noted.

Maps include the USGS maps and the Green Trails maps for all portions of the trip including the trailhead. You will need the USGS maps.

Rating is a two-part number, devised by the author, that is based on the physical effort required for a trip as well as the trip's technical difficulty. The rating may be your best source for determining if a trip is right for you. Since you may often refer to ratings, they are defined in detail in Appendix D.

Location is the jurisdiction(s), such as a National Park, National Forest, or Federal Wilderness, for all parts of a climb, including the approach on any trails, and the ranger station to contact for information. Neither maps nor guidebooks can keep up with a route's seasonal changes. When you need current trail or route information about a trip, visit or telephone the appropriate Forest Service or Park Service ranger station listed in Appendix A. There are also many useful web sites listed in Appendix A.

Permits details permit requirements and fees if any are needed. You must purchase a Northwest Forest Pass to park at the trailhead for most of the trips in this book. You can buy a pass at local outdoor equipment stores, USFS and National Park ranger stations, or many retail establishments. Mt. Rainier and North Cascades national parks are under the jurisdiction of the National Park Service. Motorized and mountain-bike travel on park trails is forbidden and horse travel is closely regulated; hunting is banned, and pets are not allowed. Backcountry permits are required for all overnight campers in national parks, and may be obtained at ranger stations on the entry roads at the ranger station closest to the start of the trip. For most of the climbs in the North Cascades National Park, the party size is limited to 6 climbers. Most wildernesses are under Forest Service jurisdiction, but the national parks also have designated wildernesses within their boundaries. Wilderness status precludes the building of roads and dams or other structures; motorized and mechanized travel is forbidden and horse travel is regulated or in some places banned. In the Alpine Lakes Wilderness, permits are required for day use as well as for overnight camping. The Enchantment Lakes are so popular that a lottery system has been initiated; you must apply for overnight permits several months in advance. Otherwise you can take your chances with the daily permit lottery—a drawing held each summer morning to determine the lucky persons who will receive on-the-spot permits. Contact the Leavenworth Ranger Station (See Appendix A) of the Wenatchee National Forest for details and current information.

We are all custodians and the ultimate defenders of the land. Always obey Leave No Trace ethics when you venture off-trail. Every person is responsible for conserving the alpine environment.

The text following the information block begins with **Summary and Highlights**, a general description of the trip and preview of what you can expect to experience along the way.

How to Get There includes driving information with distances from recognized points or towns.

Trip Description is a narrative account of the easiest route up a peak or the combination of peaks in the trip. Each description should be used only as a rough guide. You must put the whole picture together yourself, and must rely on common sense when the written description just doesn't seem to fit what you see.

Hazards and Tips describes special needs for the trip, such as glacier gear or rock protection. This section also includes the best time of year to attempt the trip and any other pertinent suggestions.

Following the text is the **GPS Waypoint Route**. These waypoints represent important points along the route that are given a Universal Transverse Mercator (UTM) reading generated from a computerized program using NAD 27 map datums. Following the UTM reading, the distance from the previous waypoint is given. For GPS (Global Positioning System) to be helpful in navigation, you must be able to correlate the GPS reading of your location to its place on the map. To do this you will need a map that is appropriately gridded to allow you to calculate distances to correspond with your reading. You will also need a ruler and a mechanical pencil—one that does not smudge when wet—to most accurately plot your location. Map stores stock special plastic UTM Grid Readers that are invaluable in coordinating your GPS measurements in the field with the topographic maps. A full description of the process and its limitations is beyond this introduction, but many textbooks explain the subject. As you become more skilled in the capabilities of GPS technology, you will lose the fear of getting lost.

Trip Times are listed for important segments of the trip. They are approximate, but they do take into account the difficulty of the terrain and the increased time needed for roped climbing. Trail travel time (or off-trail travel on easy terrain) is based on an average group with a modest 10-minute break per hour and 1000 feet of vertical gain per hour. The time to climb a technical portion of the trip is estimated for a party of two to four climbers of average rock-climbing skill and ability in the alpine environment.

Accompanying the text is a computer-generated topographic **map** using National Geographic Maps software for Washington. These maps provide only an overview of the trip; you will need the USGS maps or their equivalents to do the trip safely.

Photographs are also included to give an overview of the regions and the trips. Each season is vastly different than the next and each varies from year to year; so do not expect every photo to match the scene you encounter.

A NOTE ABOUT PERMITS
IN NORTH CASCADES NATIONAL PARK

Many climbers confuse permits and climbing registers. A backcountry *permit* is required in North Cascades National Park and recreation areas all nights of the year. In addition, there is a voluntary *climbing register* that is offered at Marblemount, Sedro-Woolley, and Glacier ranger stations as a safety option. Parties that don't have someone else tracking their return from a climb are encouraged to use this register, indicating their planned return time. *The climbing register is completely voluntary.* It is devised only for those who will be responsible to sign out, or call, the National Park Service upon completion of their trip. If you don't sign out, the National Park Search and Rescue will come looking for you. Climbers should understand that the permit is required, and that they can be fined for non-compliance.

Chris Weidner

Boston Peak

Chris Weidner

North Cascades Scenic Highway near Washington Pass

Mt. Rainier: Giant rockfall of Little Tahoma Peak on Emmons Glacier
(photo taken 1966)

CHAPTER 1
The Volcanoes

Soaring above the lesser peaks of the Cascade Range, the Washington volcanoes stand as colossal sovereigns of the sky. Each rises like a king surrounded by an entourage of lesser peaks forming a snowy cloak. The majesty of Washington's volcanoes creates a magnetic attraction, and inspires myth, mystery, and adventure, particularly for the inhabitants of Puget Sound, from the first native residents to present-day megalopolis dwellers.

The volcanoes figured significantly in Native American tradition. *Tahoma* was a generic term applied to snowy peaks, by most tribes, whereas the Puyallup, Nisqually, and Duwamish tribes had separate names for the individual volcanoes. The Lummi tribe called Mt. Baker *Koma Kulshan*, meaning broken or damaged, or in other versions, "Great White Watcher." Natives called Glacier Peak *DaKobed*, or "Great Parent," as it is the highest mountain between Mt. Rainier and the Skagit River.

The European discovery of the Washington volcanoes is in dispute. Some believe that Apostolos Valerianos, the Greek explorer known as Juan de Fuca, viewed Mt. Baker in 1592. However, though ships passed within sight of the peak from 1580 to 1780, Mt. Baker was not mentioned or noted on charts until 1790, when it appeared on Spanish maps. The first British explorer to see the volcanoes was Captain George Vancouver, who spied Mt. Rainier from his boat as he sailed through the Strait of Juan de Fuca on May 7, 1792. Captain Vancouver named the mountain after his friend Rear Admiral Peter Rainier. As Admiral Rainier was active in the war against the American colonies, the name evoked controversy. Nevertheless, it stuck. On the same voyage the cartographer Joseph Baker sighted the white cone of what is now his namesake. While zealously mapping the shores of Puget Sound, Captain Vancouver also viewed Glacier Peak.

The volcanoes are the youngest mountains in the Cascade Range. Major peaks such as Rainier, Baker, and Glacier are stratovolcanoes, built by intermittent lava flows and explosions that rapidly formed mounds of materials of variable consistency such as andesite, dacite, ash, basalt, and pyroclastic minerals. The volcanoes are far from dead; volcanic and erosive activity are still visible today, mostly in the form of massive rockfalls, such as on Mt. Rainier's Winthrop Glacier in 1989, and on the north face of Little Tahoma on the Emmons Glacier in 1963. Mt. Baker still emits steam, hinting at its dynamic interior. Indeed the cataclysmic eruption of Mt. Saint Helens in 1980 serves as a reminder that violent forces can lead to massive floods, mudslides, and suffocating ash clouds, resulting in widespread ecosystem changes.

The Washington volcanoes are massive enough to create their own weather. The conditions on the high, glaciated peaks are often drastically different than those on nearby lowlands. Storms can brew in an instant, with temperatures fluctuating from stifling heat and unrelenting sun to freezing rain and blinding snow, even in a single afternoon. Lenticular cloud caps near the summit denote wind gusts that can flatten a climber to the ground even when the approach has been calm. Rapidly changing weather is the hallmark of Cascade volcanoes, which can lead to white-out conditions resulting in confusion, hypothermia, and ultimately disaster even for the most experienced climber. Prepare for the worst, no matter what the weather report says.

Hazard Stevens and Philemon B. Van Trump made the historic first ascent of Mt. Rainier on August 17, 1870. In 1890 Fay Fuller became the first woman to reach the summit. Today, millions visit the parks and wilderness areas devoted to the volcanoes each year — most simply to gaze in wonder. To some climbers, the appeal is the wild and austere beauty of the glaciated landscape. To others, it is the physical challenge of accomplishing a difficult and strenuous climb. For most, it is also a feeling of satisfaction, knowing they have been to the top of a peak that seems to float magically above the mundane, civilized plateau below, signifying an entry into a higher, more spiritual realm.

Perhaps the defining characteristic of the Washington volcanoes is that they have the largest glaciers in the contiguous United States. The moving ice creates a wondrous landscape where otherworldly features fascinate even the most experienced climber. That also means that to scale any route on the Cascade volcanoes without a guide, you must possess solid mountaineering and crevasse-rescue skills. Although the easiest routes are within the ability of the basic-level climber (see definition page 3), fatalities regularly occur. Many accidents are caused by objective hazards such as avalanches and rock fall. Even nontechnical routes on the volcanoes have sections of unstable, rotten, and crumbly rock decimated by weather. Crevasses are the most common and most dangerous obstacles to safe travel. In early season, many crevasses are covered with tenuous snowbridges that can melt during the day. Just because you do not see a crevasse does not mean it's not there. Be cautious and vigilant. Never climb alone, and always rope up when traveling on a glacier. Practice ice-ax arrest, climb during the early morning before the sun rises, and get back to camp before the warm afternoon sun creates more hazardous conditions. If reason always overrides desire, then your journey into the commanding realm of the high volcanoes will be safe and rewarding.

As popular national treasures, Washington's volcanoes must be preserved. Wilderness areas have established quotas on the number of persons allowed on the routes at one time, and some require climbing fees. It is prohibited to drop refuse into crevasses or bury it in snow. Use composting toilets where available; otherwise you must store human waste in a well-sealed plastic bag and pack it out so it can be disposed of properly. At all times obey the Leave No Trace backcountry travel ethic to ensure that the wild and pristine experience will be preserved not only for you and your companions, but for future visitors.

Emmons Glacier, Mt. Rainier

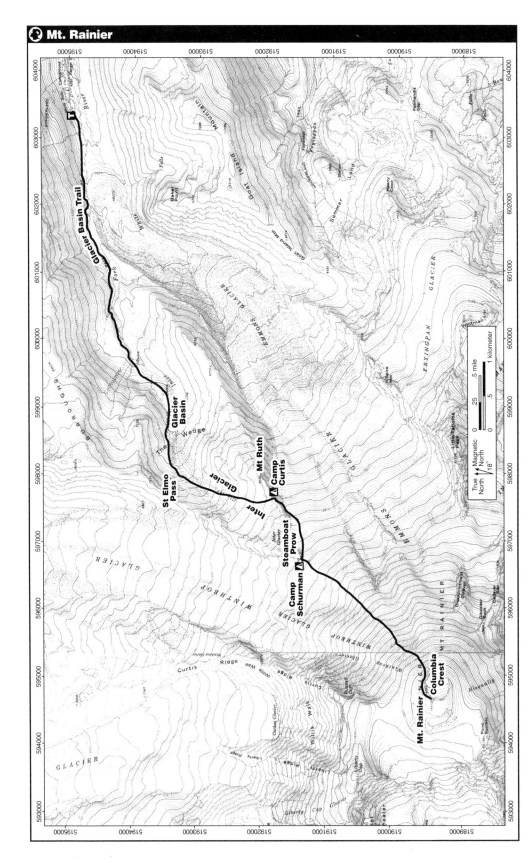

ROUTE 1

Mt. Rainier

ELEVATION: 14,410' (4392 m)

CLIMBING ROUTE: Emmons Glacier

DISTANCE: 15 miles

ELEVATION GAIN: 10,500'

DAYS: 2–3

MAPS: USGS Sunrise, Mt. Rainier East, Mt. Rainier West; Green Trails Mt. Rainier East No. 270, Mt. Rainier West No. 269

RATING: E4T3

LOCATION: Mt. Rainier National Park, White River Ranger Station

PERMITS: Permits and climbing fees are required to climb above 10,000 feet. You can make a reservation in advance. The Park Service limits the number of climbers to camp at Camp Schurman each day. Camping above Camp Schurman on the glacier at Emmons Flat is feasible, but sanitation is a problem as the only toilets are located at Camp Schurman.

SUMMARY AND HIGHLIGHTS: The undisputed king of the Cascade volcanoes, Mt. Rainier dominates the entire Puget Sound and Central Washington landscape. It is the state's highest peak and is the tallest volcano in the contiguous United States (California's Mt. Shasta is 14,161'). The massive hulk shimmers above the Seattle skyline, often shrouded in clouds but at other times brilliantly looming in the atmosphere. But do not be deceived: this colossal mountain creates its own weather, is highly dangerous, and deserves your utmost respect. Yet, for such a commanding icon, many fledgling climbers can accomplish the easiest routes up the volcano.

Mt. Rainier stands directly in the normal path of cool marine air from Puget Sound, which accounts for the high volume of snowfall on its slopes. Paradise, a National Park visitor center on the south flank of the peak, once held a world record for snowfall. Mt. Rainier's glacier system is massive, consisting of 26 major glaciers that cover more area than any other single-mountain glacier system in the lower United States. For the most intense and unrelenting glacier climbing experience in Washington, choose Mt. Rainier.

A hallmark of Mt. Rainer is its unpredictable climate. A gorgeous, sunny day on the lower Emmons Glacier can turn to dense clouds higher up, which then can deteriorate to galling winds and several feet of new, wet snow any time of the year. Thousands attempt to climb Mt. Rainier annually, only about half reaching the summit. Every year at least a few people are killed on the mountain, while many more are injured. Objective hazards such as avalanches and rockfall contribute to the risk, but most injuries are due to inexperience, poor conditioning, faulty judgment, or inadequate routefinding skills. Altitude sickness is common. You must be sure that you and your companions are in good physical condition and have the skills and judgment necessary to complete the trip.

Mt. Rainier is a physically demanding climb seen by many as an arduous trudge. The reward is a long pilgrimage through some of the most alien and austerely beautiful terrain you will ever experience. From the summit, often perched above a thick layer of clouds, the view is impressive. If you are fortunate to have good weather, sunrise over Puget Sound is a lovely sight. Go early enough in the season to avoid most of the problems associated with huge crevasses, but go late enough for more settled weather. In most years this means from July to early August, although many other times of the year are suitable depending on the weather forecast. The National Park Service provides up-to-date information about conditions on the mountain.

HOW TO GET THERE: Drive to Enumclaw via SR 169 from the north, SR 164 from the west, or SR 410 from the south. Head east from Enumclaw on SR 410 through the town of Greenwater and past the turnoff for Crystal Mountain ski area. At 34 miles from Enumclaw, reach the entrance to Mt. Rainier National Park. Continue driving for 5 more miles to a junction, then turn right on the White River (Sunrise) Road to the White River Ranger Station. Stop at the ranger station to register for the climb and pay fees as required. Continue driving to a junction at the bridge over the White River. Take the left fork and in 1.4 miles reach the White River Campground and the Glacier Basin Trailhead (4300').

TRIP DESCRIPTION: Hike on the Glacier Basin Trail for 3.0 miles to Glacier Basin (6000'). Continue for another mile to the base of the Inter Glacier (7100'). Rope up here, as the Inter Glacier has significant crevasses (fatalities of unroped climbers have occurred here). Go up the middle of the Inter Glacier, trending to the southeast, to reach the glacier rim on a ridge at Camp Curtis (8700'). Descend to the Emmons Glacier and then climb along the base of Steamboat Prow to Camp

Chris Weidner

Emmons Glacier en route to Camp Schurman

Schurman (9500'). A hut is located here but is used only for emergencies. Camp at an established site, and arrive early for a good campsite.

Start climbing during the night hours—usually just after midnight —following the snow slope called "The Corridor," which trends slightly left (southwest) between most of the crevasses on the lower half of the route. At about 12,000 feet, the Emmons Glacier becomes heavily crevassed in late season, so from here the route varies from year to year according to snow conditions. In general, go up and to the left, making your way around crevasses. Usually the route is visible from the tread of other climbers unless there has been a recent snowfall. The true summit, Columbia Crest, is on the far west side of the crater rim.

HAZARDS AND TIPS: The Emmons Glacier route is longer and requires more elevation gain than the Disappointment Cleaver route from Camp Muir on the south side of Mt. Rainier. Even though the Emmons slope is milder, fewer people attempt this route; the guided climbs up Mt. Rainier most often are from Camp Muir. The Emmons Glacier is the least technical way up, but, as mentioned, significant crevasses exist later in the season, even on the seemingly benign Inter Glacier. Glacier gear is compulsory, and you must apply the usual precautions to avoid avalanches and ice falls. A 3-day ascent makes for good acclimatization to prevent altitude sickness. Because toilet facilities are available at Camp Schurman, it is best to make a camp there, even though it is tempting to camp at Emmons Flat, at 10,200 feet, where tent sites can be dug on the

Descending at 13,000 feet on Emmons Glacier

glacier. If you are camping at Emmons Flat, be prepared to pack out any solid human waste. Also probe carefully for crevasses before making camp, and do not travel unroped beyond the area that you have established as your campsite.

GPS WAYPOINT ROUTE:

1. 10T 603238, 5194941, 4300': Glacier Basin Trailhead
2. 10T 598851, 5193413, 3.0 miles, 6000': Glacier Basin
3. 10T 597688, 5192829, 1.0 mile, 7100': Inter Glacier
4. 10T 597563, 5191834, 0.8 mile, 8700': Camp Curtis
5. 10T 596702, 5191370, 0.5 mile, 9500': Camp Schurman
6. 10T 595695, 5190214, 1.0 mile, 12,000': half way
7. 10T 594930, 5189485, 0.5 mile, 14,100': summit crater
8. 10T 594600, 5189360, 0.7 mile, 14,410': Rainier summit

TRIP TIMES:

Glacier Basin Trailhead to Camp Schurman: 5.3 miles, 5400', 8 hours
Camp Schurman to Rainier summit: 2.2 miles, 4900', 8 hours

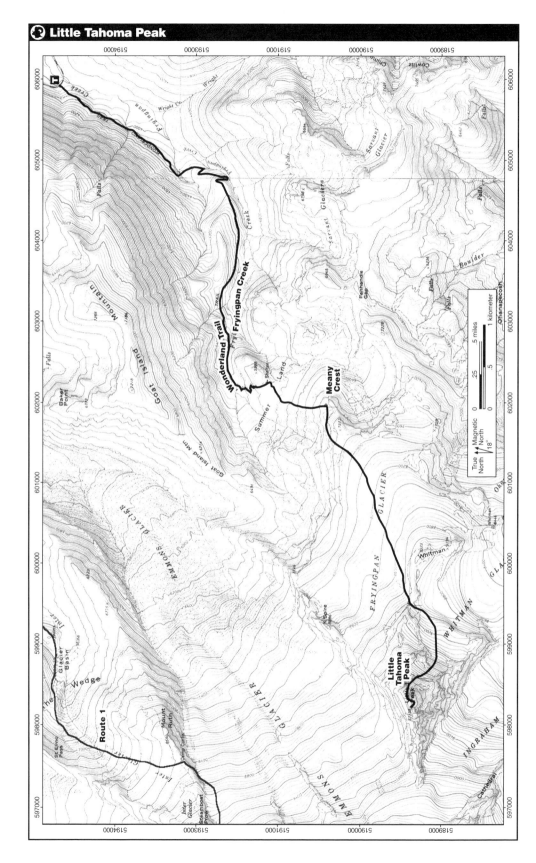

ROUTE 2

Little Tahoma Peak

ELEVATION: 11,138' (3395 m)

CLIMBING ROUTE: East Shoulder

DISTANCE: 18 miles

ELEVATION GAIN: 7300'

DAYS: 2

MAPS: USGS White River Park, Chinook Pass, Mt. Rainier East; Green Trails Mt. Rainier East No. 270

RATING: E3T3

LOCATION: Mt. Rainier National Park, White River Ranger Station

PERMITS: Permits are required and a fee is charged to climb above 10,000 feet. You can make a reservation in advance.

SUMMARY AND HIGHLIGHTS: Little Tahoma Peak is a crumbling, craggy satellite of the ancient and formerly larger Mt. Rainier. Measuring in at 11,138 feet, Little Tahoma is taller than any of the nonvolcanic summits in the Cascade Range. The summit pyramid is an isolated, triangular pinnacle that stands 3000 feet above the ice flows — the Whitman, Fryingpan, and Ohanapecosh glaciers — at the foot of its east slope. On a fine summer weekend these gentle slopes are popular sites for swooshing telemark skiers and snowboarders. But higher up the rock is unstable, as Little Tahoma forms a wedge between the massive Ingraham and Emmons glaciers, which flow from above and undercut the peak on both sides.

Little Tahoma has a relatively straightforward ascent with an excellent setting on the flank of Mt. Rainier. The approach to the climb through Summer Land on the east side of Mt. Rainier National Park is an added bonus, for here the meadows are lush in stark contrast to the ice fields above. The last push to the summit on crumbling volcanic debris can be unnerving to a party lacking good rockfall-management skills. Also be aware that at any time of year fog can obscure landmarks. You must know how to navigate competently to be able to avoid the cliffs of Meany Crest that lurk below on the way down.

HOW TO GET THERE: Drive to Enumclaw via SR 169 from the north, SR 164 from the west, or SR 410 from the south. Head east from Enumclaw on SR 410 through the town of Greenwater and past the turnoff for Crystal Mountain ski area. Thirty-four miles from Enumclaw, reach the entrance to Mt. Rainier National Park. After 5 miles more, turn right on the White River (Sunrise) Road to the White River Ranger Station. Stop at the ranger station to register for the climb and pay fees as required. Try to get a permit for camping in the Meany Crest zone at 7000 or 7400 feet rather than the Summer Land zone at 5900 feet, for camping higher will greatly facilitate completing the long approach to the summit. Continue driving west on the White River Road. At 4 miles from the White River Ranger Station, find the trailhead for the Summer Land section of the Wonderland Trail (3900').

TRIP DESCRIPTION: Hike on the Wonderland Trail along Fryingpan Creek for 5.5 miles to Summer Land Camp (5900'). Stay off meadows that are free of snow, as this is an extremely fragile alpine zone. Beyond the Summer Land campground, go left around the large meadow while skirting cliffs to the right. Next, scramble steeply up to attain Meany Crest (7100'). Just before the Fryingpan Glacier, camp at the flat, sandy, established sites on the rocky ridge and then melt snow for water. If you have more than five members in your party, you are required to camp on snow on the nearby glacier.

The next morning at sunrise, start climbing up the Fryingpan Glacier and ascend southwest toward the saddle between the Fryingpan and Whitman glaciers. Pass through the saddle at 9000 feet. Contour southwest around a rock rib. Then climb west on the Whitman Glacier. Aim toward the east shoulder of the pyramid of Little Tahoma, as it has the least severe slope. Ascend the Whitman Glacier up and left, then exit into a gully (10,500'). Climb up the gully on loose rock or snow on the east shoulder of Little Tahoma to a cleft in the rock at about 200 feet below the summit. Climb up the step (class 3), traversing to the left to gain an easy chimney system that reaches a notch just below the summit. Some parties may want to use a rope or hand line here, as the crossing is airy and exposed (class 4). The final few feet along the ridgecrest is a loose rock scramble (class 2).

HAZARDS AND TIPS: Glacier gear is required. Serious rockfall occurs from the upper Fryingpan Glacier and from above the Whitman Glacier. The scramble up the summit block is on loose volcanic debris, and helmets are recommended. A rope can cause increased rockfall in the gully system, and is therefore used primarily for the short step below the summit.

GPS WAYPOINT ROUTE:

1. 10T 605900, 5193492, 3900': Wonderland Trailhead
2. 10T 602286, 5190878, 5.5 miles, 5900': Summer Land
3. 10T 601952, 5190123, 0.5 mile, 7100': Meany Crest camp
4. 10T 599536, 5189084, 1.6 miles, 9000': saddle
5. 10T 598637, 5188906, 0.9 mile, 10,200': East Shoulder
6. 10T 598228, 5189019, 0.3 mile, 11,138': Little Tahoma summit

TRIP TIMES:

Wonderland Trailhead to Meany Crest camp: 6.0 miles, 3300', 5 hours

Meany Crest camp to Little Tahoma summit: 2.8 miles, 4000', 6 hours

Little Tahoma Peak

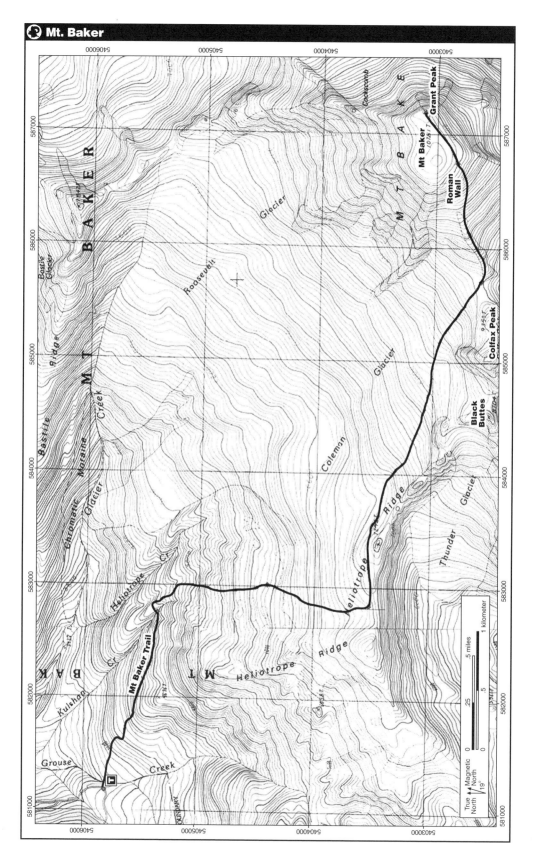

Grant Peak

Mt Baker

Roman Wall

MT. BAKER

BAKER

MT

BAKER

Bastile Ridge

Bastile Glacier

Chromatic Glacier

Roosevelt Glacier

Coleman Glacier

Moraine

Creek

Heliotrope

Cr.

Cr.

Kulshan

Grouse

Creek

Mt Baker Trail

Heliotrope Ridge

Heliotrope Ridge

Colfax Peak

Black Buttes

Thunder Glacier

Cockscomb

True North

Magnetic North

19°

0   .25   .5

0   .5   1 kilometer

.5 miles

ROUTE 3

Mt. Baker

ELEVATION: 10,781' (3287 m)

CLIMBING ROUTE: Coleman Glacier

DISTANCE: 12 miles

ELEVATION GAIN: 7100'

DAYS: 2

MAPS: USGS Groat Mountain, Mt. Baker; Green Trails Mt. Baker No. 13

RATING: E3T3

LOCATION: Mt. Baker Wilderness administered by Mt. Baker-Snoqualmie National Forest, Glacier Public Service Center or Mt. Baker Ranger District (Sedro-Woolley)

PERMITS: You are asked to sign the voluntary climbing register at the Glacier Public Service Center (no fee).

SUMMARY AND HIGHLIGHTS: Mt. Baker stands as a frozen warrior guarding the expanse of Bellingham Bay mere miles from the Canadian border. It is visible on a clear day from almost any vantage around northern Puget Sound, and its cone can be spied from Mt. Rainier more than 100 miles away. Mt. Baker sports 12 glaciers, which hold as much ice as the 26 major glaciers on Mt. Rainier. The largest are the Coleman and Roosevelt glaciers, fed by an area that extends from Heliotrope Ridge on the west to Bastile Ridge on the east. A climb up the Coleman Glacier is the most common way to reach the summit, a nearly level ice mound situated more than 1300 feet above the actual volcano crater. The Easton and Boulder glaciers on the south side also provide popular routes to the top.

Mt. Baker is still a visibly active volcano. Fumaroles (holes where vapor escapes), thermal springs, and areas of warm ground are concentrated near the crater rim. In recent years, hydrothermal activity has melted ice causing instability and intermittent release of snow, rock, and mud from Sherman Peak, a southeastern remnant of a larger crater rim. In the 1970s, Sherman Crater broke open and expelled gas and ash clouds. This activity has mostly stopped, but steam and noxious gases are still apparent. Mt. Saint Helens has outshone Mt. Baker as the most dangerous volcano of the past century, but some geologists warn that Mt. Baker may be the next to erupt.

Although crevasse-related deaths are uncommon on Mt. Baker, falls into crevasses are thought to be more common on Mt. Baker than on any other Washington volcano. The abundant marine air drops on average more than 50 feet of snow on Mt. Baker per year. (In 1999, Mt. Baker Ski Area stole the world record for annual snowfall from Mt. Rainier's Paradise.) A common weather pattern of warm, rainy conditions following snowfall keeps avalanche danger high, even on gentle slopes, during the summer months. High winds, storms, and snowfall can occur at any time of year. But because the approach to Mt. Baker is short, you can often take advantage of brief periods of settled weather to make a climb that is unparalleled in its beauty and wild appeal set close to civilization.

HOW TO GET THERE: Drive north on Interstate 5 to Bellingham. Just north of the city, drive east on State Route 542 (the Mt. Baker Sunset Highway) for 33.8 miles just past the town of Glacier. Sign the voluntary climbing register (no charge) at the Glacier Public Service Center. At one mile past town, turn right on Glacier Creek FS Road 39 and continue 8 miles to the Mt. Baker (Heliotrope Ridge) Trail No. 677 trailhead (3700').

TRIP DESCRIPTION: Hike on the Mt. Baker Trail along Heliotrope Ridge to the end of the maintained trail at 4800 feet. At timberline is the site of Kulshan Cabin, which was taken down after the area was granted wilderness status. At the junction, take the right fork on the climber's trail up the lateral moraine, called the Hogsback. At 6000 feet find a suitable campsite along the edge of the Coleman Glacier. Alternatively, go south on the western portion of the glacier to avoid most of the crevasses. At 7000 feet you can make a base camp along Heliotrope Ridge, or farther on at the bottom of the Black Buttes.

The next morning at sunrise, traverse east from base camp along the Black Buttes, remaining far enough away to avoid rockfall and avalanches. Ascend on the Coleman Glacier, bearing southeast to the saddle at 9000 feet between Colfax Peak (the east butte of the Black Buttes) and the Roman Wall, the unstable cliff at the southern edge of the Coleman Glacier headwall. A moderately steep snowfield southeast of the Roman Wall provides the least slope gradient to the summit of Mt. Baker. Climb on snow or on the rocky pumice ridge to the right (south) of the Roman Wall. Ascend steep snow past the Roman Wall to the broad summit plateau. Cross the nearly flat snow to Grant Peak, the true high point of

Ed Cooper

Mt. Baker

Mt. Baker, on the far northeast rim above the old crater and Sherman Peak.

HAZARDS AND TIPS: Because Mt. Baker is heavily crevassed, glacier gear is mandatory. At the lower elevations the snowfields and the glacier blend into each other so you must rope up on the snow above 6000 feet. Any time of year beware of rockfall off of Black Buttes and avalanches near the Roman Wall.

GPS WAYPOINT ROUTE:
1. 10U 581206, 5405820, 3700': Heliotrope Ridge Trailhead
2. 10U 582997, 5405173, 2.0 miles, 4800': trail end
3. 10U 583004, 5404342, 0.6 mile, 6000': low camp
4. 10U 582848, 5403504, 0.5 mile, 7000': high camp
5. 10U 585666, 5402607, 1.8 miles, 9000': saddle
6. 10U 586751, 5402803, 0.8 mile, 10,500': summit crater
7. 10U 587192, 5403103, 0.4 mile, 10,781': Mt. Baker summit

TRIP TIMES:
Mt. Baker Trailhead to Black Buttes camp: 3.1 miles, 3300', 6 hours
Black Buttes camp to Mt. Baker summit: 3.0 miles, 3800', 6 hours

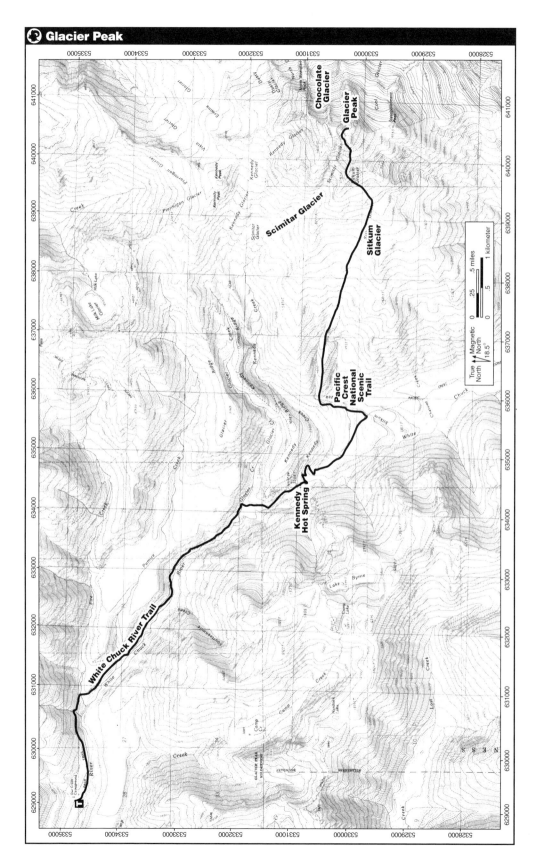

Glacier Peak

Glacier Peak

ELEVATION: 10,520+' (3207+ m)

CLIMBING ROUTE: Sitkum Glacier

DISTANCE: 22 miles

ELEVATION GAIN: 8200'

DAYS: 2–3

MAPS: USGS Mt. Pugh, Lime Mountain, Glacier Peak West, Glacier Peak East; Green Trails Sloan Peak No. 111, Glacier Peak No. 112

RATING: E3T3

LOCATION: Glacier Peak Wilderness, administered by Mt. Baker-Snoqualmie National Forest, Darrington Ranger District

PERMITS: Visitors are asked to sign the voluntary climbing register at the Darrington Ranger Station and at the trailhead.

SUMMARY AND HIGHLIGHTS: Glacier Peak is a cinder cone, much younger than the plateau upon which it stands. It has been quite active since the end of the most recent ice age, with numerous eruptions, pyroclastic flows, and mudflows. The crater is obscured by products of erosion and filled with snow and ice. The southwestern part of an older crater with an eroded rim is the true summit. Due to Glacier Peak's northern latitude and high snowfall, glaciers cover all but its southern slope. These ice rivers show great diversity, as some have advanced while others have retreated in recent years. The major central glaciers are the Chocolate, Scimitar, and Sitkum. The peripheral glaciers are the Suiattle and White Chuck, which is the largest of the Glacier Peak system. Although complex and challenging routes are available on Glacier Peak, several nontechnical routes exist for the basic-level climber (See definition page 3).

In contrast to climbing the other major volcanoes of Washington, climbing Glacier Peak is a genuine backwoods experience. The Glacier Peak Wilderness was established in 1964 with the passage of the Wilderness Act. In compliance with the designation, no roads penetrate anywhere close to the mountain, and all the approach hikes are at least 10 miles long. However, the lengthy hiking in the lush forest valleys pre-

Glacier Peak climbers near summit

pares you for the striking contrast of glacial topography. On weekends, even on the most popular routes, expect to see only a few other people, including some skiers and snowboarders. During the week, your party may be completely alone. The high camps are sublime, and the ambiance supremely adventuresome. The summit is a worthy reward for the modest effort to attain it.

HOW TO GET THERE: Drive 11 miles north of Everett on Interstate 5. Turn east on SR 530 and drive for 32 miles to Darrington. From Darrington drive south on the Mountain Loop Highway (State Route 92) for 10 miles to the bridge over the river (14 miles from Barlow Pass if you are coming from the south). Turn east (left) on the White Chuck River FS Road 23. Drive for 10.6 miles to the end of the road and the White Chuck River Trail No. 643 trailhead (2300').

TRIP DESCRIPTION: Hike on the White Chuck River Trail through dense forest. You will pass by the Meadow Mountain-Fire Mountain Trail No. 657 at 1.4 miles, and the Kennedy Ridge Trail No. 639 at an additional 3.5 miles as they exit on the left. Continue straight ahead for 0.2 mile to Kennedy Hot Spring. South of the spring, the trail becomes the Upper White Chuck Trail No. 643A. Continue ascending on switchbacks to the T-junction at 3900 feet (6.9 miles from the road). Take the left fork and hike on the Pacific Crest National Scenic Trail (Crest Trail No. 2000). In a half mile and before the footbridge over Sitkum Creek, leave the trail at 4100 feet. Go northeast, following a climber's footpath through a boulder field. Cross a creek and follow the tread east up the steep wooded ridge south of Sitkum Creek. As the path climbs sharply on the ridge, it becomes discontinuous and hard to follow. Bear south at timberline and camp at Boulder Basin (5600'). Camp only at established sites and use the outdoor toilet. Alternatively, find a campsite higher at 6900 feet on the snow at the base of the lower Sitkum Glacier.

From Boulder Basin camp, climb southeast to attain the Sitkum Glacier at 6900 feet. Avoid the right side of the Sitkum Glacier, as it has more crevasses. Climb on the lower Sitkum Glacier near the middle of the glacier, trending southeast, to the rock band that nearly transects it horizontally at about 8400 feet. Make your way upward through the break in the rock, climbing on snow or ice. Continue on the upper Sitkum Glacier traversing northeast to the saddle east of Sitkum Spire (9300'). Climb east on the pumice ridge on the south edge of the Scimitar Glacier. Choose either the north or south side of the crest, depending on the conditions. The summit is an ice-covered mound with a rocky high point at the southwest. The lowest gradient is on the north-

Chris Weidner

From Glacier Peak summit

ern slope. If you go to the south, the final snow chute that leads to the summit can be icy and dangerous.

HAZARDS AND TIPS: Glacier gear is mandatory. The summit cone is often icy, necessitating sharp crampons. The south side of the summit is prone to rockfall. Allow time to soak in the Kennedy Hot Spring on the way out or the way in — or both.

GPS WAYPOINT ROUTE:

1. 10U 629044, 5334770, 2300': White Chuck River Trailhead
2. 10U 634523, 5330965, 5.1 miles, 3300': Kennedy Hot Spring
3. 10U 635677, 5329852, 1.8 miles, 3900': Crest Trail
4. 10U 636127, 5330644, 0.5 mile, 4100': climbers trail
5. 10U 637339, 5330451, 1.1 miles, 5600': Boulder Basin
6. 10U 638229, 5330249, 0.5 mile, 6900': high camp
7. 10U 639266, 5329829, 0.5 mile, 8400': rock band
8. 10U 639730, 5330275, 0.6 mile, 9300': saddle
9. 10U 640475, 5330255, 0.7 mile, 10,520+': Glacier Peak summit

TRIP TIMES:

White Chuck River Trailhead to Boulder Basin: 8.5 miles, 3300', 7 hours

Boulder Basin to Glacier summit: 2.3 miles, 4900', 7 hours

CHAPTER 2

Northern Cascades

T he northern Cascade Range contains the wildest and most rugged
country in Washington. It is composed of the northwestern Cascade Range, which extends north from the Skagit River and Ross
Lake to the Fraser River in Canada, and the Cascade Crest, which extends south from the Skagit River and Granite Creek to the Suiattle
River. Near the Canadian border the northern Cascades climax in a dramatic series of complex and stunning peaks. This area is renowned for
its prominent hanging glaciers. Yet the landscape is diverse: lush, ever-
green forests contrast sharply with sculpted rock features that punctuate
glacial plateaus. Small lakes and tarns dot the slopes between rugged
cirques and mountain flanks. Meadows flourish beside barren rock and
moraine debris. This is a land of extremes of both gentle and harsh
beauty, but above all, the ice-clad peaks endure as a compelling presence.

The climate of the northern Cascade Range is strongly influenced by
marine airflows. Heavy precipitation pummels the western slopes, where
the winter snowpack averages 18 feet per year. The ecological zones vary
from giant western red cedars in the valleys to miniature phlox plants
above the 7000-foot alpine level. Douglas firs grow up to 200 feet tall. In
the forest shade grow all types of ferns and berries, including a generous
sprinkling of devils club. At higher altitudes, dwarf evergreens dominate
and pink heather forms an earthen patch quilt with other herbaceous
plants.

The Nooksack tribe may have settled these lowlands as early as 5000
years ago. The term *Nooksack* is derived from the bracken fern, whose
root provided a major food source. In 1670, trappers from the Hudson's
Bay Company began exploring the region. Miners followed, but little was
known about the territory for many years until both the United States
and Britain surveyed the 49th degree parallel. In 1917 the Department of
Agriculture gave Seattle City Light the right to develop the Skagit Valley
with a series of dams and electric projects, beginning with Gorge Creek
in 1924 and ending with Ross Dam, which was constructed in stages between 1937 and 1950. These manmade structures are some of the most
scenic features in the region, and they contrast elegantly with the geologic landscape.

While hunting goats, Native Americans forged most of the pathways,
such as that over Hannegan Pass. In the early 1900s the Forest Service

completed many of the principal trails with the help of local climbing clubs including the Mt. Baker Club and The Mountaineers. Today much of the northern Cascade Range falls within the Mt. Baker Wilderness and North Cascades National Park. Both prohibit the construction of new roads and only rarely create new trails. The national park has been left in a near pristine state, especially in its northern lobe, only one trail transecting it east to west.

Permits are required for all overnight stays in North Cascades National Park. They are issued in person, on the first day of the trip or the day before at the Wilderness Information Center in Marblemount or the Mt. Baker Ranger Station in Sedro-Woolley. The permit process provides an opportunity for rangers and visitors to exchange important information. Limited after-hours self-registration is provided at the Wilderness Information Center and the Sedro-Woolley ranger station for some areas that are not in high demand. Camping is permitted only at designated sites along trails. Cross-country travelers must camp at least a half mile from trails, a mile from designated campsites, and 100 feet from lakes, rivers, and streams. Fires are discouraged due to the impact caused by gathering wood; carry a stove and build a fire only in an emergency. If you end a trip early, notify a ranger to cancel your permit so others can take your place. If you find litter, pack it out.

Many peaks in this region are hard to get to, not just because they are far from any decent roads, but also because the lower elevations are thickly overgrown with vegetation that makes cross-country travel a continuous bushwhack even to the high reaches. The substantial obstacles are one reason these dazzling areas are still places of solitude. Above treeline, the blessed lack of both mosquitoes and slide alder makes for supreme alpine rambling. Naturally, the many glaciers and enormous expanses of ice in the northern Cascades present obvious dangers. But the scenery is so spectacular and the ambiance so heavenly that the effort is miniscule compared to the incomparable mountaineering opportunities.

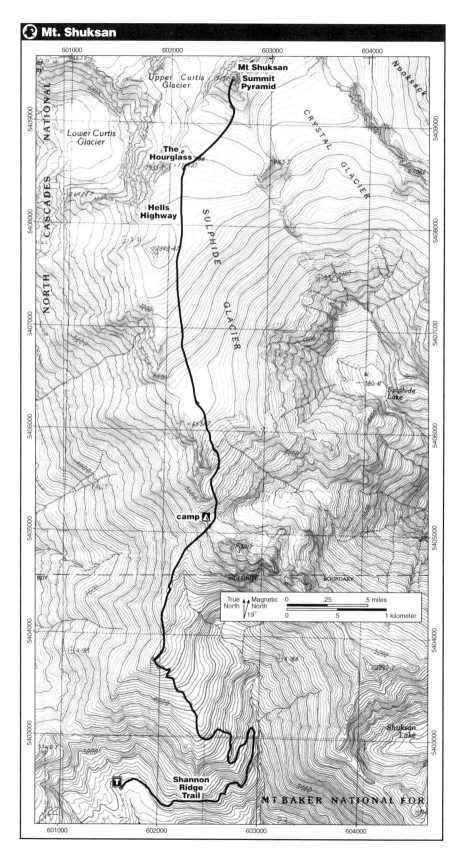

601000 602000 603000 604000

Mt Shuksan
Summit
Pyramid

Upper Curtis
Glacier

NATIONAL

Lower Curtis
Glacier

The
Hourglass

Hells
Highway

CASCADES

NORTH

SULPHIDE

GLACIER

CRYSTAL GLACIER

Nooksack

Sulphide
Lake

camp

INDEFINITE   BOUNDARY

| True North | Magnetic North 19° | 0 | .25 | .5 miles |
| | | 0 | .5 | 1 kilometer |

BDY

Shannon
Ridge
Trail

Shuksan
Lake

MT BAKER NATIONAL FOR

5409000
5408000
5407000
5406000
5405000
5404000
5403000

601000 602000 603000 604000

Mt. Shuksan

ELEVATION: 9131' (2784 m)

CLIMBING ROUTE: Sulphide Glacier

DISTANCE: 15 miles

ELEVATION GAIN: 6700'

DAYS: 2

MAPS: USGS Mt. Shuksan; Green Trails Mt. Shuksan No. 14

RATING: E2T3

LOCATION: Mt. Baker-Snoqualmie National Forest and North Cascades National Park, Mt. Baker Ranger District (Sedro-Woolley)

PERMITS: Permits are required to camp in North Cascades National Park and are limited within this cross-country zone; you are asked to register for the climb at the Sedro-Woolley Ranger Station. Permits are issued in person only on a first-come-first-serve basis on the day of your trip or the day before.

SUMMARY AND HIGHLIGHTS: Mt. Shuksan is considered by many to be the most beautiful and picturesque mountain in the Cascade Range. Arêtes and chaotic hanging glaciers coexist with immense snowfields that blanket the slopes leading up to the famed summit pyramid. In just 3 miles, the northern face drops almost 8000 feet to the North Fork Nooksack River. Additionally, Mt. Shuksan is the only nonvolcanic peak in Washington whose summit rises more than 3000 feet above treeline. On the broad southern flank lies the Sulphide Glacier, the largest ice mass on the peak. The Curtis Glacier graces the western face while the Price Glacier on the northeast flank is the steepest, with a huge icefall. The satellite peaks of Nooksack Tower, Jagged Ridge, and Cloudcap Peak are impressive, though not highly prominent amid the surrounding terrain.

A favorite with backcountry skiers and snowboarders, Mt. Shuksan provides an outstanding alpine environment for climbers, too. Its summit is within reach of the basic-level climber (see definition page 3) via the route on the Sulphide Glacier. This itinerary is the most heavily traveled, but is still supremely scenic despite the crowds. The approach is

relatively short and low camps are easily accessed at the edge of the glacier on a cozy ridge nestled in the elbow of a rock wall. The rock on the
summit pyramid is somewhat loose, but no worse than most in the region. Mt. Shuksan can be climbed in winter or early spring, but then the
rock is covered in rime ice that may plummet onto climbers below. The
best time to attempt Shuksan is in June or July, after the snow covering
the rock on the summit pyramid has melted, the avalanche risk is re-
duced, and the crevasses are mostly covered.

HOW TO GET THERE: Drive on Interstate 5 to Sedro-Woolley. Stop at
the Mt. Baker Ranger Station for a permit to camp in the North Cascades
National Park. From Sedro-Woolley drive east on Highway 20 for 17.0
miles. At the junction go north on Baker Lake-Grandy Lake Highway,
which becomes FS Road 11 upon entering Mt. Baker-Snoqualmie National Forest near Lake Shannon. Continue to Shannon Creek Campground on the north shore of Baker Lake (24.9 miles from Highway 20).
Just beyond the campground, turn left (west) on Shannon Creek FS
Road 1152. Continue on the main path for 3.0 miles to a sharp junction

Mt. Shuksan seen from Picture Lake

with FS Road 014. Follow this spur road 1.4 miles north across Shannon Creek. Where the road is blocked, begin hiking on Shannon Ridge Trail No. 742 (2800').

TRIP DESCRIPTION: Make sure you are on the proper road spur to reach the Shannon Ridge Trail No. 742 trailhead (you may see a sign). Hike on the abandoned road for about 2 miles. At 3800 feet the trail begins a series of switchbacks up to a leveled-off north-south ridge at 4600 feet. Continue on this fairly open and sparsely treed ridge to a small notch in the higher ridge to the east. Ascend a steep, small slope to the crest at 5400 feet, where a low camp can be established. You can melt snow for water here. The summit can be easily reached from this camp.

The next morning at sunrise, go north up the ridge along the western margin of the Sulphide Glacier. An alternate high camp is found at about 6400 on the glacier. From here ascend the western margin of the Sulphide Glacier to Hells Highway. Hells Highway is the opening to the Lower Curtis Glacier, located to the south of The Hourglass, which is a rent in the southwest ridge emanating from the summit pyramid. After the terrain flattens out, trend northeast up slightly steeper slopes to the base of the summit pyramid. The gully route begins to the left of the rocky ridge on the right of the triangular face and trends leftward, to the west, until just under the summit. Some parties rope up on parts of the gully route (a few class 4 moves). To return, most parties downclimb the ascent route; anchors for rappelling are not entirely trustworthy.

HAZARDS AND TIPS: Glacier gear is required and helmets are recommended for the summit pyramid. In winter or early spring, rime ice on the summit block is treacherous; the route up the summit pyramid is easiest after the snow has melted. Avalanche danger is high when going from low camp to high camp in early season. Late in the season crevasses on the Sulphide Glacier present only a moderate routefinding problem.

GPS WAYPOINT ROUTE:
1. 10U 601626, 5402497, 2800': Shannon Ridge Trailhead
2. 10U 601919, 5403735, 3.0 miles, 4600': ridge
3. 10U 602443, 5405069, 1.2 miles, 5400': low camp
4. 10U 602149, 5406340, 1.0 mile, 6400': high camp
5. 10U 601884, 5408050, 1.4 miles, 7500': Hells Highway
6. 10U 602530, 5409224, 0.7 mile, 8400': pyramid base
7. 10U 602635, 5409432, 0.2 mile, 9131': Shuksan summit

TRIP TIMES:
Shannon Ridge Trailhead to low camp: 4.2 miles, 2600', 5 hours
Low camp to Shuksan summit: 3.3 miles, 3700', 6 hours

Chilliwack Group

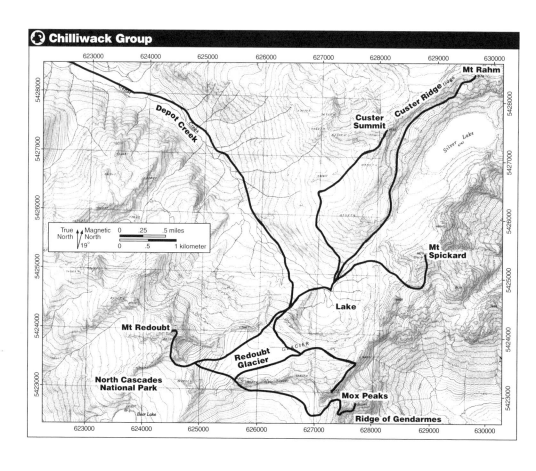

Mt Rahm

Custer Ridge

Custer Summit

Depot Creek

Silver Lake

Mt Spickard

True North / Magnetic North 19°

0   .25   .5 miles

0   .5   1 kilometer

Lake

Mt Redoubt

Redoubt Glacier

GLACIER

North Cascades National Park

Bear Lake

Mox Peaks

Ridge of Gendarmes

ROUTE 6

Chilliwack Group

Mt. Redoubt, Mox Peaks (Southeast Twin Spire and Northwest Twin Spire), Mt. Spickard, Mt. Rahm, Mt. Custer

ELEVATIONS: 8969', 8504', 8407', 8979', 8478', 8630' (2734 m, 2593 m, 2563 m, 2738 m, 2585 m, 2631 m)

DISTANCE: 38 miles

ELEVATION GAIN: 16,500'

TRIP TIME: At least 8 days

MAPS: USGS Mt. Redoubt, Mt. Spickard; Green Trails Mt. Challenger No. 15, Ross Lake No. 16

RATING: E5T5

LOCATION: North Cascades National Park, Mt. Baker Ranger District (Sedro-Woolley)

PERMITS: Permits are required for camping in North Cascades National Park. Call the Wilderness Information Center at (360) 873-4590 for a permit; you are asked to sign a register at the Canadian Border (see Appendix A: Contact Information).

SUMMARY AND HIGHLIGHTS: Situated in the Custer Ridge area north of Mt. Shuksan and the Picket Range, the Chilliwack Group of peaks rises just at the U.S. border with Canada. These jagged, towering pinnacles are the archetype of a lonesome, untamed, and otherworldly wilderness. Here the dark rock and remarkably steep profiles of the Mox Peaks (also called Twin Spires) puncture the skyline. This is a land that seems locked in time. The approach is over rough roads through Canada and across the border on a seldom traveled foot tread. A grueling ascent through dense forest leads to a thundering waterfall. You climb upward along, and sometimes through, the rushing frigid shower to emerge in the highest reaches of a lowland plateau. From there you trudge along swollen creeks and marshy bottoms, then ascend among cliffs to the splendid, icy glaciers that blanket the feet of the mountains. At sunset from camp, on a little land-locked lake, you can witness the extraordinary process of huge chunks of hanging glaciers breaking off, thundering down, and crashing onto the rocks below.

This country has an ominous and threatening nature. The rock is very loose, leading to nerve-wracking climbing as each handhold and foothold must be tested. Mt. Spickard serves as a reminder of possible tragedy: formerly named Glacier Peak, it was changed to commemorate Warren Spickard, a local physician, who met his death while descending nearby Northwest Mox Peak. Although Mounts Redoubt and Spickard are climbed often, the Mox Peaks and Mounts Rahm and Custer are less popular, partly because they consist of decaying and brittle rock. Yet each summit reveals a special vantage of the others, and Custer and Rahm offer a particularly close view of lovely Silver Lake, which glistens with an aquamarine hue during a clear summer afternoon.

Climbing all these peaks in a single outing is an extraordinary feat that requires ruthless efficiency. The region's weather is especially unsettled. The Chilliwack Group is so remote that it should be attempted only when there is a strong high-pressure system leading to ideal conditions. Most climbers find that they need to return at least several times to complete the set. But most relish the opportunity to revisit the region to experience again the solitude and wonder of being in such an intimidating and enthralling realm.

HOW TO GET THERE: Drive on Interstate 5 to Sedro-Woolley. At the ranger station obtain camping permits for North Cascades National Park. You can also obtain permits by telephone from the Wilderness Information Center in Marblemount (see Appendix A: Contact Information). Continue north to Bellingham. Take State Route 542 east to Highway 9. Drive north on Highway 9 to cross into Canada at Sumas. Continue north for 2 miles and turn right (east) on Highway 1 (exit 92 for the return trip). Drive 17 miles and take the Chilliwack/Sardis exit 119A going south. Drive 3.4 miles on this main road through town, and just before a small bridge over the river turn left onto the Chilliwack River Road. Drive about 32 miles on this main road. It turns to dirt and gets quite bumpy as you go on, with many washouts and rocks (a 4WD vehicle is recommended). About 200 yards before the Depot Creek Bridge to your right, turn left onto the narrow dirt-and-gravel Depot Creek Road (no sign). This turn is critical and difficult to find. If you have passed a small camping spot at the crossing of Depot Creek to your right, you have gone too far. Drive 2.5 miles on Depot Creek Road (stay left at the junction at 1.7 miles) and park in an open area at 2800 feet, where an intersecting side road to the right visibly leads to a broken-down bridge over nearby Depot Creek. (Note: It takes a high-clearance, 4WD vehicle to drive this final 2.5 miles on Depot Creek Road. There are a few pullouts in the first mile where a car could park or turn around. Many parties will prefer to walk on the road rather than risk damage to their car.)

TRIP DESCRIPTION: There are various ways to combine climbing the peaks of the Chilliwack Group. The following is a description of the easiest way to climb all six peaks in a single outing—an almost impossible task considering the international logistics, the effort required by the rugged terrain, the carrying of heavy equipment, and the need for sustained fine weather. But even if you do not complete the entire trip as written, you can break it up into as many outings as you need.

Approach to First Camp

From the intersection of the broken bridge on Depot Creek, continue walking on the main road. After about 200 yards, turn left and hike uphill on an intersecting road. Finding this road is critical to avoid bushwhacking. After another quarter mile, turn right at a T-junction. The road is now relatively flat for 2 miles to its end. This last 2 miles is heavily overgrown but is occasionally brushed out and suitable for hiking. From the end of the road, find a boot tread through a clearcut in the forest for about 200 yards into an old-growth forest. The clearcut is in Canada, the old growth is in the U.S., and at the border is a stone obelisk marker with a trail register. From the marker, the footpath becomes a defined but unmaintained trail southeast along Depot Creek valley. Many logs, some of which are quite large, cross the trail. Continue contouring upward through the dense forest to an opening. For 300 yards the trail goes through brush and willows just before a large waterfall. This area has been marked with cairns in the past. The way continues up along the waterfall, which may be a fine mist or raging torrent, depending on the snowmelt. To prevent soaking yourself and your pack, put on rain gear and pack cover just before arriving at the waterfall. Ascend a wet and slippery, 8-foot rocky step in the mist. Occasionally a hand line is present, on which you can pass up your pack on a prusik sling to a party member who has climbed the rock with the aid of the hand line. Quickly progress past the waterfall to dry rock. From here you can ascend on the way trail straight up into timber—a quick but slippery and slide-alder-obstructed route. Alternatively, aim diagonally up to the right on a less obvious way trail that is longer, but easier to manage. Both paths connect about 1000 feet above. The trail is better defined near the top of the waterfall where the valley flattens at 4800 feet. You can camp here in the valley next to Depot Creek.

Mt. Redoubt

The next morning begin hiking on a footpath that skirts the left edge of the valley. Rather than going to the small lake at the head of Depot Creek, cross the creek at 5100 feet, aiming for the scree- and boulder-covered hillside that angles up and then left onto the rocky buttress above the lake. This is the shortcut to attain the Redoubt Glacier at 6500 feet. Ascend rightward to attain the glacier. Rope up on the glacier and bear southwest to the saddle below the buttress of Mt. Redoubt (7800'). This low point can be walked over when the snow covers the ridge, but if the snow has melted, the crossover is a rock climb (class 5). Leave the packs at the base of the buttress and prepare a summit pack for the climb of Redoubt. After crossing through the saddle, contour west under the buttress. Look for the easiest slopes up, and then ascend moderately steep, open terrain into and up the high South Face cirque. Just above the top of the cirque is a rocky ramp, ascending gently from left to right. Follow the ramp to where it ends at a nearly vertical, shallow rock gully that is roughly 8 feet wide. Scramble up the gully system while trending to the left. At the top of the gully, exit left into a major gully and spot a cannon hole (a several-foot circular gap in the rock) through the mountain at the head of the major gully (about 100 feet away). Rope up and scramble to the cannon hole (beware of ice), and slide through it on your stomach. Come out on the steep north face very carefully, as the exposure here is precipitous with a sheer drop of

Cliff Leight

Pete Schoening and Mt. Redoubt

South side of Mt. Redoubt

nearly 3000 feet. Climb down a few feet to a ledge and walk northwest. Climb directly up to the summit on solid rock (class 4).

Some parties do not rope up on the ascent because the rock is firm and there are many obvious handholds. But most parties rappel from the summit back to the cannon hole. Make sure that you have a solid and backed-up rappel anchor. Be sure to back up the rappel slings left on the mountain with new slings while rappelling from the cannon hole over ice to the top of the ascent gully. Return down the route, pick up the packs, and continue on the Redoubt Glacier, traveling southeast to the edge of the glacier as it turns around the ridge that emanates west from Mox Peaks. At 7200 feet find a flat spot with sandy benches and water in summer. Make a camp here. If the party has the energy, continue farther east in a long traverse along the cirque on the south side of the West Ridge of Mox Peaks, and establish a camp near the remnant glacier at the col between the Mox Peaks spires.

Mox Peaks-Southeast Twin Spire

You will have to move aggressively to complete the climb of "Hard Mox" (Southeast Twin Spire) the next day. From the Redoubt Glacier camp traverse east, skirting below the rocky west ridge of Mox Peaks. Ascend the remnant glacier between the two peaks of Mox. Climb up snow or rock to the col between the two (8000'). Traverse southeast on the west face of the ridge that extends south from Mox Peaks, called the Ridge of Gendarmes. Go over the ridge. Go east along the ridge trending downward. You may see some cairns marking the way. Continue to where you can descend 180 feet down a steep gully (may have snow), then cross the rib to reach a sandy bench. Here you find the entrance to the main gully beaneath the west face of this spire. Go up 40 feet then take a right turn up the loose, dirty chimney with chockstones (class 4). Use helmets, as the rockfall danger here is extreme. Follow the system to the high notch in the ridge. From here variations exist to the top; all involve loose class 5 climbing, but areas for placing rock protection are available along the way. Climb a half rope length to where you can easily walk right. Instead, climb over the ridge to the left and continue climbing on the left side of the ridge-crest to another small notch (class 5). Walk left to the base of the steep gully (class 5) that leads to the summit. Rappel and downclimb to the base of the chockstone

SE Mox climbing route on left skyline

chimney. Retrace the route along the Ridge of Gendarmes, using short rappels as needed. Return to the Redoubt Glacier camp.

Mox Peaks-Northwest Twin Spire

Pack up camp, and prepare for the climb of the north ridge of "Easy Mox" (Northwest Twin Spire). Even though it is tempting to climb "Easy Mox" from the col between the spires of the Mox Peaks, the southeast face of "Easy Mox" is loose and treacherous. Most parties find that the longer way back over the north ridge of "Easy Mox" is more secure, and although longer in distance, is shorter in time and requires less travel on dangerously loose terrain.

Begin by traversing east from your camp, skirting the west ridge of Mox Peaks along the north margin for 1.5 miles while staying below two rock ribs. Since the glacier here is receding, it is best to climb early in the season to take advantage of snow bridges that fill some pronounced crevasses. Aim toward a low point in the northeast ridge at a snowcapped section. At the base of the snow finger that leads to the rock, take only a summit pack to finish the climb. Ascend the steep snow finger and exit to the rock; a moat may present a problem here. Climb a slab-rock pitch (class 4) to attain the ridge (7300'). Climb on the narrow ridge on relatively solid rock with blocky sections to a level area 200 feet from the summit. Descend left down a steep gully for 20 feet. Traverse to the east face directly below the summit. Climb a pitch of solid rock to a notch on the north side of the summit (class 4). A short rock pitch reaches the final summit rock.

Return to the low point on the ridge and rappel to your pack at the base of the snow finger. Set up camp at the lake at the headwaters of Depot Creek by retracing your steps onto the Redoubt Glacier and down the buttress on the southwest cirque above the lake. Carefully pick your way down an improbable route, descending northeast on small ledges to the lake (class 3). Either walk around the lake on the north side or, if the water is low, wade across the lake near its outlet, but beware: the water may be chest-deep here. Establish a camp on the northeast side of the lake on flat, sandy benches (5700').

Mt. Spickard

To climb Mt. Spickard the next morning, hike northeast from camp toward a pass that leads to Silver Lake. Well before the pass, at about

Dave LeBlanc

7000 feet, turn right and ascend the right side of a steep, rocky buttress onto a series of glacial moraines. Continue climbing on moderately steep snow slopes toward a low point in the south ridge of Spickard. Cross the saddle (8000') and descend about 50 feet. Traverse east across a large snowfield, keeping high to cross another rib, rounding the shoulder of the south ridge. Find a short, easy rock slope to cross onto the wide-open southeast slope. Ascend easy, then steep, open slopes that progress to gullies. Bring crampons for possible ice. The summit, on the north end of the ridge, can be reached through one of several gully systems (class 3). Return to the camp at the lake.

Climber on south side of Mt. Spickard

Dave LeBlanc

Mox Peaks

Mt. Rahm

Rahm and Custer can be combined in a single day, but the rough terrain can lead to a marathon of many hours. The trip is more leisurely if Rahm and Custer are done as two separate day trips. For Mt. Rahm, head up the gully trending northeast from camp to the glacier along the outlet of Silver Lake, then ascend to the relatively flat plateau along the lake's northwest edge. This ascent can be steep and on rotten rock, and requires some routefinding for the best path. Traverse at about 7500 feet, contouring above Silver Lake. At a break in the cliffs two thirds of the way along Silver Lake, attain the bowl below the summit of Rahm using a gully route that is extremely loose, and requires an airy step to enter when the snow is low (class 4). Climb up talus or snow into a small glacier bowl. The final push to the summit is on talus (class 2). Return to camp.

Mt. Custer

For Custer, from the lake travel northeast until about 6000 feet and then northwest below Point 8205 feet on the USGS map around the south shoulder of Custer Ridge. Enter a large basin at 6800 feet and then trend northeast to a higher basin at 7700 feet. From the upper basin, scramble north on loose talus to attain the ridge leading east to the summit of Custer (class 3).

HAZARDS AND TIPS: This multi-peak trip requires endurance, patience, and fortitude. Glacier gear and rock gear are both required. The terrain is rough and in many places very loose and treacherous. Helmets are mandatory on "Hard" Mox. The rappel descent off "Easy " Mox can be complicated by a moat. This trip should be attempted only in good weather. The best time for the trip is late July to mid-August, when the snow cover is adequate but most of the rock routes are free of snow. Due to its remote location, parties must be prepared to deal with emergencies since outside rescue could take days. Be sure to pack enough food.

GPS WAYPOINT ROUTE:

1. 10U 622294, 5428554, 1.5 miles, 2800': Canadian border
2. 10U 626418, 5425296, 4.0 miles, 5100': cross Depot Creek
3. 10U 626346, 5424632, 0.8 mile, 6500': Redoubt Glacier
4. 10U 624493, 5423949, 2.0 miles, 8969': Redoubt summit
5. 10U 625556, 5423077, 1.0 miles, 7200': Redoubt Glacier camp
6. 10U 627435, 5422625, 1.5 miles, 8000': Ridge of Gendarmes
7. 10U 627735, 5422833, 0.8 mile, 8504': "Hard" Mox (SE) summit
8. 10U 627719, 5423512, 4.0 miles, 7300': Mox Peaks northeast ridge
9. 10U 627318, 5422997, 0.5 mile, 8407': "Easy" Mox (NW) summit
10. 10U 627185, 5424759, 2.0 miles, 5700': lake camp
11. 10U 628535, 5424888, 1.5 miles, 8000': Spickard south ridge saddle
12. 10U 628861, 5425384, 0.7 mile, 8979': Spickard summit
13. 10U 629663, 5428455, 5.3 miles, 8478': Rahm summit
14. 10U 627009, 5426385, 4.3 miles, 6800': lower Custer basin
15. 10U 628138, 5427496, 1.2 miles, 8630': Custer summit

TRIP TIMES:

Cross Depot Creek to Redoubt summit: 2.8 miles, 3900', 6 hours
Redoubt Glacier camp to "Hard" Mox (SE) summit: 2.0 miles, 1600', 9 hours
Redoubt Glacier camp to "Easy" Mox (NW) summit: 2.2 miles, 1200', 6 hours
Lake camp to Spickard summit: 2.2 miles, 3300', 5 hours
Lake camp to Rahm summit: 3.1 miles, 2800', 6 hours
Lake camp to Custer summit: 2.4 miles, 2900', 5 hours

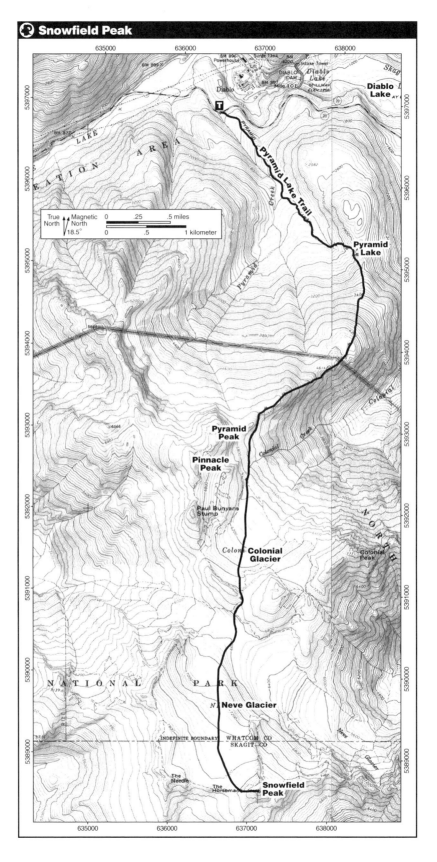

ROUTE 7

Snowfield Peak

ELEVATION: 8347' (2544 m)

CLIMBING ROUTE: Neve Glacier

DISTANCE: 15 miles

ELEVATION GAIN: 7600'

DAYS: 2

MAPS: USGS Diablo Dam, Ross Dam; Green Trails Diablo Dam No. 48

RATING: E3T3

LOCATION: Ross Lake National Recreation Area and North Cascades National Park, Marblemount Ranger Station

PERMITS: Permits are required to camp in Ross Lake National Recreation Area and North Cascades National Park; register for the climb at the Wilderness Information Center at the Marblemount Ranger Station.

Snowfield Peak from the north

Paul Bunyan's Stump, Pinnacle and Pyramid peaks

SUMMARY AND HIGHLIGHTS: Snowfield Peak is the triangular-shaped apex of the sub-range of the Cascade Crest just southwest of Diablo Lake. A small but distinctive group of peaks, the sub-range contains the familiar faces of Pyramid and Colonial peaks and Paul Bunyan's Stump, all visible from North Cascades Scenic Highway. The approach to Snowfield Peak along the Pyramid Lake Trail is steep but short. The entry into this high alpine region is therefore relatively straightforward, and there's excellent camping along the ridge of Pyramid Peak.

The Neve Glacier extends high on the northern slope of Snowfield Peak. The trek on the glacier is sustained, but moderate. A scramble finishes the final push to the summit. From the top of Snowfield you can view the panorama of the major giants of the region—from Buckner Mountain and Forbidden Peak in the background to Austera Peak, Dorado Needle, and Eldorado Peak in the foreground. This trip is best done early in the season when snow covers some of the brush along the approach. A weekend trip allows most climbers to explore the surrounding circle of interesting formations before returning home.

HOW TO GET THERE: From Interstate 5 head east on Highway 20 and stop at the Marblemount Ranger Station to register and obtain a camping permit. Continue east past Newhalem for 6.4 miles on Highway 20 to the Pyramid Lake Trail No. 770 trailhead (1100').

TRIP DESCRIPTION: Follow the Pyramid Lake Trail to Pyramid Lake. Although a climber's trail goes around each side of the lake, a more defined path is on the western side. From the south end of the lake, ascend south to join a ridge trending southwest toward Pyramid Peak. At 5400 feet find good campsites. Alternatively, continue to about 5900 feet to camp higher on the Colonial Glacier, although it may be hard to find a better campsite on the steep slope. Be sure to pack out human waste.

The next morning continue south on the Colonial Glacier to a pass at 6900 feet. Descend about 300 feet to the Neve Glacier. Aim toward The Horseman, a notable rock spire to the south. At about 7700 feet attain the west ridge of Snowfield Peak. Scramble up the west ridge to 8200 feet and go north into a gully. Go up the gully about half way and exit on the left (north) side. Climb up a ramp to a notch in the ridge. Here move to the south to attain the summit block (class 4). The final path is easy to the summit.

HAZARDS AND TIPS: Glacier gear is required. The summit block is exposed and a rope is recommended.

GPS WAYPOINT ROUTE:

1. 10U 636518, 5396658, 1100': Pyramid Lake Trailhead
2. 10U 638170, 5395048, 2.1 miles, 2600': Pyramid Lake
3. 10U 638184, 5393821, 1.0 mile, 4400': ridge
4. 10U 637278, 5393109, 0.8 mile, 5400': low camp
5. 10U 636992, 5392162, 0.7 mile, 5900': high camp
6. 10U 636945, 5390744, 1.0 mile, 6900': pass
7. 10U 636888, 5388396, 1.5 miles, 7700': west ridge
8. 10U 637236, 5388378, 0.4 mile, 8347': Snowfield summit

TRIP TIMES:

Pyramid Lake Trailhead to low camp: 3.9 miles, 4300', 6 hours
Low camp to Snowfield summit: 3.6 miles, 3000', 5 hours

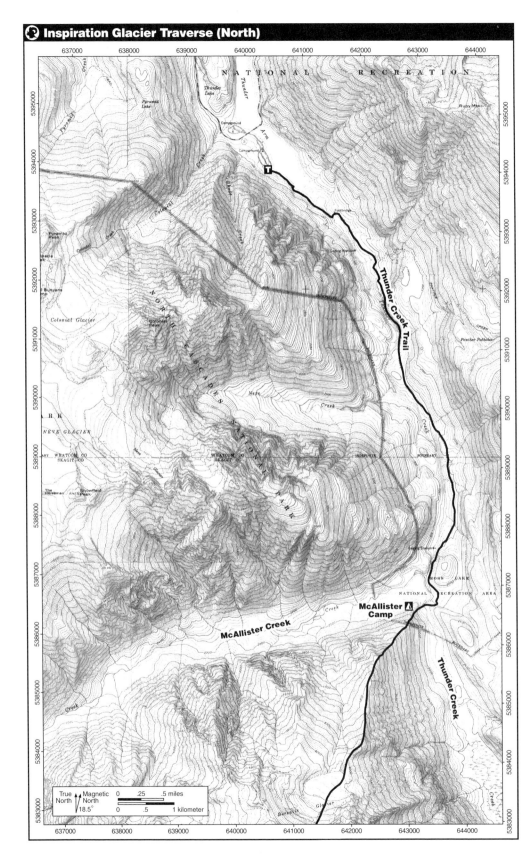

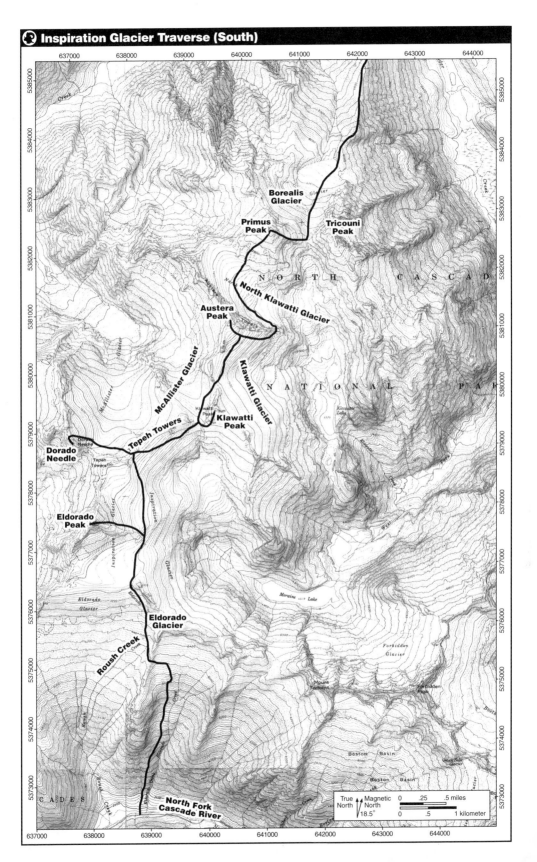

Inspiration Glacier Traverse (South)

Borealis
Glacier

Primus
Peak

Tricouni
Peak

N O R T H   C A S C A D

North Klawatti Glacier

Austera
Peak

McAllister Glacier

Klawatti Glacier

N A T I O N A L   P A

Klawatti
Peak

Tepeh Towers

Dorado
Needle

Tepeh
Towers

Eldorado
Peak

Inspiration Glacier

Eldorado
Glacier

Moraine Lake

Forbidden
Glacier

Roush Creek

Mount
Torment

Forbidden
Peak

Boston Basin

Boston Basin

C A D E S

North Fork
Cascade River

True Magnetic | 0   .25   .5 miles
North North |
       18.5° | 0   .5   1 kilometer

ROUTE 8

Inspiration Glacier Traverse

Primus Peak, Austera Peak, Klawatti Peak, Dorado Needle,
Eldorado Peak

ELEVATIONS: 8508', 8334', 8485', 8440+', 8868' (2593 m, 2540 m, 2586 m, 2573+ m, 2703 m)

DISTANCE: 23 miles

ELEVATION GAIN: 11,600'

DAYS: At least 6

MAPS: USGS Ross Dam, Forbidden Peak, Eldorado Peak, Cascade Pass; Green Trails Diablo Dam No. 48, Cascade Pass No. 80

RATING: E5T5

LOCATION: Ross Lake National Recreation Area and North Cascades National Park, Marblemount Ranger Station

PERMITS: Permits are required to camp in Ross Lake National Recreation Area and North Cascades National Park; register for the climb at the Wilderness Information Center at the Marblemount Ranger Station.

SUMMARY AND HIGHLIGHTS: The expansive sheets of ice that form the Inspiration, Klawatti, and McAllister glaciers of the Cascade Crest region create a mountainous setting as savage and pristine as any in Washington. An extended outing following ridgelines and then traversing the course of these multiple glaciers is an experience not soon forgotten. Intense alpine glaciation has resulted in many cols between pinnacles in the plateau, where constantly active ice and weather sculpt the landscape into otherworldly forms. It is a realm of staggering brilliance, of stark contrast between the blackness of the protruding, serrated rock crests and the seemingly endless and blinding expanse of white glacier and snow.

A major portion of the trip follows the course of the Inspiration Glacier, which occupies the large accumulation basin east of Eldorado Peak and drains into the West Fork of Thunder Creek. Climbing the series of summits along the way can be accomplished with a series of peak-bagging days, interspersed with rest days at scenic, elevated camps on glacial terrain among nunataks (protuberances of rock through the ice) and towers. The difficulty ranges from Primus Peak, a moderately sloping, glacier-clad mound offering few technical difficulties, to Dorado Needle, a pyramidal rock formation with technical portions and an exposed but short *cheval* (a travel technique involving mounting a knife-ridge as if riding a horse) pitch to reach the summit. But to most, Eldorado, with its breathtakingly exposed snow crest at the summit, is the most compelling experience. A tale among mountaineers says that should a slip occur here, the only way to arrest the fall of a rope team member is for another member to jump off the other side of the knife-ridge to counterbalance the weight of the falling climber.

The best way to tackle this extended high traverse is to begin with a strenuous bushwhack up the extended northeast ridge of Tricouni Peak, and end with a descent from Eldorado Peak down the Eldorado Glacier to the Cascade River. This way the boulder-hopping between the high country and the road is done on the way down rather than the way up, and routefinding on this segment is kept to a minimum—although in recent years the climber's trail has become better defined.

The Inspiration Glacier Traverse takes time as well as a car shuttle. The logistics are more complicated than for most trips, but the prolonged and challenging routefinding over massive ice fields creates a classic and highly memorable glacier trek. While you negotiate the vast expanse of the glaciers, the panorama of the entire Cascade Crest unfolds from

Keith Wilson

On Inspiration Glacier with Mt. Logan in background

Canada to Mt. Rainier. The view from the trek affords a vantage of
Forbidden Peak and Buckner Mountain immediately to the southeast,
with the sharp pyramid of Goode's summit hovering in the background.
Across the deep hole of Thunder Creek to the east sits massive Mt.
Logan, while to the south you can see the peaks along the Ptarmigan
Traverse. The power of the landscape, compounded by elegant travel
over highly glaciated terrain, is most extraordinary.

HOW TO GET THERE: A car shuttle is required, leaving one vehicle at
the terminus. Drive on Interstate 5 just north of Mount Vernon. Turn
right on the North Cascades Scenic Highway (State Route 20). Drive east
47 miles to Marblemount. Stop at the Marblemount Ranger Station to
register for the climb and obtain permits. From Marblemount head east
on the Cascade River Road for 19.8 miles and park one vehicle in the
large, flat clearing (downslope from the Roush Creek basin) on the right
side of the road (2100'). Return in one vehicle to Marblemount. Drive
east on the North Cascades Highway for 23 miles to Colonial Creek
Campground. Park here and find the Thunder Creek Trailhead (1200').

TRIP DESCRIPTION: Hike on Thunder Creek Trail for 6.4 miles. Turn
right and cross Thunder Creek on the bridge that leads to McAllister
Camp (1900'). Execute a southwest ascent along the top of the long,
brushy ridge to timberline. Make a camp near the snout of the Borealis
Glacier on a knob at 6000 feet. This long approach is difficult and requires some navigation around cliff bands to reach the top.

Primus Peak

To attain Primus Peak, pack up your gear in the morning and ascend
the Borealis Glacier at its eastern edge to avoid an icefall near the center.
Climb to the saddle between Primus Peak and Tricouni Peak, called
Lucky Pass (7200'). Anyone with extra energy can climb Tricouni Peak
from Lucky Pass (class 3). From Lucky Pass ascend west with full packs
directly up to the summit of Primus Peak (class 2). Descend southwest
onto the North Klawatti Glacier. Cross the glacier, heading southeast to
a low point on the east ridge of Austera. Cross the ridge at 7200 feet.
Descend slightly to find a camp on rock or snow above the lower portion of the North Klawatti Glacier. Alternatively, in good weather you
can camp at Lucky Pass or on the summit of Primus.

Austera Peak

From camp the next day, ascend the Klawatti Glacier to the south
slope of Austera Peak (additional good camps here). At about 8200
feet, drop the packs in favor of a daypack with a rope and a small rack
for rock protection. Climb the snow slope to its highest point and then

ascend left (northwest) to the south ridge. Follow the ridge, dropping into a sandy notch just below the summit. Climb a short chimney with a chockstone (class 5), then 25 feet of rock to the summit (class 3). An alternative to the chimney is to circle counterclockwise out of the sandy notch and up around a small pinnacle, which has good hand holds but ample exposure (class 4), to complete a corkscrew, ending at a point above the chockstone. Some parties may want a hand line or a short rappel on the descent. Return to the packs and continue south along the Klawatti Glacier to the col on the north ridge of Klawatti Peak (7900'). You can find a good camp here or, alternatively, cross over to the McAllister Glacier and travel south to the saddle between Klawatti Peak and Tepeh Towers (7800'). A camp can be made here at Klawatti Col on snow, on a bench, or on granite, with nearby running water.

Klawatti Peak

The next day bring only a daypack with a rope and a small rock-climbing rack for scaling Klawatti Peak. Travel east on the Inspiration Glacier, skirting the south slope of Klawatti. Climb the highest snow above the glacier, which is steep and prone to avalanches in spring and early summer, to the south face (8100'). In late season the face may be blocked by a moat. Ascend the snow, or cross the moat to climb up a short pitch to get onto the south face (class 5). Scramble leftward (westward) on steep snow or loose scree. Alternatively, go straight up a steep gully (class 4) that is filled with snow in early summer. At the summit ridge scramble on blocks to the top (class 3). Return to camp at Klawatti Col.

Dorado Needle

The next day traverse southwest, then west along the Inspiration Glacier below the Tepeh Towers to a broad, flat saddle (8000'). Leave your packs and prepare a daypack for the climb of Dorado Needle with a rack for rock protection. Drop down 600 feet onto the McAllister Glacier, then make an ascending traverse to the northwest. Climb up on steep snow to the north ridge of Dorado Needle. In late summer, a moat may present an obstacle getting onto the rock. Climb up the rock of the north ridge to a notch at 8300 feet (class 5). The interesting feature of the ridge route is the rising, 20-foot, knife-edged cheval with striking exposure on both sides. You may want to straddle it to maintain your balance. A mantle move over a 7-foot pedestal puts you onto the summit block (class 3). Rappel or downclimb the route and return to your packs. Travel south on the Inspiration Glacier to make a camp at the base of the east ridge of Eldorado Peak (7500'). Rock outcrops provide fine camps in summer.

Eldorado Peak

Start early the next day. Traverse west on the Inspiration Glacier and then ascend the broad, snow-covered ridge to the top of Eldorado. The last push is a classic knife-edge of snow that leads to the summit, then down a few feet to the safer rocks beyond. Descend to camp and pack to go out.

To the Shuttle Car

The route descends south across the Eldorado Glacier; stay just west of Point 7733 and its south ridge. Drop down the snow slopes along the rocky ridge into the upper Roush Creek basin. At about 6100 feet, look for a

Dorado Needle Basecamp, east of Eldorado on Inspiration Glacier

climber's trail that ascends steeply to the left onto the ridge where it levels out below a large buttress. Scramble east about 100 feet up and over the ridge and drop into Eldorado Creek basin. Descend snow, talus, or heather to the break in the short cliffs, then go down through scrubby trees and past waterfalls on a faint trail. Severe erosion on the route between 5100 and 5500 feet has led park rangers to reroute boot traffic away from this section and to replant the eroded gullies. The new route is marked by a large cairn at both top and bottom. It is critical that you use the new route to give the newly planted and fragile alpine greenery a chance to establish itself. At approximately 5100 feet there is a large, flagged cairn near an obvious waterfall section, marking the suggested place to cross the creek as you leave the subalpine zone and begin the upper talus section. Follow the trail down along brush into the huge field of blocks and talus. This region usually has cairns and flags. Descend talus, and then go down a steep trail in timber within earshot of Eldorado Creek until it levels out as it approaches the North Fork

Cascade River. Finally, go right (west) to a large log that crosses the river. The crossing is sometimes marked and is noted by a clump of three trees on the other side. After crossing, go upstream about 90 feet along the road to find the parking area.

HAZARDS AND TIPS: The trip as described is strenuous and demanding. But it can be broken down into portions to make it more manageable. Very few parties have the time, good weather, or endurance to complete the entire agenda. However, this description is the shortest and most economical (in time and effort) way to attain all the peaks. Glacier and rock-climbing gear are required as well as accomplished routefinding skills on glacial terrain. Snow sluffs and small avalanches are common on Klawatti before the snow has consolidated. The boulder-field descent from Eldorado Peak is treacherous and slippery when wet.

GPS WAYPOINT ROUTE:
1. 10U 640462, 5394027, 1200': Thunder Creek Trailhead
2. 10U 643282, 5386642, 6.4 miles, 1900': Thunder Creek bridge
3. 10U 641994, 5383742, 2.2 miles, 6000': Borealis Glacier
4. 10U 641480, 5382393, 1.0 mile, 7200': Lucky Pass
5. 10U 640831, 5382540, 0.5 mile, 8508': Primus summit
6. 10U 640911, 5380853, 1.4 miles, 7200': Austera east ridge
7. 10U 640163, 5381013, 0.6 mile, 8334': Austera summit
8. 10U 639919, 5379921, 0.9 mile, 7900': Klawatti north ridge
9. 10U 639626, 5379273, 0.5 mile, 7800': Klawatti Col
10. 10U 639983, 5379315, 0.2 mile, 8100': Klawatti south face
11. 10U 639957, 5379466, 0.3 mile, 8485': Klawatti summit
12. 10U 638541, 5378721, 1.4 miles, 8000': saddle
13. 10U 637358, 5378989, 0.8 mile, 8300': Dorado Needle ridge
14. 10U 637453, 5378878, 0.2 mile, 8440+': Dorado Needle summit
15. 10U 638756, 5377266, 2.0 miles, 7500': Eldorado east ridge
16. 10U 637801, 5377507, 0.7 mile, 8868': Eldorado summit
17. 10U 638357, 5375446, 1.9 miles, 6100': Roush Creek basin
18. 10U 638558, 5372562, 2.0 miles, 2100': Cascade River Road

TRIP TIMES:
Thunder Creek Trailhead to Borealis Glacier: 8.6 miles, 4800', 10 hours

Borealis Glacier to Primus summit: 1.5 miles, 2500', 4 hours

Austera East Ridge to Austera summit: 0.6 mile, 1200', 3 hours

Klawatti Col to Klawatti summit: 0.5 mile, 700', 4 hours

Klawatti Col to Dorado Needle summit: 2.0 miles, 1000', 6 hours

Eldorado East Ridge to Eldorado summit: 0.7 mile, 1400', 3 hours

Chris Weidner

In the moat next to the couloir on Forbidden Peak

CHAPTER 3
Cascade Pass

Cascade Pass is one of the most historic and visually stirring mountain regions in Washington. As the entryway to the core of the North Cascades, the pass begins the rhythm of peaks and valleys that unfolds in every direction. Though deep in the heart of the range, it is relatively easy to access by driving the Cascade River Road for 22 miles from the town of Marblemount to the start of the Cascade Pass Trail. Rising on moderate switchbacks in 4 miles to 5392-foot Cascade Pass, the tread then descends through the upper Stehekin River valley to Cottonwood Camp. A road connects the camp to Stehekin on Lake Chelan, thus completing a scenic overland hiking connection from the western to the eastern side of the mountains. Cascade Pass is also the starting point for the famous Ptarmigan Traverse, a popular high route along multiple glaciers to the south.

For centuries Native Americans used Cascade Pass as a thoroughfare. Unfortunately, much of their culture and history regarding the pass has vanished. The first well-documented non-native crossing of Cascade Pass occurred in 1877 by an expedition organized by Otto Klement to investigate a gold claim in the Methow Valley. He commented on "mountains piled upon mountains, stretching away in every direction." Explorers and fur traders later traversed the Cascades using the pass. But the area wasn't thoroughly explored until 1889, when prospectors George L. Rowse (also spelled Rouse), John C. Rouse, and Gilbert Landre explored the Cascade River district. While tracing ledges etched by the glaciers of Horseshoe Basin and then along the rim of Doubtful Basin, they established the claim that was to become the Boston Mine. Little prospecting was done near Cascade Pass until trails were built in the early 1890s, opening a route for horses. After that, mining flourished in Boston Basin, on Johannesburg Mountain, along the Middle Fork of the Cascade River, and in Horseshoe Basin, where the Black Warrior Mine operated until 1948. Mining buffs can still find relics in the region, though some believe the mines were little more than a boondoggle for money and jobs with little prospect of actually producing a profit.

Here great peaks stand solitary or in compact, isolated groups. The terrain is known for vast and wild glaciers, which contrast sharply with sublime alpine meadows. Most spectacular is a massive glacier that occupies a broad cirque between Forbidden Peak and Buckner Mountain—

Dave LeBlanc

Sahale Arm near Cascade Pass

the Boston Glacier, the largest single glacier in the North Cascades. Every peak is clad in some degree of glaciated splendor, creating a striking scene of brilliant ice patches among grand and rugged terrain. There is also a dramatic contrast between the jagged alpine slopes dotted with small, picturesque stands of hemlock flanking mountain parapets, and the forested depths of the Cascade River watershed, clad with Douglas fir, western red cedar, and Pacific silver fir, all typical of a maritime forest.

Today the Cascade Pass area is protected by the North Cascades National Park. Permits are required for all overnight stays in the backcountry. They are issued in person only, on the day before or the first day of the trip, at the Wilderness Information Center at the ranger station in Marblemount. Self-registration is not allowed for heavily used areas. During July and August, the Cascade Pass area fills quickly on weekends. If possible, plan your trip here on weekdays or after Labor Day. Be flexible; have alternatives in mind in case you are not able to get a permit for the climb you planned. Camping is not allowed at Cascade Pass, Sahale Arm, Mix-up Arm, or Doubtful Basin. Once the insulating snow blanket disappears in summer, the sparsely vegetated alpine soils are highly vulnerable to erosion. Therefore every climber must carefully observe Leave No Trace camping ethics, and follow the rules of the national park.

Because so many climbers come safely to this region, you may underestimate the seriousness of some of the alpine routes and their potential hazards. In recent decades the Cascade Pass area has seen an

Ed Cooper

Mt. Formidable, Cache Col and Gunsight Notch

increasing number and variety of accidents, with fatalities occurring on almost every peak. Many climbs in this sector can be accomplished with basic-level skills (see definition on page 3), but some require more extensive experience and competence. Do not attempt a peak that is too difficult for your ability level, and always be prepared to deal with the potential harshness of the unforgiving alpine environment.

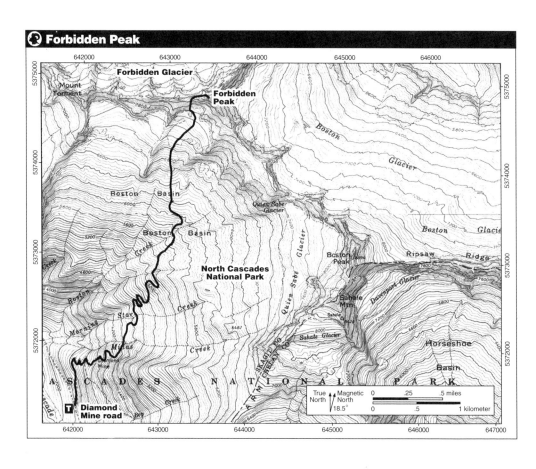

Forbidden Peak

Forbidden Glacier

Mount Torment

Forbidden Peak

Boston Basin

Boston Basin

Boston Creek

North Cascades National Park

Boston Glacier

Quien Sabe Glacier

Quien Sabe Glacier

Boston Glacier

Boston Peak

Ripsaw Ridge

Davenport Glacier

Sahale Mtn

Sahale Glacier

Horseshoe Basin

Midas Creek

Star Creek

Morning Star

CASCADES   NATIONAL   PARK

Diamond Mine

Diamond Mine road

Cascade Creek

Boston Creek

True North   Magnetic North   18.5°

0   .25   .5 miles

0   .5   1 kilometer

Forbidden Peak

ELEVATION: 8815' (2687 m)

CLIMBING ROUTE: West Ridge

DISTANCE: 10 miles

ELEVATION GAIN: 5700'

DAYS: 2–3

MAPS: USGS Cascade Pass, Forbidden Peak; Green Trails Cascade Pass No. 80, Diablo Dam No. 48

RATING: E2T5

LOCATION: North Cascades National Park, Marblemount Ranger Station

PERMITS: Permits are required to camp in North Cascades National Park and are issued in-person only, on the first day of the trip or the day before. Permits for the Cascade Pass area must be obtained at the Wilderness Information Center at the Ranger Station in Marblemount during operating hours. Because permits for this area are in demand during the summer months, try to plan your trip for weekdays to more easily obtain a permit to camp in Boston Basin.

SUMMARY AND HIGHLIGHTS: The climbs in the watershed of the North Fork Cascade River are some of the most popular in Washington due to their relatively easy access and splendid alpine landscape. The most outstanding example is Forbidden Peak. The rock is firm and the summit is one of the finest and most favored in the range. Forbidden Peak is known for its angular appearance, with three sharp ridges emanating from its spiked top. A monster mountain, Forbidden is set apart from the mass of ice and jagged spires at its sides by an impressive amount of airy exposure.

There are several common routes to the top, but the most traveled is the West Ridge, a moderate rock climb within the ability of many climbers. To some the crux is the 40- to 50-degree snow couloir on the approach that qualifies as a "no-fall" zone. After early summer, a bergschrund at the end of the snow finger can prevent easy access to the rock portion of the route. In addition, there is no simple way down Forbidden

Peak. Most parties choose to downclimb the West Ridge while the leader is on belay. Many climbing parties also choose to rappel the snow couloir rather than plunge-step down the steep slope, particularly when the snow condition is poor. Forbidden demands skill and quick responses. More than a few parties have been forced to bivouac when time ran out. Because of the hazards, scaling this peak is a substantial accomplishment and highly worth considering.

HOW TO GET THERE: Drive north on Interstate 5 to the North Cascades Scenic Highway (State Route 20). Drive east 47 miles to Marblemount. Stop at the Marblemount Ranger Station to register for the climb and obtain permits. In the town at the junction, go right (east) on Cascade River Road for 21.7 miles to a fork in the road about 0.5 mile from the road's end. There is limited parking here for the trail to Boston Basin (3200').

TRIP DESCRIPTION: Hike on the abandoned Diamond Mine road. In less than a mile a well-defined climber's trail leaves the road to the right and then ascends steeply through open slopes, then through trees. The trail traverses north over potentially difficult stream crossings. In 2002 the route was nearly destroyed in parts by avalanche debris—large trees and rocks to crawl over. You reach Boston Basin at 5600 feet. Campsites and a toilet are behind the moraine. Continue on the trail, going north past a grassy moraine. At the upper basin find established camps on a flat sandy bench equipped with a composting toilet (6200'). You may camp in Boston Basin as long as you are on rock or snow and not on vegetation of any type. The established camps are highly recommended because of the nearby toilets. Otherwise, you are requested to pack out your solid waste in plastic bags.

The next morning from your camp in Boston Basin, ascend the unnamed glacier to the cirque beneath the 500-foot couloir leading to the West Ridge. In early season the couloir is a 40- to 50-degree snow slope. In later season, a bergschrund or ice may force you to bypass the lower portion of the couloir by using steep gullies to its left to eventually attain the upper snow finger or the lower west ridge (class 4). Either snow or a gully then leads to the ridgecrest. Attain the West Ridge near the notch where the couloir joins the ridge. If you are planning to descend the climbing route on your return, you can put on climbing shoes and leave your boots here. The climbing on the ridge is exposed, but generally solid and blocky with adequate stances for belays and anchors (class 5). Eight pitches of roped climbing are common, although some parties use running belays. Bypass towers and gendarmes (spiky pinnacles on the ridge) by crossing to the north face. This is particularly right for the

Chris Weidner

Rappelling down the couloir on Forbidden Peak

Ed Cooper

Forbidden Peak from Sahale Peak

tower that is about 175 feet below the summit. A piton protects the north side of the tower and leads to a belay station at the top of the step. From the west high point farther along the ridge, drop north into a small notch and bypass the west peak (class 5). You can bypass the tower, the step, and the west peak by traversing lower on the north face (class 4). From the notch between the summits, scramble to the true east summit.

Although Forbidden has several descent routes, the best is to descend back down the West Ridge. The East Ridge descent route on the east face is quicker but leads to a series of ledges that can be difficult to navigate. By descending down the West Ridge climbing route, the party is familiar with the route and can climb the ridge in rock shoes, leaving boots behind to be picked up on the return. Use a combination of down-climbing with belays and short rappels. Rappel the entire West Ridge couloir to the glacier using two double rope rappels. Alternatively, rappel the gully to the west of the couloir to attain the glacier.

HAZARDS AND TIPS: Camp only on snow, rock, or established campsites in Boston Basin. Plan in advance to be at the ranger station in Marblemount early in the morning of the first day of your climb or the afternoon before in order to obtain a permit. Glacier gear and a rack for low class 5 rock climbing are required. Helmets are essential. Due to the bergschrund and potential moat problems at the couloir, this trip is best done early in the season (late June to the end of July) just after the road is open to the trailhead. Expect difficult stream crossings in Boston Basin. Major parts of the boot path may be obstructed or destroyed by avalanche debris. Double ropes are recommended for the rappel down the snow couloir on the return. If you attempt this climb in late season, the rappel anchors for the couloir may be too high to reach due to melted snow. You may want to plan a leisurely three days for the trip due to the time that is required to negotiate the couloir and downclimb the West Ridge. However, most experienced parties will find that two days are sufficient.

GPS WAYPOINT ROUTE:
    1. 10U 642018, 5371237, 3200': Diamond Mine road
    2. 10U 643099, 5372904, 3.2 miles, 5600': Boston Basin low camp
    3. 10U 643173, 5373628, 0.6 mile, 6200': high camp
    4. 10U 643311, 5374636, 0.8 mile, 7800': couloir
    5. 10U 643346, 5374773, 0.2 mile, 8300': West Ridge
    6. 10U 643487, 5374798, 0.4 mile, 8815': Forbidden summit

TRIP TIMES:
    Diamond Mine road to high camp: 3.8 miles, 3000', 5 hours
    High camp to Forbidden summit: 1.4 miles, 2600', 7 hours

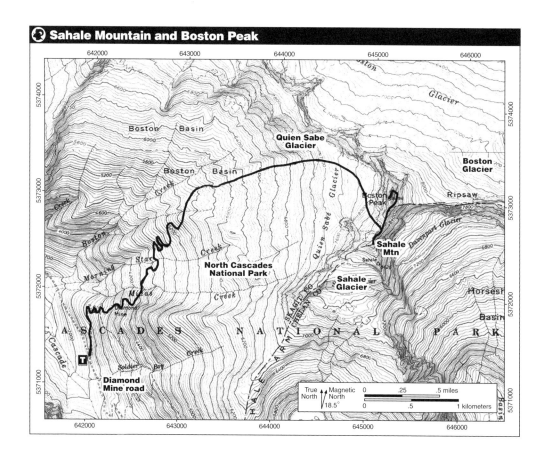

Sahale Mountain and Boston Peak

Boston Basin

Quien Sabe
Glacier

Boston
Glacier

Boston Basin

Glacier

Creek

Boston
Peak

Ripsaw

Quien Sabe Glacier

Boston

Creek

Sahale
Mtn

Davenport Glacier

Star

Creek

North Cascades
National Park

Sahale
Glacier

Horsesh

Morning

Creek

Midas

SKAGIT CO
CHELAN CO

Basin

Mine

CASCADES

NATIONAL

PARK

Cascade

Creek

Soldier

Boy

T

Diamond
Mine road

True
North

Magnetic
North

18.5°

0   .25   .5 miles

0   .5   1 kilometers

Sahale Mountain and Boston Peak

ELEVATION: 8680+', 8894' (2646+ m, 2711 m)

CLIMBING ROUTES: Sahale: Quien Sabe Glacier; Boston: Northeast Ridge

DISTANCE: 12 miles

ELEVATION GAIN: 6200'

DAYS: 2

MAPS: USGS Cascade Pass; Green Trails Cascade Pass No. 80

RATING: E2T4

LOCATION: North Cascades National Park, Marblemount Ranger Station

PERMITS: Permits are required to camp in North Cascades National Park and are issued in-person only, on the first day of the trip or the day before. Because permits for this area are in demand during the summer months, you must plan in advance to arrive early in the morning the day of your climb or the afternoon before at the ranger station in Marblemount to obtain a permit to camp in Boston Basin. Alternatively try to schedule your trip for midweek.

SUMMARY AND HIGHLIGHTS: Sahale Mountain is one of the most popular summits in the North Cascades not only because it is relatively simple and safe to climb, but also because it provides stunning views of the Cascade Pass region. Sahale is climbed either from the Sahale Arm, which extends north from Cascade Pass, or from Boston Basin, the wide alpine meadow north of Sahale Arm. Connected to Sahale by a broad saddle, Boston Peak is even more massive and impressive. The name of the mountain was derived from the Boston Mine and the largest glacier in the region—the Boston Glacier—which occupies the huge cirque to the north and east. Boston Peak is not climbed as often as Sahale, mainly because the rock on the steep summit section on the southern flank is extremely loose (proving fatal for one climber). But you can find easier terrain if you circle around the summit and reach it via the north ridge. Because you can readily reach the Sahale-Boston col from the summit block of Sahale or the false summit of Boston, a combination of both

Ed Cooper

Boston Peak from Sahale Peak

mountains on an extended summit day is desirable, as they use the same approach from Boston Basin to the col.

HOW TO GET THERE: Drive north on Interstate 5 to the North Cascades Scenic Highway (State Route 20). Drive east 47 miles to Marblemount. Stop at the Marblemount Ranger Station to register for the climb and obtain permits. In the town at the junction, go right (east) on Cascade River Road 21.7 miles to a fork in the road about 0.5 mile from the road's end. There is limited parking here for the trail to Boston Basin on the abandoned Diamond Mine road (3200').

TRIP DESCRIPTION: Use the Forbidden Peak approach (see Trip 9) into Boston Basin to set up camp at 5600 feet.

Sahale Mountain

The easiest ascent route is to climb the left side of the Quien Sabe Glacier to the base of Sharkfin Tower, a striking rock formation along the ridge rimming the glacier. Traverse to your right along the base of the rock face until the glacier steepens at the col between Boston and Sahale.

Climb to the col, avoiding crevasses that form at the base of the slope. Go to your right toward the summit block of Sahale on a short and exposed snow traverse. Be careful to avoid the cornice that forms on the north side and lasts into summer. Attain the summit block at the ridge and climb on loose rock to the summit (class 3).

Boston Peak

From Sahale Mountain rappel and downclimb back to the col between Sahale and Boston. Continue northwest up the ridge and climb over the false summit of Boston and then immediately drop over to the north face and trend downward on a ledge that leads to the tip of the Boston Glacier on the east side of the peak (class 3). Descend north for about 200 vertical feet on steep snow on the western edge of the Boston Glacier to a rib where the rock is not as steep. A bergschrund or moat may present a problem here. Attain the northeast ridge on large, blocky, loose rocks and travel south on the exposed ridge back to the south end of the summit block (class 3). From the summit, rappel straight off to the high point of the Boston Glacier, using three single-rope rappels. Return to camp by retracing your steps over the false summit of Boston Peak and then to the col between Boston and Sahale.

HAZARDS AND TIPS: Glacier gear is required. The rock on Boston is particularly loose and hazardous, and helmets are mandatory.

GPS WAYPOINT ROUTE:
1. 10U 642018, 5371237, 3200': Diamond Mine road
2. 10U 643099, 5372904, 3.2 miles, 5600': Boston Basin low camp
3. 10U 644403, 5373404, 1.0 mile, 7400': Quien Sabe Glacier
4. 10U 645095, 5372716, 0.9 mile, 8500': col
5. 10U 645012, 5372545, 0.2 mile, 8680+': Sahale summit
6. 10U 645240, 5372973, 0.5 mile, 8500': Boston Glacier
7. 10U 645184, 5373044, 0.4 mile, 8894': Boston summit

TRIP TIMES:
Diamond Mine road to Boston Basin low camp: 3.2 miles, 2400', 4 hours

Boston Basin low camp to Sahale summit: 2.1 miles, 3100', 5 hours

Sahale summit to Boston summit: 0.9 mile, 700', 4 hours

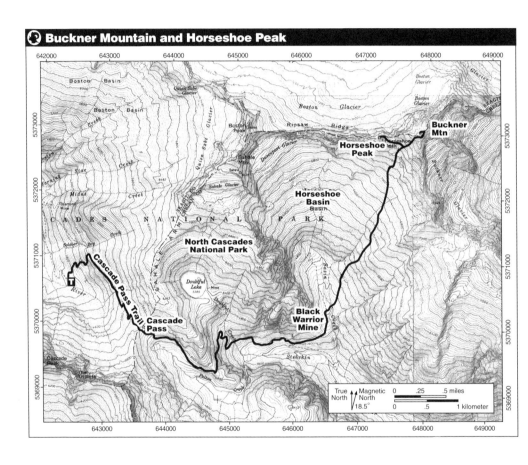

Buckner Mountain and Horseshoe Peak

Boston Basin

Boston Basin

Boston Glacier

Glacier

Boston Glacier

Boston Glacier

Buckner Mtn

Boston Peak

Ripsaw Ridge

Horseshoe Peak

Sahale Mtn

Horseshoe Basin

C A D E S   N A T I O N A L   P A R K

North Cascades National Park

Doubtful Lake

Black Warrior Mine

Cascade Pass Trail

Cascade Pass

Stehekin

True North | Magnetic North | 18.5°

0   .25   .5 miles

0   .5   1 kilometer

ROUTE 11

Buckner Mountain
and Horseshoe Peak

ELEVATION: 9112+', 8480+' (2778+ m, 2585+ m)

CLIMBING ROUTES: Buckner: Southwest Face; Horseshoe: East Face

DISTANCE: 20 miles

ELEVATION GAIN: 9500'

DAYS: 3

MAPS: USGS Cascade Pass, Goode Mountain; Green Trails Cascade Pass No. 80, McGregor Mountain No. 81

RATING: E4T4

LOCATION: North Cascades National Park, Marblemount Ranger Station

PERMITS: Permits are required to camp in North Cascades National Park; register for the climb at the Wilderness Information Center at the Marblemount Ranger Station.

SUMMARY AND HIGHLIGHTS: Located at the eastern end of the enormous cirque that holds the Boston Glacier, Buckner Mountain stands less angular and ominous than many of the surrounding peaks but is still imposing and impressive. Its southwest peak is estimated to be just 2 feet higher than its northeast peak. The north face sports popular snow and ice routes, but the easiest way to the summit is from the southwest. For some climbers, steep snow in early summer or loose rock in late summer makes this section undesirable. Even so, the southwest face consists of scrambling and climbing that is within the ability of the basic-level climber (see definition on page 3). Ripsaw Ridge is the backbone of spires above Horseshoe Basin connecting Sahale Mountain to the summit of Buckner Mountain. Horseshoe Peak is the highest spire on the ridge. (The crux of this climb may be identifying the appropriate spire, which is difficult to pinpoint on the USGS map.) For both Buckner and Horseshoe summits, the reward is the outstanding vista of the surrounding Cascade Pass region, including the horn of Forbidden Peak, the massive Eldorado ice cap, and the jagged spires of Goode and Logan.

The approach to Buckner and Horseshoe through Horseshoe Basin may be longer than that from the Sahale Arm, but it is safer and more interesting if mining relics and waterfalls appeal to you.

HOW TO GET THERE: Drive north on Interstate 5 to the North Cascades Scenic Highway (State Route 20). Drive east 47 miles to Marblemount. Stop at the Marblemount Ranger Station to register for the climb and obtain permits. In the town at the junction, go right (east) on Cascade River Road for 22.2 miles to its end and the Cascade Pass Trailhead (3600').

TRIP DESCRIPTION: Hike on the Cascade Pass Trail for 3.7 miles to Cascade Pass (5392'). Descend on the trail for 3.0 miles to a trail junction (3600'). Take the left fork (Horseshoe Basin Trail). Continue into the lower basin; from here the way is sketchy and difficult to find. Before you get to the Black Warrior Mine — the large cone of mining tailings at the head of Horseshoe Basin that may be covered by snow in early season — cross Basin Creek at the lower east side of the cirque (4000'). The walls of the basin are steep and cliffy. Slide alder lines waterfalls and brush fills the spaces in between. You can pick your way through this area using the right side of the basin, which has the least slope angle. Alternately, try to find an old steel cable that runs from beside the creek up through rocky sections of the head of the basin. Stay to the right of the cable, where the terrain is the most forgiving. Above you are the rocky nose buttress and small patches of cedar and meadow. Work your way upward until you finally reach open heather slopes. Make a camp at 6400 feet on the east side of Horseshoe Basin. An alternative spot for camping is at the top of a rock knob in the middle of the upper basin at about 7100 feet.

Buckner Mountain

To attain Buckner from the upper basin the next day, start climbing northeast on talus or snow to a steep snow finger that reaches toward a small saddle on the south ridge at 8900 feet. The final push on the east face to the north summit ridge is blocky and easy (class 3). Circle back south to the southwest peak of Buckner, the true summit, directly above Buckner Glacier.

Horseshoe Peak

From the face of Buckner descend steep snow or scree trending southwest for 0.4 mile into a small basin at the low point of Ripsaw Ridge (8200'). Just below the rock ridge, leave behind all but a daypack and a rope, long runners, and rock protection. Many of the spikes on Ripsaw Ridge can be difficult to identify from a distance. Horseshoe Peak is the spire to the far left that you can see to the west when you are in the basin. The next peak east is the false summit of Horseshoe, and the next peak east of it is Lick of Flame, a sharp-pointed peak named for its appearance when viewed from the southwest. Scramble to the col between Lick of Flame and the false summit of Horseshoe. Continue scrambling west on the shoulder of the false summit of Horseshoe, where you cross a small, steep snow finger on its south side. Continue a short distance, then climb down into a sandy gully, and scramble up loose rock to another sandy spot 20 feet from the col between the two summits of Horseshoe. Rope up and climb a left-slanting ledge about 60 vertical feet (class 4) to the point where you can stand just under the final summit move. Two major protection points provide solid rock protection: the first is about 20 feet from the belay (1.25-inch cam) and the second is at head level about 5 feet before the crux (1.5-inch cam). Small cam units and stoppers can protect in other places. Climb the crux (class 5) over the notch; the summit cairn is to the right and the summit register is to the left. Take some long runners to make a safe rappel anchor. A 20-foot runner can be put around a large section of the summit block to the right of the crux, perhaps the only solid section. Rappel straight down to the gully; a single rope is adequate.

For the descent from the camp in upper Horseshoe Basin, instead of retracing your steps you may want to trend to the left (east) where the slope angle is the most moderate. This area on the edge of the cirque is

Chris Weidner

Moonrise on Buckner Mountain

Dave LeBlanc

Buckner Mountain and Ripsaw Ridge

covered in thick brush and riddled with gullies. You may have to rappel short sections, despite limited vision, to reach the lower basin.

HAZARDS AND TIPS: A small rack for class 5 climbing on Horseshoe is recommended, although some parties may use the rope only for the rappel. Helmets are essential due to rockfall on Horseshoe. Routefinding from lower to upper Horseshoe Basin is frustrating and requires some bushwhacking. If you do not find the cable, you can still pick your way up through the cliffs using ledge systems to gain the upper basin.

GPS WAYPOINT ROUTE:

1. 10U 642393, 5370649, 3600': Cascade Pass Trailhead
2. 10U 643562, 5369907, 3.7 miles, 5392': Cascade Pass
3. 10U 645961, 5369751, 3.0 miles, 3600': Horseshoe Basin Trail
4. 10U 646553, 5370344, 1.0 mile, 4000': Basin Creek
5. 10U 647318, 5372438, 1.8 miles, 7100': Horseshoe Basin camp
6. 10U 647759, 5372959, 0.6 mile, 8900': Buckner ridge
7. 10U 647878, 5372989, 0.2 mile, 9112+': Buckner summit
8. 10U 647264, 5372919, 0.6 mile, 8480+': Horseshoe summit

TRIP TIMES:

Cascade Pass Trailhead to Horseshoe Basin camp: 9.5 miles, 5300', 14 hours

Horseshoe Basin camp to Buckner summit: 0.8 mile, 2000', 4 hours

Buckner summit to Horseshoe summit: 0.6 mile, 400', 3 hours

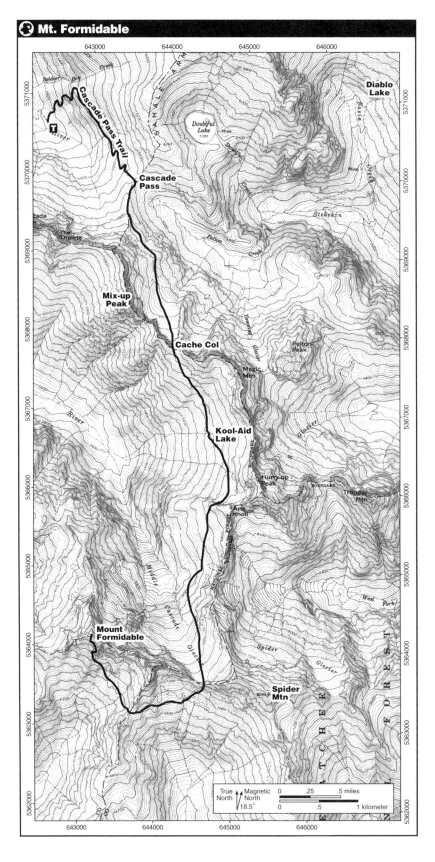

Diablo
Lake

Soldier Boy
Cascade Pass Trail
Doubtful
Lake

Cascade
Pass

Stehekin

The
Triplets

Mix-up
Peak

Cache Col

Felton
Peak

Magic
Mtn

Kool-Aid
Lake

Hurry-up
Peak

Trapper
Mtn

River

Art's
knoll

West
Fork

Mount
Formidable

Spider

Spider
Mtn

True
North
Magnetic
North
18.5°
0   .25   .5 miles
0   .5   1 kilometer

ROUTE 12

Mt. Formidable

ELEVATION: 8325' (2537 m)

CLIMBING ROUTE: South Face

DISTANCE: 20 miles

ELEVATION GAIN: 7800'

DAYS: 3

MAPS: USGS Cascade Pass; Green Trails Cascade Pass No. 80

RATING: E3T3

LOCATION: North Cascades National Park and Glacier Peak Wilderness administered by Mt. Baker-Snoqualmie National Forest, Marblemount Ranger Station

PERMITS: Permits are not required but you are asked to register for the climb at the Wilderness Information Center at the Marblemount Ranger Station.

SUMMARY AND HIGHLIGHTS: Mt. Formidable's name comes from Hermann Ulrichs, an early mountaineer who in 1934 scouted the climb of the mountain and described its fearsome north slope. Notwithstanding, Mt. Formidable is less memorable than many of the well-known peaks in the Cascade Pass region, despite its status as one of the local titans. Although there are several northern routes to the summit that require ice-climbing skills, the easiest way up, on the South Face, can be accomplished by a basic-level climber (see definition on page 3).

The best approach to Mt. Formidable is from the Ptarmigan Traverse. The name of this classic, high-alpine trek comes from the Ptarmigan Climbing Club, several of whose members pioneered the high route. The full trip begins at Cascade Pass and crosses glaciers with steep portions and high cols, winding past several peaks: Magic, Mix-up, Spider, Formidable, Le Conte, Sentinel, Spire, and Dome. Each peak can be climbed individually along the way, but the traverse typically takes from five to seven days just by itself. You can reach Mt. Formidable from the first-day camp of the Ptarmigan Traverse at Kool-Aid Lake, a small tarn surrounded by dramatic ice-clad pinnacles.

HOW TO GET THERE: Drive north on Interstate 5 to the North Cascades Scenic Highway (State Route 20). Drive east 47 miles to Marblemount. Stop at the ranger station to register for the climb. In the town at the junction, go right (east) on the Cascade River Road 22.2 miles to the road end and the Cascade Pass Trailhead (3600').

TRIP DESCRIPTION: Hike on the Cascade Pass Trail for 3.7 miles to Cascade Pass (5392'). At the pass, leave the main trail and travel on the climber's trail south toward Mix-up Peak. When the snow is gone, you will see the path that is worn into grass and scree on the ridge's eastern slope. Attain the Cache Glacier and ascend to Cache Col, the eastern and higher of the two cols (6900'). Descend on snow or talus to Kool-Aid Lake (6100'). Camp at an established site or camp on snow.

From Kool-Aid Lake continue south to a spur (called Arts Knoll) and cross a finger of steep snow to enter the Red Ledge, which traverses across the cliffs. In late season there may be a moat here. Continue contouring slightly downward across meadows and then rocky ribs to a spot above the snout of the Middle Cascade Glacier (6500'). Climb up talus and snow to the glacier above the main icefall. Ascend the glacier to the Spider-Formidable col (7400') 100 yards east of the most visible low spot. Descend snow on the south slope (may be hard and icy). At 300 feet below the col, traverse west to the first rock rib that emanates south off the ridge connecting the col to Formidable. Cross the rib at a notch

Red Ledge on Mt. Formidable

(7000'). Attain a snow basin and traverse across the snowfield to a second rib. Cross the rib to a high snow patch just south of the summit pyramid and go either up or around the snow to the top left corner. Find a ledge that leads you to the South Face (class 4). From here climb directly upward to the summit (class 3).

HAZARDS AND TIPS: In late season moats may be problematic at Cache Col, at the Red Ledge, and on the Middle Cascade Glacier. Some parties may prefer to continue to Yang Yang Lakes for a better camp rather than camping at Kool-Aid Lake, but this makes for a longer two-day approach with some backtracking. You can also camp just after crossing the Red Ledge.

GPS WAYPOINT ROUTE:

1. 10U 642393, 5370649, 3600': Cascade Pass Trailhead
2. 10U 643562, 5369907, 3.7 miles, 5392': Cascade Pass
3. 10U 644067, 5367824, 1.5 miles, 6900': Cache Col
4. 10U 644611, 5366746, 0.9 mile, 6100': Kool-Aid Lake
5. 10U 644682, 5365850, 0.6 mile, 6800': Red Ledge
6. 10U 644487, 5364324, 1.0 mile, 6500': Middle Cascade Glacier
7. 10U 644573, 5363563, 0.6 mile, 7400': Spider-Formidable Col
8. 10U 643642, 5363184, 0.5 mile, 7000': notch
9. 10U 643135, 5363932, 0.7 mile, 7600': high snow patch
10. 10U 643118, 5364148, 0.3 mile, 8325': Formidable summit

TRIP TIMES:

Cascade Pass Trailhead to Kool-Aid Lake: 6.1 miles, 3400', 7 hours
Kool-Aid Lake to Formidable summit: 3.7 miles, 3000', 7 hours

CHAPTER 4
Washington Pass

Before the North Cascades Highway was built in the 1970s, Washington Pass was so remote that it was barely visited. Only after an arduous trek were climbers able to enjoy some of the best rock climbing in the North Cascades. Today the highway provides excellent access to the backcountry (except during its winter closure due to high avalanche activity), including the highest peaks surrounding Washington Pass: Ragged Ridge and Black Peak to the west in North Cascades National Park; Tower Mountain, Golden Horn, and Azurite Peak to the north in the Okanogan National Forest; Silver Star Mountain and Big Snagtooth to the east in the Okanogan National Forest; and Reynolds Peak to the south in the Lake Chelan-Sawtooth Wilderness.

Topographically, the Washington Pass area varies from gently sloping, glacier-carved valley floors to sheer cirque walls ending in striking rock pinnacles. These are some of the most dramatic and unusual geologic formations in the Cascades. A visual fantasy unfolds as you ascend from placid flood plains and evergreen-covered foothills to raw, heavily glaciated crags and rutted alleys laced with flowery meadows or high alpine vegetation. The area north of Washington Pass is characterized by

Dave LeBlanc

Black Peak from Goode Mountain

88

rugged, high granite peaks, broadly rounded ridgecrests, and low, trough-shaped passes strewn with boulders stranded by ancient ice fields. Here many peaks are high enough to have escaped the glacial forces of the ice ages. There are extensive spires on ridges surrounding Golden Horn, the youngest granitic body in the Cascades, on Kangaroo Ridge, Snagtooth Ridge, Silver Star Mountain, and the Liberty Bell group. In contrast, the Methow region south of Washington Pass has been greatly affected by both alpine glaciation and ancient ice-sheet movement. One of the most recent ice sheets entered this region from Canada from the northwest, spilled over Harts Pass, and engulfed the entire Methow Valley. Unlike alpine glaciers that erode rock in virtually any direction, the ice sheet deepened valleys aligned specifically northwest and southeast. The ice sheet left in its wake leveled-off ridgecrests and unusual U-shaped troughs across divides.

The climate changes dramatically within a relatively short distance around Washington Pass. In only a few miles the heavily forested, moisture-rich west slope gives way to the dry, coniferous habitat that is characteristic of eastern Cascade slopes. The Methow region remains dry due to the rainshadow effect. East-slope precipitation is still a substantial 50 to 80 inches annually, but most of it comes as snow in winter and spring, whereas the summers are usually hot and arid. Sparse forests of primarily ponderosa pine dominate the lower east-slope elevations. At medium altitudes Pacific silver fir and western larch abound, while at higher altitudes subalpine fir and Englemann spruce are prominent. At timberline, particularly around Washington Pass, Lyall's subalpine larch is notable—a favorite tree due to its delicate needles, which in autumn give to the sparsely vegetated landscape a golden, shimmering hue.

More avalanches occur in the Cascades than in any other mountain range in the western U.S.. The Washington Pass area is particularly susceptible, and many persistent and dangerous avalanche paths have been identified along the North Cascades Highway. Avalanche risk commonly increases when warm, rainy weather follows a colder, snowy period. Wind-slab conditions and slopes with weak layers can remain unstable for long periods, and new snow or a warming trend may also increase risk. The most dangerous slabs form on slopes of greater than 30 degrees, especially where there is substantial variation in density between the snow surface layer and the consolidated bed layer. All these conditions are common in the Washington Pass region. Therefore you must know the avalanche potential for the location you plan to visit before going there in the winter or spring. Alternatively, plan your outing during summer, when the snow pack has consolidated and deep-slab instability is seldom a danger beyond a few days after a storm.

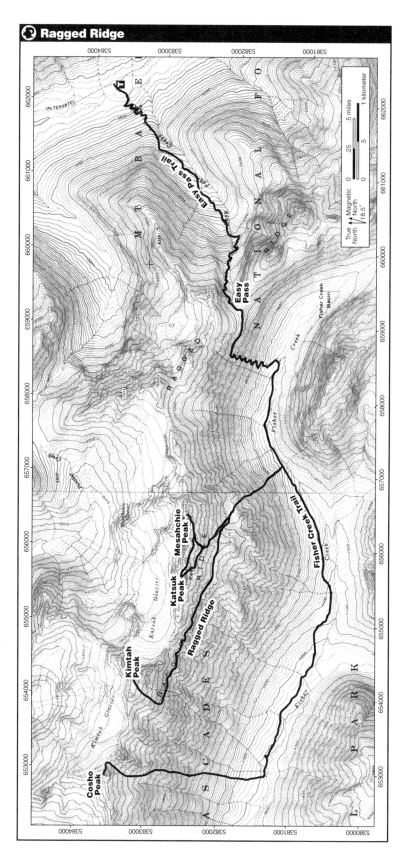

Ragged Ridge

Ragged Ridge
Cosho Peak, Kimtah Peak, Mesahchie Peak, and Katsuk Peak,

ELEVATIONS: 8332', 8600+', 8795', 8680+' (2540 m, 2621+ m, 2681m, 2646+ m)

DISTANCE: 30 miles

ELEVATION GAIN: 13,200'

DAYS: At least 5

MAPS: USGS Mt. Arriva, Mt. Logan, Green Trails Mt. Logan No. 49

RATING: E5T3

LOCATION: Mt. Baker-Snoqualmie National Forest administered by Okanogan National Forest, and North Cascades National Park, Marblemount Ranger Station

PERMITS: Permits are required to camp in North Cascades National Park; register for the climb at the Wilderness Information Center at the Marblemount Ranger Station.

SUMMARY AND HIGHLIGHTS: Ragged Ridge consists of a series of airy mountaintops trending northwest between Fisher Creek and Panther Creek. The ridge is 10 miles long but the major summits span only about 3 miles along the crest. Although the Fisher Creek Trail along the valley is frequented by backpackers and hikers, the high, rugged alpine country towering above is lonesome and seldom visited. This is partially because upward travel here requires a strenuous bushwhack through notoriously dense brush and slide alder. But once above timberline, the going is easier, although significant rutting and steep, loose talus prevent quick progress.

Mesahchie Peak, named after the Chinook word meaning "wicked," is located at the southeastern terminus of Ragged Ridge and is the highest point of the chain. The substantial Mesahchie Glacier abuts on the precipitous north face, whereas the south face is covered with talus and broken rock and is more moderate. Katsuk Peak is second highest and next in line near the center of Ragged Ridge. Here the Katsuk Glacier, the largest in the area, extends northward. Next, Kimtah Peak is noted for a row of jagged pinnacles on its southern slope called Grotesque Gen-darmes. Situated last in line at the northwestern end of Ragged Ridge is Cosho Peak, sometimes called the Ragged End.

These four neighboring mountaintops can be tackled in a variety of ways. A sustained push along the ridgecrest is appealing, although for most parties the terrain is too rough, with corrugated gullies and rock ribs, to accomplish all four summits in a day. Instead the trip described here requires several days, first scaling Cosho from the valley floor, then the remaining three as a high traverse with an overnight alpine camp.

HOW TO GET THERE: Drive north on Interstate 5 to the North Cascades Scenic Highway (State Route 20). Drive east 47 miles to Mar-blemount. Stop at the Marblemount Ranger Station to register and ob-tain a camping permit. Continue northeast on Highway 20 to Newhalem. At 32 miles past Newhalem turn onto a short, paved spur west to the Easy Pass Trail No. 741 trailhead (3700').

TRIP DESCRIPTION: Hike up switchbacks for 3.6 miles to Easy Pass (6500'). Enjoy sweeping views of Mts. Logan and Arriva from the alpine meadow. Descend on Fisher Creek Trail 1.5 miles and 1300 feet to Fisher Camp. Continue along Fisher Creek for 4.1 miles and camp in the for-est at Cosho Camp (3800'). Water is easily available from Fisher Creek.

Cosho Peak

Continue west on Fisher Creek Trail from camp. In 0.2 mile, before the trail crosses Fisher Creek to the south, start off-trail up the brushy and treed slope. Stay to the right of the main stream coming down be-tween Cosho and Thieves Peak, the satellite 8120-foot point southeast of Cosho summit. Approach the end of the creek system at 7000 feet. Bear northeast to the saddle (7900') between Cosho and Thieves Peak. Climb on heather and rock on the east ridge to the summit (class 3). Descend back down the slope, aiming to intersect the trail on the north shore of Fisher Creek and east of Cosho Camp. Turn right (west) and return on the trail to Cosho Camp.

Kimtah Peak

The next day, from Cosho Camp, hike east on Fisher Creek Trail for 3 miles. Leave the trail at 4900 feet and start northwest upslope. Find a high camp on the south shoulder of Mesahchie in a flat basin at 6700 feet that has snow late in summer.

The next morning, prepare a daypack for the climb of Kimtah Peak. Starting from the basin camp, ascend talus and scree westward to 7200 feet. Traverse west across minor ribs and gully systems to the east shoul-der of Kimtah staying between 7000 and 7400 feet (class 3). The terrain

Keith Wilson

Grotesque Gendarmes on Kimtah

is steep and rocky requiring navigational skills and patience. Use a ledge system to traverse below the Grotesque Gendarmes—the spiky towers southeast of Kimtah's summit. Ascend to the summit on ledges in a series of steps on the south face (class 3–4). From Kimtah summit, return to the 7000-foot level and traverse east back to the high camp in the basin on Mesahchie.

Mesahchie Peak

From camp ascend the west side of the basin to attain the ridgecrest above the prominent ridge buttress at 7430 feet. Climb the ridge, staying on the crest or just west of the crest. Scramble over big blocks, then across ledges and headwalls, up loose troughs and across steep ribs. At 8200 feet you may see a cairn on a huge block; go to the right here to traverse downsloping boilerplates to reach the 8200-foot col between Katsuk and Mesahchie. From the col traverse north 100 feet and look to the right for a steep, hidden chimney that runs up to a notch on the southwest ridge of Mesahchie. Look at the top of the ridge to locate the path. Go up the chimney 40 feet and then angle left up a shallow, gray trough that tops out at the right edge of a large, winding couloir. Ascend the couloir to its top and climb up a short chimney to the summit ridge. Move on the exposed knife edge very carefully for 40 feet east to the true summit (class 3).

Keith Wilson

Katsuk Peak with Kimtah Peak in the background

Katsuk Peak

From Mesahchie, descend to the col and cross the boilerplates, then drop past a huge block and turn right to make a rising traverse across several steep ribs on the south side of Katsuk until you reach the east summit ridge. Wind along the ridgecrest, passing each short pinnacle on the side that you judge will offer the least trouble, until you get to the summit. The summit register still contains the original note left on the first ascent of Katsuk on August 22, 1968. From the summit of Katsuk, descend southeast back to the basin camp. The next day return to the Fisher Creek Trail, cross over Easy Pass, and return to the trailhead.

HAZARDS AND TIPS: The above itinerary has Cosho as a separate leg because the combination of Cosho and Kimtah is complicated and long enough that many parties must bivy to complete the two in a single day. Routefinding in the deep forest on the east face of Cosho requires identifying the proper stream system and gully to follow, as you will find it difficult to climb over steep rock ridges between the streams to find the proper gully (class 4). These four peaks can be combined in many variations. The most aesthetic is a high traverse that connects all four. The high traverse for the three eastern peaks is feasible in two days from a high camp. Climbing all four in a single weekend is a near-heroic feat.

GPS WAYPOINT ROUTE:

1. 10U 662212, 5383768, 3700': Easy Pass Trailhead
2. 10U 659227, 5381858, 3.6 miles, 6500': Easy Pass
3. 10U 653169, 5381299, 5.6 miles, 3800': Cosho Camp
4. 10U 652914, 5382275, 1.0 mile, 4900': Cosho south face
5. 10U 652888, 5383252, 0.7 mile, 7000': Cosho basin
6. 10U 653074, 5383562, 0.3 mile, 7900': saddle
7. 10U 652882, 5383654, 0.2 mile, 8332': Cosho summit
8. 10U 657192, 5381253, 5.3 miles, 4900': leave trail
9. 10U 656479, 5381928, 0.6 mile, 6700': basin camp
10. 10U 653840, 5382757, 2.0 miles, 7100': Kimtah south face
11. 10U 654174, 5383233, 0.4 mile, 8600+': Kimtah summit
12. 10U 656439, 5382557, 3.0 miles, 8795': Mesahchie summit
13. 10U 655602, 5382599, 0.7 mile, 8680+': Katsuk summit

TRIP TIMES:

Easy Pass Trailhead to Cosho Camp: 8.6 miles, 2800', 7 hours
Cosho Camp to Cosho summit: 2.2 miles, 4500', 8 hours
Basin camp to Kimtah summit: 2.4 miles, 1900', 6 hours
Basin camp to Mesahchie summit: 0.6 mile, 2100', 3 hours
Mesahchie summit to Katsuk summit: 0.7 mile, 600', 2 hours

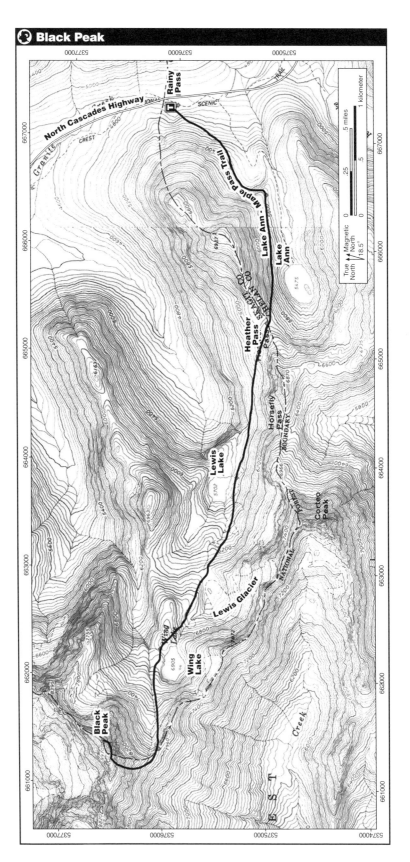

ROUTE 14

Black Peak

ELEVATION: 8970' (2734 m)

CLIMBING ROUTE: South Face

DISTANCE: 12 miles

ELEVATION GAIN: 4700'

DAYS: 1–2

MAPS: USGS Washington Pass, Mt. Arriva, Green Trails Washington Pass No. 50, Mt. Logan No. 49

RATING: E1T3

LOCATION: North Cascades Scenic Highway Corridor, Mt. Baker-Snoqualmie National Forest administered by Okanogan National Forest; North Cascades National Park, Marblemount Ranger Station

PERMITS: Permits are required to climb and camp in North Cascades National Park. Black Peak is on the park boundary; you do not need a permit to camp at Wing Lake.

SUMMARY AND HIGHLIGHTS: Black Peak is an imposing and important landmark, situated between Mt. Arriva to the north and Corteo Peak to the south. Yet it represents a straightforward alpine ascent with characteristic features of this section of the Cascade Range. On Black Peak easy snowfield, talus, and moraine give way to a more complex rock scramble to the summit, yielding an impressive vantage of the myriad peaks of the North Cascades in every direction. An additional bonus is the hike along the Lake Ann-Maple Pass Trail, a lovely enough trip by itself. Nestled in a hollow in the basin southeast of the mountain, Wing Lake is also an enjoyable stop along the way to the summit block. Because Black Peak is one of Washington's highest alpine climbs that you can do in a single day, this is a good trip for those times when you want to carry only a daypack.

HOW TO GET THERE: Drive north on Interstate 5 to the North Cascades Scenic Highway (State Route 20). Drive east 47 miles to Marblemount. You can stop at the ranger station to get information on current conditions in North Cascades National Park. Continue east on

Highway 20 to Diablo Dam. At 32 miles past Diablo Dam you will come to Rainy Pass. Turn right on the spur road on the west side of Highway 20 and continue past the picnic area. Find parking for the Lake Ann-Maple Pass Trail No. 740 trailhead (4800').

TRIP DESCRIPTION: Hike on the Lake Ann-Maple Pass Trail for 1.4 miles. At a junction the left fork continues down to Lake Ann. Instead take the right fork to Heather Pass (6100'). Cross the pass and traverse along the north shoulder of Corteo Peak on rockslide boulders or snow to the outlet of Lewis Lake. You can go around Lewis Lake to the right (north) on a bench above the basin containing the stream that feeds Granite Creek. Or, to avoid crossing the outlet, go around Lewis Lake to the left (south) on snow slopes. Trend northwest along the moraine to Wing Lake along the northeast margin of the Lewis Glacier. Go around Wing Lake to the right (east), and begin the ascent to the col on the south flank of Black Peak (7900'). If the final push on the perennial snowfield below the col is too steep, you can bypass the snow by climbing up boulders to the north. Cross through the col and ascend broken rock and talus on the south face toward the false summit. Trend leftward in the loose gully systems that get steeper as you climb (class 3–4). Just before the summit block start a traverse to the east (8800'). The final gully to the summit is on the east face (class 3).

HAZARDS AND TIPS: A climber's trail is visible most of the way from Heather Pass, and the route through the boulders has cairns. Some portions on the peak are exposed and loose; helmets are recommended. Although this trip is feasible in a day, the area around Wing Lake makes for a beautiful overnight camp. It is best to do this trip earlier in the season as the snow then covers extensive talus fields that, when exposed, might slow your progress.

GPS WAYPOINT ROUTE:
1. 10U 667350, 5376148, 4800': Lake Ann-Maple Pass Trailhead
2. 10U 666740, 5375282, 1.4 miles, 5500': trail junction
3. 10U 665299, 5375115, 0.7 mile, 6100': Heather Pass
4. 10U 664010, 5375349, 1.0 mile, 5700': Lewis Lake
5. 10U 662398, 5375851, 1.2 miles, 6900': Wing Lake
6. 10U 661315, 5376081, 0.9 mile, 7900': col
7. 10U 661399, 5376583, 0.8 mile, 8970': Black summit

TRIP TIME:
Lake Ann-Maple Pass Trailhead to Black summit: 6.0 miles, 4500', 6 hours

Eve Kaiyala

Black Peak

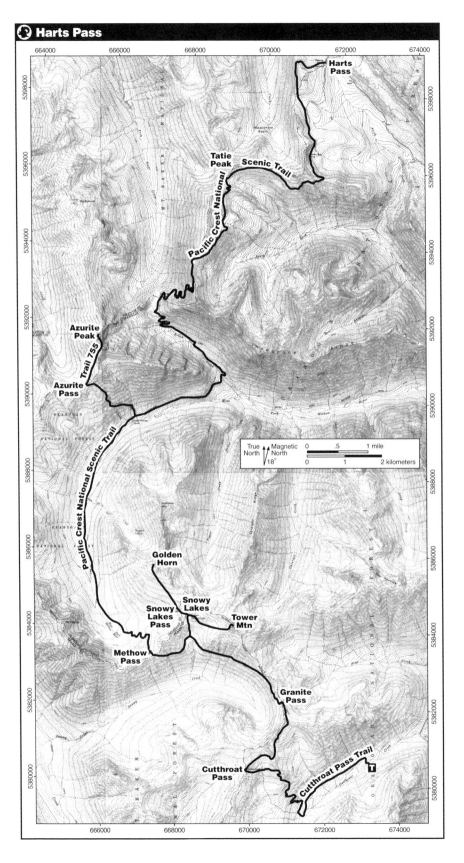

ROUTE 15

Harts Pass

Tower Mountain, Golden Horn, and Azurite Peak

ELEVATIONS: 8444', 8366', 8400+' (2574 m, 2550 m, 2560+ m)

DISTANCE: 44 miles

ELEVATION GAIN: 12,500'

DAYS: At least 5

MAPS: USGS Washington Pass, Mt. Arriva, Azurite Peak, Slate Peak; Green Trails Washington Pass No. 50, Mt. Logan No. 49

RATING: E4T3

LOCATION: Okanogan National Forest, Methow Valley Visitor Center

PERMITS: None; you must register at the trailhead.

SUMMARY AND HIGHLIGHTS: These three summits are the highest points above the Pacific Crest National Scenic Trail (Crest Trail No. 2000 in Washington) as it winds from Cutthroat Pass north to Harts Pass. Typical of the arid region east of the Cascade Crest, the countryside appears barren in comparison to the wetter, more glaciated slopes just a few miles to the west. Sometimes the terrain appears bizarre and surreal as the austere slopes open to huge vistas and endless horizons.

The Harts Pass group is best done as a one-way trek with a car shuttle. Although you can go in either direction, the most logical choice is from south to north, as it simplifies the car shuttle (you will have to drive past the trailhead at the southern terminus to leave a car at Harts Pass for the return). The Crest Trail provides the path to the summits as it undulates up and over multiple clefts in the ridges: Cutthroat, Granite, Methow, Azurite, Glacier, Grasshopper, and Harts passes. Tower Mountain and Azurite Peak are distinctive but contain much shattered rock. Their faces hold mysterious labyrinths of gullies and ribs that lead to their summits. Golden Horn, with a striking appearance that forms the basis of it name, is the most solid of the threesome. Rounding the Crest Trail just below this landmark you are exposed to an airy, open traverse with jagged peaks soaring upward over gently flowing basins and valleys. At the base of Golden Horn a large larch grove surrounds Snowy Lakes, an exceptional site for a camp along the way.

HOW TO GET THERE: This trip requires a car shuttle. Drive to the town of Mazama, either from the west via Highway 20 or from the south via State Route 153 plus 20. From Mazama, drive for 18.5 miles on Lost River Road 9140 (becomes Harts Pass FS Road 5400) to Harts Pass and park a car for the return trip. Drive back to Mazama, then go west on Highway 20 for 13 miles to Road 400 that exits to the right. Take this spur for a mile to the Cutthroat Creek Campground. Find parking for Cutthroat Pass Trail No. 483 trailhead (4500').

TRIP DESCRIPTION: Hike on Cutthroat Pass Trail for 5.5 miles to its end at Cutthroat Pass (6800'). From the pass, go north on the Pacific Crest National Scenic Trail (Crest Trail No. 2000). Descend to Granite Pass (6200') and continue contouring west below the face of Tower Mountain. At 1.8 miles past Granite Pass the trail loops to the north in the basin below Snowy Lakes. Leave the trail at 6200 feet and go north to Snowy Lakes. Make a camp at the lakes below Snowy Lakes Pass on the western rim of the lakes (6800').

Tower Mountain

The next morning from camp, trek cross-country southeast toward Tower Mountain. Traverse around the southwest ridge at about 7200 feet. Scramble up the southwest ridge on its south side. Contour left through a short, sharp notch onto the west face. Scramble directly up broken rock and gullies. Near the summit rocks, ascend counter-clockwise around the summit to its top (class 3).

Golden Horn

From the camp at Snowy Lakes, trek northwest while gently ascending talus or snow toward the summit block. Near the top you will encounter boulders with some easy crack systems. From the south, climb for 20 or 30 feet on the last boulders to the top (class 4).

Azurite Peak

From Snowy Lakes camp, return cross-country to the Crest Trail. Continue west on the trail over Methow Pass (6600'). Descend 2200 feet while hiking beside the West Fork Methow River. At 5.4 miles from Methow Pass, Trail No. 756 to Meebee Pass exits to the left. Continue on the Crest Trail for 0.5 mile to the junction with unmaintained Trail No. 755 that leads north to Azurite Pass. This trail junction (4400'), about 200 yards north of the spur to Horse Heaven Camp, is not accurately shown on the USGS map. Furthermore, it is difficult to locate in high grasses.If you look carefully, you might see a cairn on the Crest Trail marking the junction, but you may need to go higher to find the trail in open meadow if necessary. After you locate the trail go back to the Crest Trail and find a place to camp along the West Fork Methow River.

Steve Fry

East face of Tower Mountain

The next morning for Azurite, hike on Trail No. 755 to Azurite Pass (6700'). From the pass, descend about 200 vertical feet, then contour north, crossing a deep summit gully. You will have to cross many black ridges defining smaller gullies along your way. Ascend the second deep summit gully. A solid rock dike ascends rightward to the summit (class 3–4). Either gully will work. Many other variations exist to attain the summit ridge. Be careful, as many of the small downsloping ledges and granite slabs are covered by treacherous gravel and the rock is very loose. The summit is only a few feet higher than the satellite north peak. Return to camp.

To the Car Shuttle

Continue northeast on the Crest Trail. At 2.0 miles the West Fork Methow Trail No. 480 exits to the right following the West Fork Methow River. Stay on the Crest Trail (the left fork) and hike northwest along Brush Creek. Ascend 1300 feet to Glacier Pass (5600'). The trail rises another 1400 feet to traverse around the south face of Tatie Peak at 7000 feet. After hiking for12.7 miles from the West Fork Methow Trail junction, make the final descent to Harts Pass (6200'), where your car awaits.

HAZARDS AND TIPS: If you are climbing only Azurite, it can be more easily approached from the West Fork Methow Trail No. 480. This trail has been refurbished, is well-maintained, and has a new bridge on it. The trail goes from the end of River Bend Campground Road—off Harts Pass Road—to the Crest Trail 2.0 miles east of the Azurite Pass Trail, yield-

Climbers on southwest face of Azurite Peak

ing 1600 feet of elevation gain in 8 miles of easy travel. You can exit the trip on the West Fork Methow Trail instead of at Harts Pass if you leave a car at the trailhead for the return. You may be overwhelmed by the variety of choices in your routefinding on Tower and Azurite. Although the gully and rib systems are complex, they will generally funnel you into the proper final gully to the summit rocks if you persevere and systematically trend upward. The rock is loose and the gullies are dirty; helmets are mandatory. Keep your party size small (two to four climbers) to minimize rockfall danger. You will also need excellent rockfall-management skills. Some climbers will want a rope with modest rock protection for the final summit boulders of Golden Horn.

GPS WAYPOINT ROUTE:

1. 10U 673144, 5380583, 4500': Cutthroat Pass Trailhead
2. 10U 669795, 5380318, 5.5 miles, 6800': Cutthroat Pass
3. 10U 668315, 5383690, 4.5 miles, 6200': leave trail
4. 10U 668198, 5384328, 0.5 mile, 6800': Snowy Lakes
5. 10U 668916, 5383747, 0.7 mile, 7200': southwest ridge
6. 10U 669401, 5384049, 0.6 mile, 8444': Tower summit
7. 10U 667237, 5385662, 2.3 miles, 8366': Golden Horn summit
8. 10U 666561, 5389450, 8.6 miles, 4400': Azurite Pass Trail
9. 10U 665302, 5390222, 2.2 miles, 6700': Azurite Pass
10. 10U 665643, 5391527, 1.0 mile, 8400+': Azurite summit
11. 10U 668948, 5390641, 5.2 miles, 4300': trail junction
12. 10U 671467, 5398875, 12.7 miles, 6200': Harts Pass

TRIP TIMES:

Cutthroat Pass Trailhead to Snowy Lakes: 10.5 miles, 3000', 8 hours
Snowy Lakes to Tower summit: 1.3 miles, 1600', 5 hours
Snowy Lakes to Golden Horn summit: 1.1 miles, 1600', 4 hours
Azurite Pass Trail to Azurite summit: 3.2 miles, 4000', 7 hours

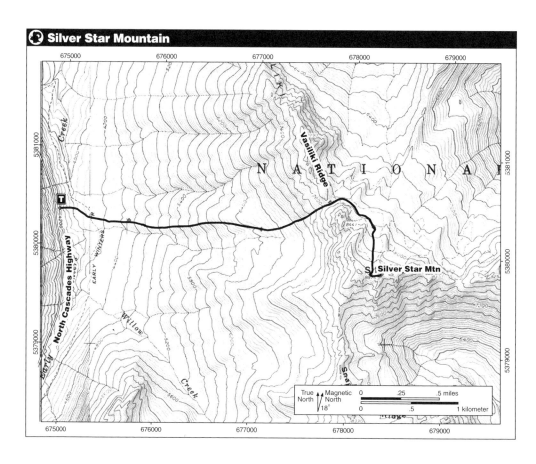

Silver Star Mountain

ELEVATION: 8876' (2705 m)

CLIMBING ROUTE: Silver Star Glacier

DISTANCE: 7 miles

ELEVATION GAIN: 5200'

DAYS: 1–2

MAPS: USGS Washington Pass, Silver Star Mountain, Green Trails Washington Pass No. 50

RATING: E1T3

LOCATION: North Cascades Scenic Highway Corridor; Okanogan National Forest, Methow Valley Visitor Center

PERMITS: None

SUMMARY AND HIGHLIGHTS: Silver Star Mountain is a renowned landmark clearly visible from North Cascades Highway. The chaotic western face reveals deeply rutted erosion joints and a seemingly sheer facade. To the north you can plainly see the "Wine Spires": Burgundy, Chianti, Pernod, and Chablis. Due to their solid rock and striking alpine setting, these needle-like pinnacles are fashionable intermediate to advanced rock climbs. Though the ridgecrest appears ominous, do not be disheartened: On the backside, hidden from view from the highway, is a moderate glacier route to the summit.

Silver Star Mountain is a favorite early-season alpine climb when snow coats the steep slope to Burgundy Col, which is covered with infamously loose scree later in summer. You can chose to camp overnight at a high alpine tarn, but you can also summit Silver Star Mountain in a relatively easy day from North Cascades Highway.

HOW TO GET THERE: Drive east on North Cascades Highway 20 from Marblemount. About 4 miles past Washington Pass (mile marker 166), park on the wide shoulder area near a sign that points to Silver Star Mountain. This spot is near the confluence of Early Winters Creek and Burgundy Creek, the large stream that is fed by the Vasiliki Ridge and Burgundy Spire to the east.

Silver Star Mountain above the North Cascades Highway (Highway 20) just west of Washington Pass

TRIP DESCRIPTION: From the parking spot on the highway, descend about 200 feet to Early Winters Creek and cross on a log. Head eastward up the slope and locate the climber's trail at about 4400 feet. Continue up the treed slope north of the creek draining off the Wine Spires. Go to the bench at 6400 feet that makes for a suitable camp if staying overnight. Otherwise, continue up steep snow in early season, or scree after the snow has melted, to Burgundy Col (7800'). From Burgundy Col, descend for 200 feet on moderate snow to the backside of Silver Star Mountain. Go east and down around Burgundy Spire. Then descend slightly to round a large buttress at the glacier's margin. Connect to the upper Silver Star Glacier and ascend moderately steep snow to a col (8600') between the smaller west peak and the larger and more complex east peak summit block. Go east of the col, then trend rightward to find the scramble route on the ridge to the summit (class 3). The last few moves to the top of the summit rock may be more challenging (class 4).

HAZARDS AND TIPS: Glacier gear is recommended, although some parties do not rope up on the glacier. As the route is often icy, you should bring crampons. This trip is best done when snow covers the steep scree slope to Burgundy Col. A bergschrund may prevent easy access to the summit block col in late season.

GPS WAYPOINT ROUTE:
1. 10U 674943, 5380369, 4200': parking at Highway 20
2. 10U 675077, 5380493, 0.2 mile, 4000': Early Winters Creek
3. 10U 675609, 5380254, 0.4 mile, 4400': climber's trail
4. 10U 676956, 5380318, 0.8 mile, 6400': bench camp
5. 10U 677758, 5380539, 0.6 mile, 7800': Burgundy Col
6. 10U 678072, 5380440, 0.4 mile, 7700': Silver Star Glacier
7. 10U 678208, 5379814, 0.6 mile, 8600': col
8. 10U 678316, 5379812, 0.3 mile, 8876': Silver Star summit

TRIP TIMES:
Highway 20 to Silver Star summit: 3.3 miles, 5100', 7 hours

Climber on summit ridge of Silver Star Mountain

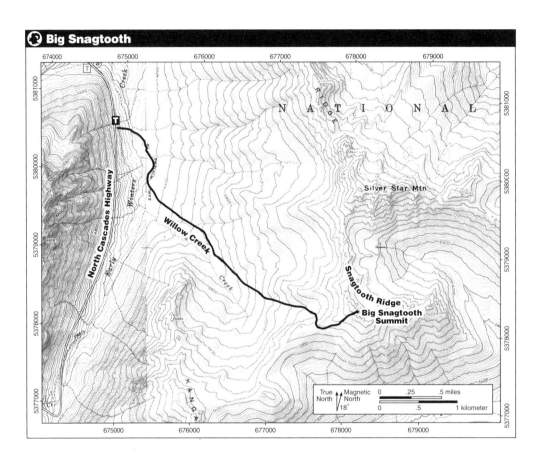

Big Snagtooth

Big Snagtooth

ELEVATION: 8330+' (2539+ m)

CLIMBING ROUTE: South Face

DISTANCE: 7 miles

ELEVATION GAIN: 4600'

DAYS: 1

MAPS: USGS Washington Pass, Silver Star Mountain, Green Trails Washington Pass No. 50

RATING: E1T4

LOCATION: North Cascades Scenic Highway Corridor; Okanogan National Forest, Methow Valley Visitor Center

PERMITS: None

SUMMARY AND HIGHLIGHTS: Big Snagtooth is the southernmost and highest point on Snagtooth Ridge, a blocky, ragged crest just to the south of Silver Star Mountain (Trip 16). The ridge forms a toothy grin composed of Big Snagtooth and its companion peaks: Willow, Cedar, Decayed, Red, Dog, Split, and Last Tooth. The landscape is quintessential Washington Pass: reddish-toned needles towering above expanses of treeless talus and scree from which all glaciers have vanished. The rock portion of the ridge is moderate; extensive, barren slopes blend downward from the south face to meet the forest adjoining North Cascades Highway. The ridge itself is riddled with widely spaced notches etched out by weathering. The granite that makes up the startling towers of Snagtooth Ridge is more friable than neighboring formations, perhaps due to differential cooling that affected its texture. In addition to extensive scree that can slow forward progress, Big Snagtooth is notable for its remarkable view not only of Silver Star Mountain, but also of also nearby Kangaroo Ridge, renowned for its quality climbing. The summit of Big Snagtooth sports an airy perch that often requires the leader to stand on the shoulder of another climber to reach the very top.

HOW TO GET THERE: Drive east on the North Cascades Highway 20 from Marblemount. At 4 miles past Washington Pass (mile marker 166), park on the broad shoulder near a sign that points to Silver Star Mountain.

TRIP DESCRIPTION: From the parking spot on the highway, descend 200 feet and cross Early Winters Creek on a log. Head south and ford Burgundy Creek, the large stream that is fed by the west slope of Silver Star Mountain and the Wine Spires. Pass into the Willow Creek drainage and ascend the steep slopes north of the creek by hiking cross-country on a climbers trail. On approaching the waterfall area, head up to the left and enter the basin under the west side of Snagtooth Ridge. (For a two-day trip you can find late-season water and small tent and bivy sites about a half mile directly north of the waterfalls on upper Willow Creek, at about 6100 feet.) At the head of the basin at 7000 feet, zigzag to the right up through black, rocky outcrops on loose scree and talus (beware rockfall danger here) to a saddle at 7500 feet on the southwest ridge. From the saddle travel close on the ridge on the Cedar Creek side, heading to the left of the right-hand block of crags, which include the summit. Scramble eastward up the ridge toward the summit formation on the right.

The huge summit block is now clearly visible: it is about 40 feet wide and 15 feet tall, sloping 15 degrees to the right. Climb up through short chimneys and blocks to reach the summit ridge at the base of the summit block (8300'). Trend slightly east into the large notch south of the summit. Avoid the gully at the middle of the summit formation, as it would lead to more difficult climbing. Scramble upward around the left base of the summit block to the northwest corner. Climb up onto a 3-foot-high detached block whose 2-foot-wide top slants down toward the summit block. A friable crack here can provide placements for cams ($\frac{3}{4}$" – $1\frac{1}{2}$") to lend some stability and a solid anchor for the shoulder stand. There are a couple of 2–4 inch ledges for foot placements, but no easily reachable solid handholds for making the move up over the edge of the block (class 5). At the top of the summit you will find an anchor and slings to rappel down the summit block and the summit ridge.

HAZARDS AND TIPS: For a shorter start to Big Snagtooth, park on the highway across from the Willow Creek drainage. However, the crossing of Early Winters Creek may be more difficult to locate than starting farther north on the highway at the traditional start to Silver Star Mountain and the Wine Spires, which provides a well-traveled creek crossing. The summit rock is difficult to protect until an anchor can be placed at the top. Most climbers use rock shoes to attain the summit, and include a shoulder stand on another party member. You can avoid this move by

Steve Fry

Snagtooth Ridge

crossing thin ledges beyond the shoulder-stand block and using an un-
protected friction technique up a steep, 8-foot detached boulder that un-
derpins the final summit rock (class 5.7). Extensive scree slopes impede
progress below the summit ridge after the snow has melted.

GPS WAYPOINT ROUTE:
1. 10U 674943, 5380369, 4200': parking at Highway 20
2. 10U 675301, 5379609, 0.8 mile, 4300': Willow Creek drainage
3. 10U 677427, 5378294, 1.5 miles, 7000': basin
4. 10U 677564, 5378076, 0.3 mile, 7500': southwest ridge
5. 10U 678047, 5378315, 0.6 mile, 8330+': Big Snagtooth summit

TRIP TIMES:
Highway 20 to Big Snagtooth summit: 3.2 miles, 4300', 7 hours

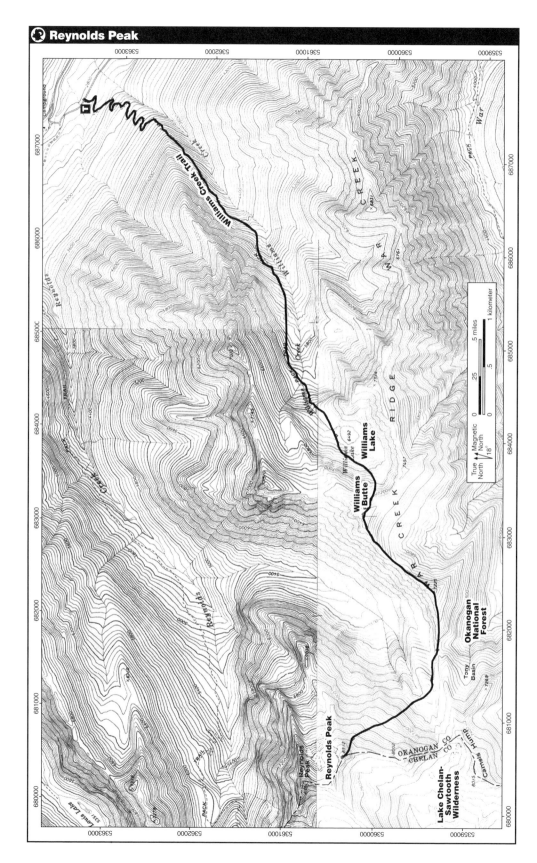

ROUTE 18

Reynolds Peak

ELEVATION: 8512' (2594 m)

CLIMBING ROUTE: Southeast slope

DISTANCE: 20 miles

ELEVATION GAIN: 7300'

DAYS: 2–3

MAPS: USGS Midnight Mountain, Gilbert, Sun Mountain; Green Trails Buttermilk Butte No. 83, Stehekin No. 82

RATING: E3T1

LOCATION: Okanogan National Forest and Lake Chelan-Sawtooth Wilderness administered by Okanogan National Forest, Methow Valley Visitor Center

PERMITS: None

SUMMARY AND HIGHLIGHTS: Located south of Washington Pass and east of Lake Chelan, Reynolds Peak is the highest formation in this part of the Methow Mountains. Many more of Washington's tallest mountains are situated here on the Chelan-Sawtooth Crest, but they are gentler in nature and can be scrambled on class 2 routes. Reynolds is more complex and steep, earning the ranking of "alpine climb," although many parties will choose not to use a rope to attain the summit.

Reynolds Peak has two distinct high points separated by a prominent saddle. Both are marked on the USGS map. The south peak, a large rock pyramid with three ridges, is the higher. The easiest way to reach this summit is on its moderate southern slope from War Creek Trail, or as a shorter trip via Williams Creek Trail. You can climb Reynolds in an exhausting, one-day marathon or in a leisurely weekend. The lowland panorama of the Sawtooth Ridge reveals hulking yet rounded mounts that yield easy and unrivaled highland rambling on the sparsely timbered slopes. The view from the top encompasses the nearby Lake Chelan-Sawtooth Wilderness with its other "Big Boys," all reaching above 8300 feet: Mt. Bigelow, Raven Ridge, and Martin, Hoodoo, Star, and Oval peaks.

Reynolds Peak from Reynolds Creek

HOW TO GET THERE: Drive to the town of Twisp, either from the north via Highway 20 or from the south via State Route 153. Drive west on the Twisp River County Road 9114, which becomes FS Road 44 upon entering the Okanogan National Forest. At 15 miles from Twisp reach the War Creek junction. Take the south fork and cross the Twisp River on the bridge. Drive north on FS Road 4430 for 0.5 mile past a spur road that leads to the War Creek Trail. Continue on FS Road 4430 for 3 miles more to the Williams Creek Trail No. 407 trailhead (2800').

TRIP DESCRIPTION: Hike on Williams Creek Trail No. 407 for 6.8 miles to Williams Lake (6500'). You can find a reasonable camp here (although a horse camp is nearby). Go around the northern shore of Williams Lake and veer southwest to the head of the basin. Climb up to Williams Butte in open meadows. Go along War Creek Ridge toward Camels Hump, avoiding the steep, northern wall of the basin of the south fork of Reynolds Creek. Trend northwest above Tony Basin (located below the east shoulder of Camels Hump) and cross north over War Creek Ridge at the saddle at 6700 feet. Descend downward in a gully about 200 feet into the head of the basin of the south fork of Reynolds Creek. Ascend the moderate and open southeastern slope of Reynolds Peak, aiming toward the near southern summit. Scramble up a gully to attain the southeast ridge at 7900 feet. From here go up on solid rock to the top of the summit horn (class 3).

HAZARDS AND TIPS: An alternate approach from the north via Reynolds Creek Trail No. 402 seems shorter, but leads to more difficult climbing than the path from the south. This trip is very strenuous if done in a single day. If a two-day trip is desirable, you can camp at Williams Lake and take only a summit pack on the summit day. You can make a longer trip, with less elevation gain, by using the War Creek Trail.

GPS WAYPOINT ROUTE:
1. 10U 687510, 5363445, 2800': Williams Creek Trailhead
2. 10U 683998, 5360543, 6.8 miles, 6500': Williams Lake
3. 10U 683163, 5360212, 0.6 mile, 7500': Williams Butte
4. 10U 681736, 5359346, 1.2 miles, 6700': War Creek Ridge saddle
5. 10U 680748, 5360243, 1.0 mile, 7900': southeast slope
6. 10U 680548, 5360351, 0.3 mile, 8512' Reynolds summit

TRIP TIMES:
Williams Lake Trailhead to Williams Lake: 6.8 miles, 3700', 7 hours
Williams Lake to Reynolds summit: 3.2 miles, 3200', 5 hours

CHAPTER 5
Pasayten Wilderness

The Pasayten Wilderness encompasses nearly half a million acres of undeveloped country laced with only a few trails, stretching east of North Cascades National Park along the Canadian border for 50 miles. The major portion covers the Okanogan Range, which joins the main Cascade divide at Harts Pass. Many of the highest points are scrambles: Robinson and Lake mountains; Monument, Lost, Osceola, Ptarmigan, and Windy peaks; and Mounts Carru, Lago, and Remmel. But several of the giants—Cathedral Peak, Jack, Amphitheater, and Blackcap mountains—require basic-level climbing skills (see definition on page 3). The Pasayten Wilderness is a dry and sometimes waterless land, popular with horse riders who can cover long stretches of territory between water sources. But for the climber who plans the trip well, or who goes in early season when snow provides water to drink, this region is rewarding for its unfettered high-country roaming and expansive horizons of sweeping, guileless skies.

Dave LeBlanc

Jack Mountain south face

118

The climate ranges from alpine forests in the western half to semiarid sagebrush desert in the east. Between 75 and 80 inches of precipitation fall annually near Ross Lake, but only 16 inches fall at the eastern margin. At higher elevations moisture falls mostly as snow, and the summers are short and dry, with large daily temperature fluctuations and infrequent severe thunderstorms. The forests of this inland region reflect the scant moisture: dense in the shaded valleys, sparse on most sunny slopes.

The word *Okanogan*, used by trappers and traders in various forms, stands for "rendezvous." Native Americans gathered for potlatches at various locations, bringing supplies of fish and game. The important streams of the region all had tribal names, some of which have been preserved in Anglicized form. The fur trade led to a need to explore routes from the interior to the coast. Early on, the region was claimed by the powerful nations of the era: Great Britain, the U.S., Spain, and Russia. When Spain and Russia ceded rights to the territory, Great Britain and the U.S. jointly occupied the region. In 1846 a treaty between both governments settled the boundary along the 49th parallel from the eastern slope of the Rocky Mountains to the middle of the channel separating the continent from Vancouver Island. Still, the territory along this line in the Cascades was completely unknown, and even native information on drainages proved flawed. After Lewis and Clark made their historic exploration, maps of the region were still marred by sketchy information.

In 1858 Great Britain and the U.S. agreed to implement a ground survey. Because of the difficult terrain and great cost, they agreed to determine points only at convenient and necessary intervals. Between 1857 and 1862 the boundary was first marked on the ground by teams representing both governments. Today a broad, clear-cut swathe runs like a straightedge through dense timber along the northern boundary of the Pasayten Wilderness. This precise marking of the 49th parallel looks as though a mammoth hand drew a larger-than-life knife blade over the countryside as far as the eye can see.

Okanogan National Forest manages the Pasayten Wilderness, which was first protected by legislation in 1934. Today newer regulations have made it the largest area without roads in the Cascade Range. Most of the villages in the Methow and adjacent valleys have kept their rustic charm. The Pasayten Wilderness remains a throwback to less civilized times. Travel is allowed only by foot or on horseback and only handsaws can be used for trail maintenance. Yet this outstanding area is still subject to land development and activities that do not protect or preserve the landscape. For the present at least, the Pasayten Wilderness remains an uncluttered, approachable backcountry destination where you can walk for days through all kinds of terrain—often completely alone.

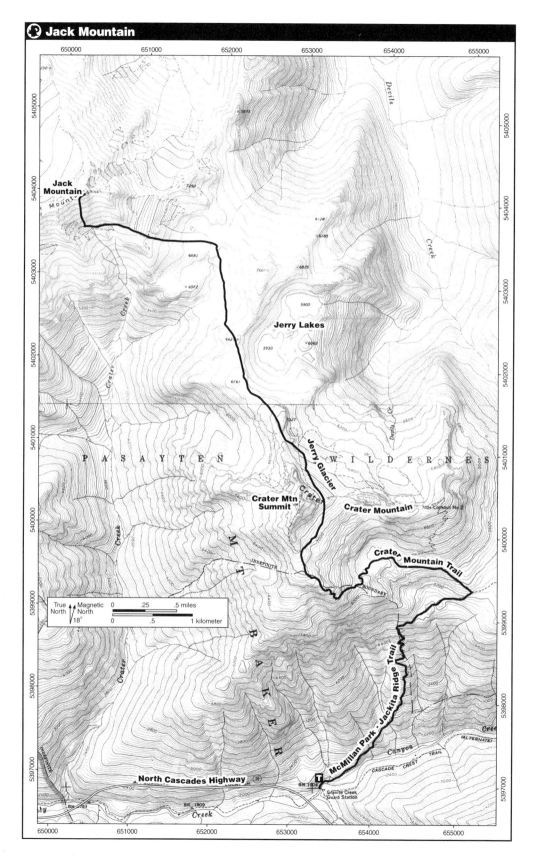

Jack Mountain

Jerry Lakes

Jerry Glacier

Crater Mtn Summit

Crater Mountain

Crater Mountain Trail

P A S A Y T E N   W I L D E R N E S S

M T   B A K E R

McMillan Park - Jackita Ridge Trail

North Cascades Highway

True North / Magnetic North 18°

0   .25   .5 miles
0   .5   1 kilometer

Jack Mountain

ELEVATION: 9066' (2763 m)

CLIMBING ROUTE: South Face

DISTANCE: 21 miles

ELEVATION GAIN: 9600'

DAYS: 3

MAPS: USGS Crater Mountain, Jack Mountain; Green Trails Mt. Logan No. 49, Jack Mountain No. 17

RATING: E3T4

LOCATION: North Cascades Scenic Highway Corridor, Pasayten Wilderness; Mt. Baker-Snoqualmie National Forest administered by Okanogan National Forest, Methow Valley Visitor Center

PERMITS: None; you must register at the trailhead.

SUMMARY AND HIGHLIGHTS: Jack Mountain stands alone like a citadel, big and mean-looking, dominating all the peaks nearby. One of the 10 non-volcanic peaks in Washington State over 9000 feet high, Jack towers above Ross Lake as a sheer profile in the sky rising nearly 8000 feet in just three miles. There is no easy way up this colossal hulk; indeed it has the reputation of being one of the most demanding and nerve-wracking ascents in the entire Cascade Range. Jack has therefore been relegated to the category of "nasty peak" and is less often climbed than many of its cohorts.

Despite its location in the rainshadow of the Picket Range, Jack Mountain sports large glaciers on both its northwest and northeast flanks. Here sharp moraines and hummocky groundcover extend below glaciers into partly timber-covered talus slopes. One approach to the summit along the north ridge is on relatively firm rock, but also contains an airy, icy traverse across the Nohokomeen Glacier, with a difficult portion near the summit block that has turned back even experienced climbers. The approach on the south face requires bold climbing as well, due to steep and rotten rock, but it is regarded by some climbers who have been on both routes as the less technical route to the top.

HOW TO GET THERE: Drive north on Interstate 5 to North Cascades Highway 20. Drive east on the highway to the town of Newhalem. Continue driving east 21.9 miles to an open area on the highway and a large parking lot (mile marker 141). Park here to find the footbridge crossing of Granite Creek (1900') at the Canyon Creek Trail No. 754 trailhead.

TRIP DESCRIPTION: From Highway 20, hike east to cross Granite Creek on a footbridge. Then hike downstream to cross Canyon Creek. Immediately after the crossing find a T-junction. Go right and hike northeast on McMillan Park-Jackita Ridge Trail No. 738, which climbs steeply for 3.7 miles to another trail junction (5300'). Take the left fork and hike on Crater Mountain Trail No. 738B for 0.7 mile. At a junction at 5800 feet just before Crater Lake go left (west) on a boot tread toward the western Crater Mountain summit (8128'). Hike on the unmaintained trail until you reach 7100 feet. Leave the trail and traverse northeast to Jerry Glacier (7400'). Rope up and traverse the glacier to a ramp beyond a cliff band. Climb and attain the north ridge of Crater Mountain at the saddle (7100'). Alternatively, go to the low point of Jerry Glacier to reach Jerry Lakes. Continue northwest past Jerry Lakes up and over a ridge into a basin east of Crater Creek. Make a camp in the flat basin at 6000 feet.

The next day scramble west to the southeast ridge at 7300 feet. Continue traversing on a northwest contour past Crater Creek. Scramble west on scree or snow to beyond a cliff band. Continue traversing at about 7500 feet on a relatively flat bench until you are on the south face directly below the summit of Jack. Go up for about 1000 feet on the south face, climbing in steep, dirty gullies that are filled with snow until late summer (class 3–4). There are many variations here, but in general stay in the center of the face. Aim toward a gully just west of the summit that leads to the southwest ridge. Some parties choose to scramble the last bit on the exposed ridge, but it is loose enough that others prefer to directly climb the face to the top. On all parts of the face beware of rotten rock and intense exposure. Manage your party well and wear helmets. You may want a small rope to use for a hand line and short rappels, but expect little belayed climbing due to extreme rockfall danger.

HAZARDS AND TIPS: The south face route is notorious for extraordinarily loose rock and has provided a dicey ascent for many climbing parties. This trip may be best done when the face is mostly free of snow, but not too late in the summer when the face is dry, forcing you to carry excess water. Jack can also be climbed from the north ridge over the Nohokomeen Glacier. Some parties believe that this route provides more

Jack Mountain (left) and Crater Mountain (right), from the south

solid rock to climb. However, a steep step and an airy glacier traverse under the summit block have turned back some parties, particularly when the snow conditions are poor. The north ridge route also requires coordination with Ross Lake Resort to arrange for boat transportation to the east shore of Ross Lake for the cross-country start.

GPS WAYPOINT ROUTE:
1. 10U 653316, 5396665, 1900': Granite Creek
2. 10U 655197, 5399334, 3.9 miles, 5300': Crater Mountain Trail
3. 10U 654180, 5399708, 0.7 mile, 5800': trail junction
4. 10U 653060, 5399667, 1.5 miles, 7100': leave trail
5. 10U 652792, 5401126, 0.8 mile, 7100': saddle
6. 10U 651733, 5403454, 1.9 miles, 6000': basin camp
7. 10U 650805, 5403581, 0.6 mile, 7300': southeast ridge
8. 10U 650233, 5403598, 0.5 mile, 7500': South Face
9. 10U 650255, 5404010, 0.5 mile, 9066': Jack summit

TRIP TIMES:
Granite Creek to basin camp: 8.9 miles, 5400', 9 hours
Basin camp to Jack summit: 1.6 miles, 3100', 7 hours

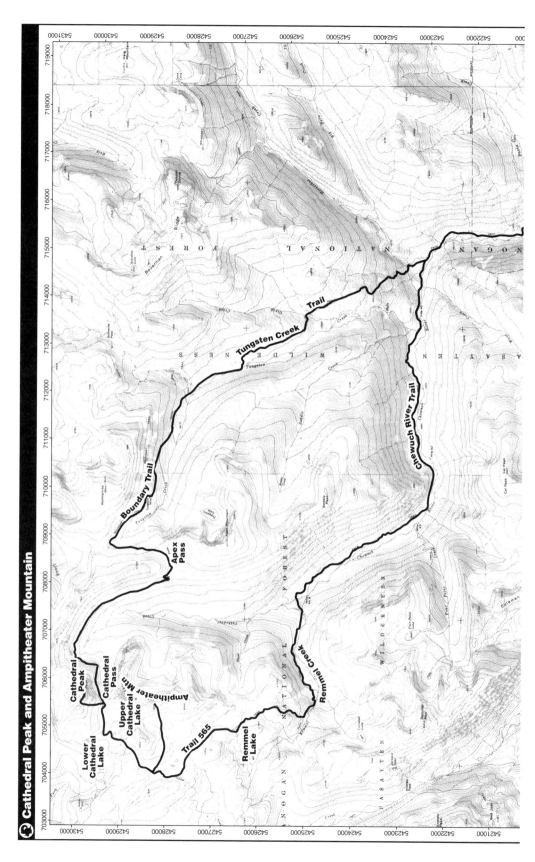

Cathedral Peak and Ampitheater Mountain

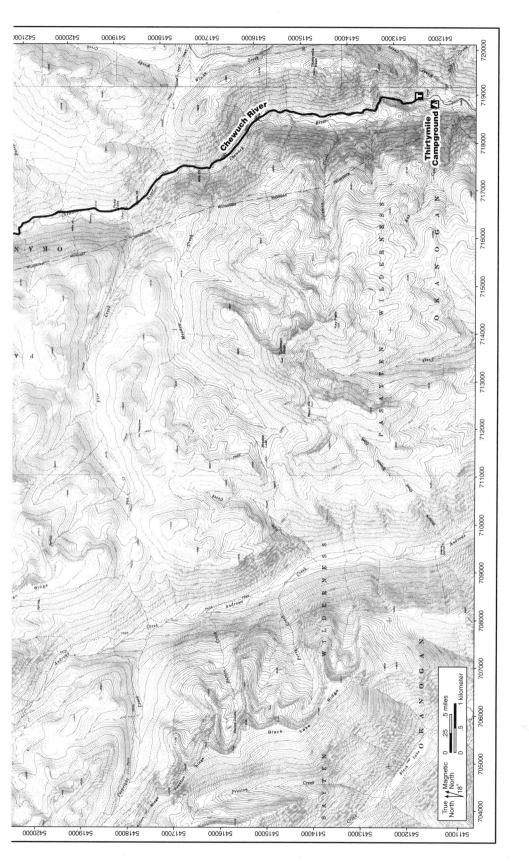

Cathedral Peak and Amphitheater Mountain

ELEVATIONS: 8601', 8358' (2622 m, 2548 m)

CLIMBING ROUTES: Cathedral: West Ridge; Amphitheater: West Face

DISTANCE: 49 miles

ELEVATION GAIN: 6700'

DAYS: At least 4

MAPS: USGS Coleman Peak, Bauerman Ridge, Remmel Mountain; Green Trails Coleman Peak No. 20

RATING: E4T4

LOCATION: Pasayten Wilderness, administered by Okanogan National Forest, Methow Valley Visitor Center

PERMITS: None; you must register at the trailhead.

SUMMARY AND HIGHLIGHTS: This duo resides deep in the core of the Pasayten Wilderness. Reaching them requires miles of lowland hiking from any direction, but the splendid locale is your prize for the lengthy journey. Blocky peaks jut above the green, rolling terrain, creating high artistic contrast and stirring visual drama. Cathedral Lakes, tucked away in the belly of the surrounding peaks, are as pretty an alpine milieu as any in the monster-crag region of the Cascade Crest.

South of Cathedral Pass stands Amphitheater Mountain, a remnant of the original dome-shaped peak named for the glacial sculpting that left great cirques between long spurs of rock. The central point of the huge, sprawling formation is also the highest. Cathedral Lakes are nestled in ice scours in an adjacent meadow. Nearby Cathedral Peak is named for its resemblance to a Gothic church. Its fine granite and elegant, 1000-foot face are celebrated among rock climbers. But less experienced mountaineers can still attain the summit of this important mountain by an easier way, which requires only basic-level climbing skills (see definition page 3).

HOW TO GET THERE: Drive to the town of Winthrop, either from the west on Highway 20 or from the south on State Route 153 plus 20. Just west of Winthrop and west of the Chewuch River (Chewack River on the USGS map) find the West Chewuch Road. Drive north on this road, which becomes FS Road 51 upon entering the Okanogan National Forest and FS Road 5160 at Camp 4. Continue driving on this main road to Thirtymile Campground (29 miles from Winthrop) and the parking area for the Chewuch River Trail No. 510 trailhead (3600').

TRIP DESCRIPTION: Hike on the Chewuch River Trail for 8.7 miles to a Y-junction (4700'). Take the right fork and hike northwest on the Tungsten Creek Trail No. 534 for 6.2 miles to a T-junction (6800'). Hike left (west) on the Boundary Trail No. 533 over Apex Pass for 5.0 miles to Cathedral Pass (7600'). Continue another 0.7 mile to a camp at Upper Cathedral Lake (20.6 miles from Thirtymile Campground). Most parties will need two days to get to Upper Cathedral Lake.

Cathedral Peak

The next day, hike east on the trail back to Cathedral Pass. Scramble up heather and scree toward the notch on the west ridge of Cathedral Peak. At the base (8300') of the summit cliffs, stay right and scramble over the first rock ridge at a small gap. Drop a few feet into a narrow passageway between the rock ridge and the next ridge and go east about 40 feet. Climb north onto the second ridge and scramble to the highest

Keith Wilson

Cathedral Peak

Keith Wilson

Amphitheater Mountain summit

point. Drop again into a notch to the south. Some parties will require
rock protection and a short rope to execute an exposed, airy step above
a 20-foot drop to cross the gap of several feet to gain the final summit
block (class 4). From the last rocky block the final portion is a walk to
the summit. Retrace your steps through Cathedral Pass back to camp at
Upper Cathedral Lake.

Amphitheater Mountain

On either the same day or the next day, hike southwest from Upper
Cathedral Lake on Boundary Trail No. 533 for about 1.3 mile to the pass
at 7300 feet at the base of the west shoulder of Amphitheater Mountain.
Leave the trail and hike east in open country. Scramble up the easy west
slope to the broad summit ridge. The central peak that is a mile south of
Cathedral Pass is the highest.

For a pleasing loop trip on the hike out, from Upper Cathedral Lake
go southwest on Boundary Trail No. 533 for 0.5 mile to the pass at the
base of the west shoulder of Amphitheater Mountain. Then go south on
unmaintained Trail No. 565 for 3.2 miles past Remmel Lake to Remmel
Creek (6600'). Here take the left branch of the main trail and hike southeast on the Chewuch River Trail No. 510 for 8.0 miles to the junction
with Tungsten Creek Trail at 4700 feet. Continue south on the Chewuch
River Trail for 8.7 miles to the trailhead (20.4 miles from Upper
Cathedral Lake to Thirtymile Campground).

HAZARDS AND TIPS: A short rope and runners with a few pieces of rock protection are recommended for the step across the gap on Cathedral Peak just below the summit. Crossing the west spur of Amphitheater from Cathedral Pass leads to class 5 climbing. Going around the west spur allows you to reach the summit of Amphitheater on the easy west slope. This trip has many miles of trail and can be combined with climbing other peaks in the area for an extended outing.

GPS WAYPOINT ROUTE:
1. 10U 718915, 5412432, 3600': Chewuch River Trailhead
2. 10U 715124, 5422905, 8.7 miles, 4700': Tungsten Creek Trail
3. 10U 704772, 5429052, 11.9 miles, 7400': Upper Cathedral Lake
4. 10U 705474, 5429909, 1.2 miles, 8300': notch
5. 10U 705747, 5429860, 0.2 mile, 8601': Cathedral summit
6. 10U 705503, 5429421, 0.7 mile, 7600': Cathedral Pass
7. 10U 704134, 5428354, 2.0 miles, 7300': Amphitheater west shoulder
8. 10U 705543, 5428330, 1.3 miles, 8358': Amphitheater summit

TRIP TIMES:
Upper Cathedral Lake to Cathedral summit: 1.4 miles, 1200', 4 hours

Cathedral summit to Amphitheater summit: 4.0 miles, 1100', 4 hours

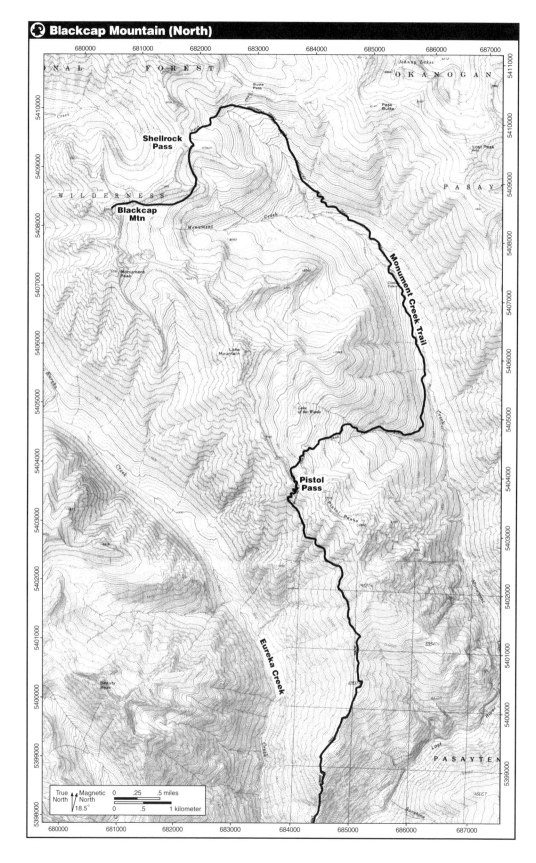

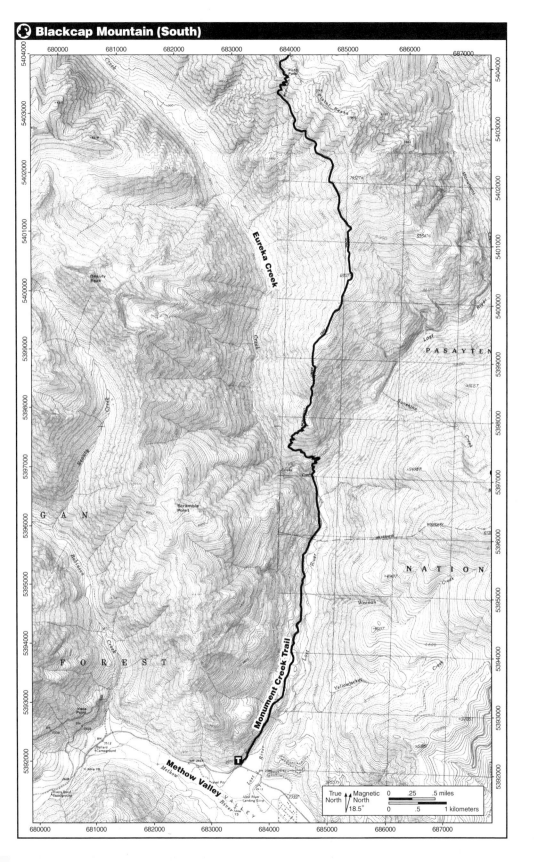

Eureka Creek

Beauty Peak

PASAYTEN

Scramble Point

G A N

Monument Creek Trail

N A T I O N

F O R E S T

Methow Valley

Methow River

True North / Magnetic North 18.5°

0 .25 .5 miles

0 .5 1 kilometers

ROUTE 21

Blackcap Mountain

ELEVATION: 8397' (2559 m)

CLIMBING ROUTE: Northeast Ridge

DISTANCE: 38 miles

ELEVATION GAIN: 12,700'

DAYS: 3–4

MAPS: USGS Robinson Mountain, McLeod Mountain, Lost Peak, Mt. Lago; Green Trails Washington Pass No. 50, Mazama No. 51, Billy Goat Mountain No. 19, Pasayten Peak, No. 18

RATING: E4T1

LOCATION: Pasayten Wilderness, administered by Okanogan National Forest, Methow Valley Visitor Center

PERMITS: None; you must register at the trailhead.

SUMMARY AND HIGHLIGHTS: Wild, alien, and lonely. The alpine countryside near Blackcap Peak is a place few people visit because it takes so much work to get there. Parts of the trail are not well-maintained. Furthermore, the route to Pistol Pass gains nearly 5000 feet on parched and waterless ground. But part of the incentive is the stretch along the Monument Creek Trail as it passes through the dramatic confluence of two gorges carved by Eureka Creek from the west and Lost River from the east. Lonely Blackcap Peak has its own innate dignity in the barren Pasayten Wilderness—a last living link to a simpler past.

The dark face of Blackcap Mountain stands above rough cirques that hold residual patches of ice, yet the ridge to the summit requires only modest climbing skills. From the top you can nearly reach out and touch nearby scramble-worthy peaks of more than 8300 feet of elevation: Lake Mountain; Mounts Lago and Carru; and Osceola, Monument, and Lost peaks. In this Wilderness you can immerse yourself in freedom of motion and worldly abandon.

HOW TO GET THERE: Drive to the town of Mazama, either from the west on Highway 20 or from the south on State Route 153 plus 20.

Steve Fry

Blackcap Mountain with mounts Carru and Lago in the distance

Continue on Harts Pass County Road 9140 (becomes FS Road 5400) for 7.2 miles to the Monument Creek Trail No. 484 trailhead (2400').

TRIP DESCRIPTION: Hike north on the Monument Creek Trail (also called the Lost River-Monument Creek-Ptarmigan Creek Trail), which begins in the Methow River Valley just to the west of Lost River. At 4.0 miles at the falls, Eureka Creek joins the Lost River, and the huge chasm of the Lost River Gorge enters from the northeast. Continue for 6 miles up the steep and waterless slope to Pistol Pass (7000'). Descend 2400 feet to Monument Creek. The trail then climbs to a junction at 6600 feet. Monument Creek Trail No. 484 continues north along Ptarmigan Creek, but instead take the left fork and continue upward along Trail No. 484A toward Shellrock Pass. At about 6800 feet find a suitable camp away from the trail on the east side of the pass.

The next morning, hike up the trail to its southernmost point (7300') at the last large switchback. Here leave the trail and traverse rock or snow, trending south. Cross over the east spur of Blackcap Mountain at 7300 feet. Drop into the broad, eastern basin of Monument Creek where the terrain is open. Go upward and attain the northeast ridge at a saddle at 7700 feet (class 3). Scramble on the ridgecrest or its northwest side to the summit on relatively firm rock.

HAZARDS AND TIPS: This is a strenuous trip with many miles along the trail. Pistol Pass faces south and is intensely hot in the summer sun.

Be sure to carry enough water to comfortably reach the pass, as there is not a reliable water source until you cross over into the Monument Creek drainage. You can also climb Blackcap Mountain from the west side of Shellrock Pass by travelling south and reaching the northeast ridge at the saddle. Because the Monument Creek Trail between Pistol Pass and Shellrock Pass is not maintained, the going may be slow due to blowdowns on it. An alternative method is to start from Slate Pass, going past Osceola, Carru, and Lago, to reach Shellrock Pass from the west. When wet, black lichen that coats the higher rocks of Blackcap creates a surface slick as ice.

GPS WAYPOINT ROUTE:

1. 10U 683421, 5392026, 2400': Monument Creek Trailhead
2. 10U 683860, 5403830, 10.0 miles, 7000': Pistol Pass
3. 10U 681878, 5409399, 7.3 miles, 7300': leave trail
4. 10U 681974, 5408761, 0.5 mile, 7300': east spur
5. 10U 680875, 5408465, 0.8 mile, 7700': northeast ridge
6. 10U 680517, 5408317, 0.4 mile, 8397': Blackcap summit

TRIP TIMES:

Monument Creek Trailhead to camp: 17.0 miles, 7100', 12 hours
Camp to Blackcap summit: 2.1 miles, 2300', 4 hours

CHAPTER 6
Lake Chelan

L ake Chelan stretches for nearly 50 miles from the small city of Chelan to the resort hamlet of Stehekin. Its name is derived from a Native American phrase meaning "clear water," though its actual jade-green color results from the inflow of silt from the highly glaciated peaks of the Cascade Crest to the northwest. This crest region at the upper end of Lake Chelan is known for its lush coniferous forests, considered unique even for already lush Western Washington. Here the deep alluvial soil feeds several species of giant trees—up to 200 feet high—for up to 500 years. A particularly impressive stand grows on rich, moist benches near the confluence of Thunder and McAllister creeks. Although Douglas fir is the most common tree, this area is called a Western Hemlock Forest Zone. Also in this zone is vine maple, a shrubby tree that chokes avalanche paths and, unfortunately, impedes cross-country travel (but also has vibrant autumn leaves). Lowland plants—twinflower, marsh marigold, skunk cabbage, and bunchberry—join foamflowers and assorted ferns that cloak the valley bottoms and prosper in the cool, dry summers.

Well above shoreline flora gives way to the alpine zone, where meadows replace upright trees due to the harsh environment and lingering snowpack. Dwarf juniper grows on exposed rock outcrops. Red heather and blue-leaf huckleberries coexist. The huckleberry brings remarkable orange and red hues in fall. Its berries are a delicate and flavorful prize to bears and humans alike. Chickweed, lupine, phlox, cinquefoil, and avalanche lily are all present at high elevations, growing in dwarfed forms together with heaths.

Native Americans roamed and paddled along Lake Chelan's shores for millennia, but the first recorded reference to the uncharted lake was in 1811 by Alexander Ross, an early explorer for the Pacific Fur Company. John A. Tennant and D.C. Linsley were the first non-natives to voyage up Lake Chelan, canoeing to its headwaters in 1870 to explore the Stehekin River and Agnes Creek drainages for possible railroad routes. From 1897 to 1899, USGS parties under W.T. Griswold and R.A. Farmer surveyed Lake Chelan's shoreline and the entire span of the Methow Mountains. Fur traders were the first white men to settle the region, and miners soon followed. The now-abandoned Holden Mine on Railroad Creek where it feeds into the western shore of Lake Chelan was

Dave LeBlanc

South side of Goode Mountain

the largest copper producer in the history of Washington State during its 20 years of operation. Its legacy is a blight of unsightly yellowish residue with poisonous tailings that threatens water quality even today.

The entire Lake Chelan region is served by an extensive trail network, much of which follows the former routes of prospectors and shepherds. The National Park Service in the form of Lake Chelan National Recreation Area and North Cascades National Park administers the northern portion of the region. Wenatchee National Forest manages the remainder of the mountainous terrain as part of the Glacier Peak and Lake Chelan-Sawtooth wildernesses. The only settlements along Lake Chelan are Holden on the west side of the lake and Stehekin on the north shore. Both villages are landlocked and can be reached only by boat, floatplane, or foot. From Lucerne—a boat landing on the western lakeshore—hikers, climbers, and visitors can ride on a school bus shuttle up a steep, short road to the religious retreat at Holden. Here you can enjoy a nutritious, communally prepared meal for a small fee; you can also visit the ice cream bar, which is open most afternoons during the summer. There are trails emanating from the small settlement to other backcountry sites and climbs. Stehekin is similar in that many hiking trails lead from it, and that hikers and climbers can shuttle on the Stehekin Valley Road on the way to the Cascade Pass Trail.

Private concessionaires operate the bus service in the lower Stehekin River valley while the National Park Service (NPS) operates the shuttle bus in the upper valley past High Bridge Camp. Schedules and busses vary depending on the time of the year. Reservations are not needed on the Lower Valley bus. The upper valley NPS shuttle runs several times daily during the summer. Because the van is crowded in summer with visitors in North Cascades National Park who stay at campsites along the route, you should reserve your place in advance. To make reservations call the NPS at (360) 856-5700 Ext. 340, then dial Ext. 14 for reservations. The fare for the Lower Valley bus is $4 per person each way. The fare for the NPS shuttle is $6 per person each way. Carry some small bills, as the National Park Rangers who drive the NPS Shuttle can accept only cash, and often run out of change.

The northern reaches of Lake Chelan are accessed by the *Lady of the Lake*, a local pedestrian ferry, from the town of Chelan or from Fields Point Landing farther up the lake. This is one of the unique experiences of Washington. As you move away from the brazen condominiums and resorts that swarm the southern shores of the lake and move toward remote Lucerne and eventually the rustic and backwoods ranger station at Stehekin, it feels as if you are going backward in time. As the boat ride progresses, you venture deeper into wild country, where higher and ever more rugged ice-clad pinnacles plunge to the glacier-fed waters. Some climbers think of the boat ride as a time-consuming obstacle. But for others, the relaxing and serene journey up the lake is a welcome chance to meditate on the adventures to come.

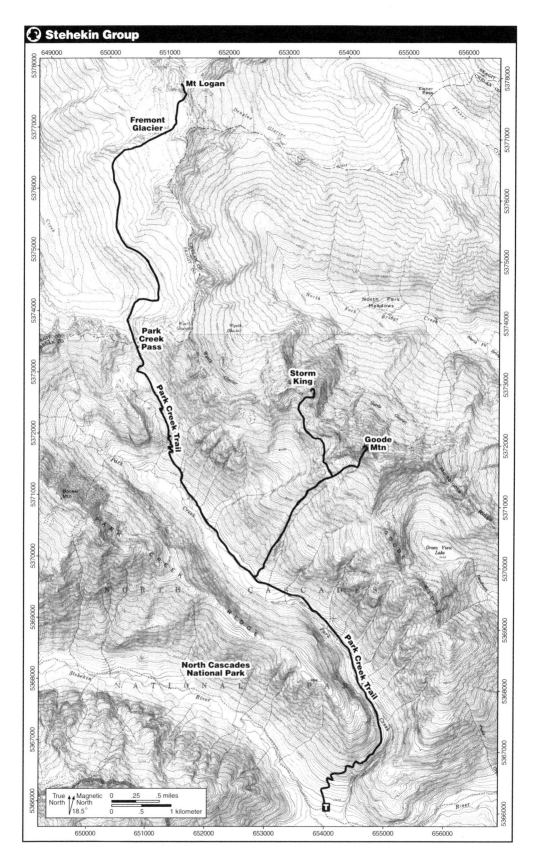

ROUTE 22

Stehekin Group
Goode Mountain, Storm King, and Mt. Logan

ELEVATIONS: 9200+', 8515', 9087' (2804+ m, 2596 m, 2770 m)

CLIMBING ROUTES: Goode: Southwest Couloir; Storm King: Southeast Ridge; Logan: Fremont Glacier

DISTANCE: 31 miles

ELEVATION GAIN: 13,900'

DAYS: At least 5

MAPS: USGS Goode Mountain, Mt. Logan; Green Trails McGregor Mountain No. 81, Mt. Logan No. 49

RATING: E5T4

LOCATION: North Cascades National Park, Stehekin Ranger Station

PERMITS: Permits are required for camping in North Cascades National Park; NPS shuttle-bus reservations are recommended for the road past High Bridge Camp; contact the Sedro-Woolley Ranger Station to connect with the National Park Service in Stehekin for information and reservations by calling (360) 856-5700 ext. 341 then ext. 14.

SUMMARY AND HIGHLIGHTS: Goode Mountain, Storm King, and Mt. Logan are some of the largest monster crags in the North Cascades. This Stehekin Group forms the backbone of the Cascade Crest amid surrounding ice-clad spires. Goode Mountain dominates the entire wave of mountains between the head of Lake Chelan and the Skagit River, but is so tucked away in the wilderness that it is virtually hidden from view from the surrounding valleys. Its northeast buttress forms a long, well-known, intermediate rock-climbing route to the horn-shaped summit. But the southwest face of Goode has blocky breaks that provide a less technical route to the top. Situated between Park Creek Pass and Goode Mountain, Storm King is less massive, yet is another local titan. The location of the actual summit can cause some confusion. The summit area consists of a long, east-west hogback culminating in sharp needles and then two tall, slender towers at the eastern end. The true summit is the eastern of the two prominent towers. Mt. Logan rounds out the threesome. It is a broad, ice-covered massif with three major glaciers: the Banded, the Douglas, and the Fremont. It also has three major summits, the north summit being the highest. Mt. Logan can be approached from most directions on any of these glaciers, but the southeast approach from Park Creek Pass along the Fremont Glacier is the shortest and easiest path to the summit.

Reaching the Stehekin group calls for commitment and energy, and climbing it requires modest technical skills. This is one of the most remote regions in the entire Cascade Range. The journey through this fragile yet stunning terrain above treeline and into the stark alpine world is an experience you will treasure.

HOW TO GET THERE: Drive to north Wenatchee either from the west via Highway 2 or from the south using Interstate 90 and then Highway 97 over Blewett Pass. From north Wenatchee drive north on Alternate Highway 97 on the west side of the Columbia River. At 9 miles past the town of Entiat go north on Navarre Coulee Road (State Route 971) at the sign for Fields Point Landing. Continue to Lake Chelan State Park, situated on the southern shore of Lake Chelan. Go left (north) on South Lakeshore Road for 8 miles along the shore of Lake Chelan until you reach Fields Point Landing. Here find a huge space for parking and the ticket station for the *Lady of the Lake*. Be sure to get here early enough to catch the daily boat that leaves at 9:45 A.M. You can also pay more money and catch a faster boat that leaves a half hour earlier.

TRIP DESCRIPTION: Take either boat to Stehekin at the headwaters of Lake Chelan. Obtain your required permit to camp in the national park and register for the climb at the information station. Reserve space at either the Twomile or the Fivemile Camp on Park Creek. Take the Lower Valley bus to High Bridge Camp. Connect with the NPS shuttle to Park Creek Camp and the Park Creek Trail No. 1270 trailhead at 2300 feet (18.5 miles from Stehekin). Hike north on the trail to your selected camp for the first night. Very strong parties and those who choose to stay the first night at the North Cascades Stehekin Lodge (to make reservations call (509) 682-4494) or other accommodations and catch the early shuttle the next morning may pack to sites high on the ridge that drops down southwest of Goode. The sites range in elevation: From 5600 feet later in the season when water is available from a stream coming down from the Goode-Storm King col, to 6500 feet on benches with snow-patch water in early season; or to 7200–7400 feet on or just under the bench directly below Goode's southwest side, where water is always available from higher, permanent snowfields.

Descending Goode Mountain

Leave the Park Creek Trail about 3.8 miles past Park Creek Camp just after hiking through a wide brush patch and into timber (4000'). Because the slope above is waterless, fill your bottle here. You cannot see the climber's trail, but the site may be marked with a cairn that shows the starting point just before you cross a small stream 0.1 mile after entering the woods. Ascend through trees, moving left if you encounter thick brush. After 300–400 feet of elevation gain you can find a foot tread on the crest of the timber-covered rib that runs down along the left side of the stream, which comes from the 7400-foot bench on the southwest slope of Goode. The slope, above and northwest of the deep streambed, is too steep to descend to get water. When the track peters out at 5500 feet continue upward and to the left on open slopes. Continue up the crest of the ridge through broken cliffs, or skirt directly below them trending toward the outlet stream on the right. You can camp at level spots at 6500 or 6800 feet using snow patches for water. But continue upward if time permits. At 7000 feet scramble to the right (east) of a rocky buttress. Cross the bench at 7200 feet directly under the southwest face. You will find beautiful campsites here with water throughout the year.

Goode Mountain

To attain Goode the next day from camp, go up the right side of the long southwest couloir to the pocket glacier on the southwest face of Goode. Scramble up snow or loose talus to the ridge of the surrounding cirque. Ascend the rocky face, aiming toward the high, white towers on the southeast ridge. At the top of the rock scramble, at the far upper-left-hand corner at the base of the summit cliff, kiss the cliff (go up until you nearly touch it) and walk easily north on a big ledge into the upper half of the deep southwest couloir. Climb up the gully on the left side to 8800 feet below a notch in the summit ridge. At this point the white tower of Goode summit is to the left, while the Black Tooth (a dark pointed tower on the southeast ridge) is to the right. Here find a 40-foot downsloping slab (rappel slings are visible at the top of the slab). Begin the first pitch of climbing here.

Climb a few moves up a rightsloping crack high on the left side of the white slab (class 5), then traverse right on the slab, step across a narrow gully, and step around a blind rock corner to a good belay stance. For the second pitch, climb upward and left (class 4) to a gap called Black Tooth notch. From the notch on the crest, cross over the ridge onto a sandy ledge above the east face and go left (northwest). Downclimb 8 feet at the end of the ledge and continue. In about 100 feet encounter a minor ridge that can be seen from the sandy ledge. This ridge is part of the northeast buttress. From here climb two additional pitches obliquely upward and to the right in steep slots to the summit (class 4). Rappel down the ascent route and return to camp.

Storm King

If you camped at 6500 or 6800 feet, start trending north up the same rib used for the Goode approach. Then veer west scrambling up the steep buttress to avoid the talus. Aim toward the stream in a heather patch and arrive at a meadow basin (7400') where the buttress levels out after 700 feet of scrambling. Alternatively, if you camped at 7200 feet, traverse northwest at 7400 feet to the same meadow basin. At the 7400-foot bench, go left up and across the red ledge and contour northwest across talus slopes and snow benches. Then scramble over a heather-covered buttress and a longer snowfield to reach the huge scree-talus field below the two tall, slender eastern towers—the West Peak (8515') is lower and the tower to the right (east) has the summit. Climb the talus or snow slope on the right side (or scramble up the buttress to avoid the talus) to a notch just right of the twin towers. Some parties may wish to rope up here or fix the end of a hand line. Find the ledge system leading across the northeast face of the summit tower by crossing through the notch and downclimbing 5 feet. Make an exposed, awkward step left (class 4) to get onto the wide ledge. Find good cracks for placing protection while traversing the ledge, with one more awkward, crouching move to cross a thin area under an overhanging block. The ledge ends at a minor rib after 150 feet.

Ascending the wind cirque to attain the ridge of Mt. Logan

Continue walking around the summit block formation for another 200 feet. Ascend a rib about 30 vertical feet to a good belay position. Rope up and climb left toward the notch between the twin towers (class 4). Drop down (west) through the notch about 10 feet and cross downsloping slabs for about 20 feet above a major chimney. Climb left directly up a shallow chimney with good hand and foot holds for about 30 vertical feet to reach a good belay point (rappel slings left on the mountain mark the site) just below the summit blocks (class 5). Climb the final rocks to the summit.

Rappel the ascent route or, if two ropes are available, rappel directly down onto the wide ledge. Return across the ledge system to the notch at the end of the summit block formation and descend the snow or talus slopes. Return to camp by the wide ledges and snowfields used on the ascent or directly down the nasty scree fields south of Storm King to hit the tree-covered rib that leads to the low camp at 6500 feet. Contour around to the climber's track and descend to the Park Creek Trail.

Mt. Logan

To attain Logan hike northwest on the trail to Park Creek Pass at 6100 feet (3.4 miles from the climber's trail to Goode Mountain). A quarter mile past the pass, just before the switchbacks descend steeply to Thunder Creek, leave the trail at 5900 feet and climb east up the terminal moraine of the Wyeth Glacier to a large, sandy bench with nearby water to camp (6400'). The next day traverse northwest at 6600 feet for 2 miles across ribs and streams, heading parallel to the ridge that connects Logan with Storm King and Goode to the south. Go nearly to the base of a major buttress that trends west from the middle of the Fremont Glacier. Then angle up (east) along the base of the buttress across boulder fields, heather benches, and snowfields to reach the Fremont Glacier at about 8000 feet. Snow may fill all the crevasses in early season but by August expect to negotiate crevasses and blue ice.

Cross the glacier northeast to below the huge buttress that juts out from the middle summit. Ascend the glacier, angling left, aiming to reach the low point on the ridge (8700'). Approach the rock on the snow crest of a wind cirque. Scramble up a gully to a notch in the ridge and scramble north on the east side of the ridge to avoid obstacles (class 4).

Chris Weidner

Mt. Logan

Traverse north for 0.3 mile, bypassing a false summit on its right side, to approach the final summit block. Climb a short chimney and work upward past a solid chockstone to attain the summit (class 4). Return to camp via the ascent route and, if time allows, pack and hike back down the Park Creek Trail to stay at Fivemile Camp. On the following day hike on the trail to Park Creek Camp. Take the NPS shuttle and the Lower Valley bus back to Stehekin and then the boat back to the parking spot.

HAZARDS AND TIPS: Rock protection and a moderate rack (cams and stoppers) are required for all three mountains. Glacier gear is required for Logan. This is a long trip but it is the easiest way to reach all three summits.

GPS WAYPOINT ROUTE:
1. 10U 653966, 5366020, 2300': Park Creek Camp
2. 10U 652646, 5369776, 3.8 miles, 4000': leave trail
3. 10U 653945, 5371408, 1.5 miles, 7200': Goode-Storm King camp
4. 10U 654305, 5371559, 0.4 mile, 8100': Goode southeast ridge
5. 10U 654432, 5371894, 0.3 mile, 9200+': Goode summit
6. 10U 653568, 5372087, 1.1 mile, 7400': upper basin bench
7. 10U 653605, 5372702, 0.7 mile, 8000': Storm King notch
8. 10U 653570, 5372824, 0.3 mile, 8515': Storm King summit
9. 10U 650550, 5373538, 6.2 miles, 6100': Park Creek Pass
10. 10U 650653, 5376777, 3.2 miles, 8000': Fremont Glacier
11. 10U 651328, 5377572, 0.9 mile, 8700': Logan south ridge
12. 10U 651252, 5377771, 0.4 mile, 9087': Logan summit

TRIP TIMES:
Goode-Storm King camp to Goode summit: 0.8 mile, 2000', 5 hours
Goode-Storm King camp to Storm King summit: 1.3 miles, 1300', 4 hours
Moraine camp to Logan summit: 4.3 miles, 2700', 6 hours

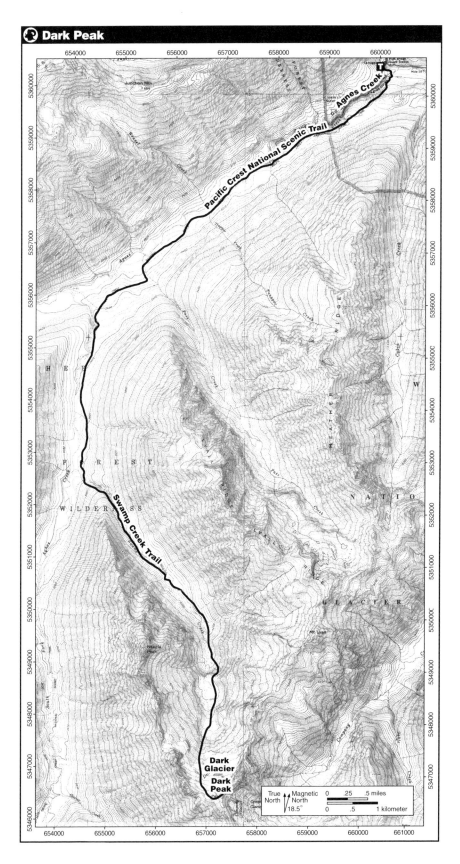

Pacific Crest National Scenic Trail

Agnes Creek

Swamp Creek Trail

WILDERNESS

Dark Glacier

Dark Peak

| True North / Magnetic North 18.5° | 0 | .25 | .5 miles |
| | 0 | .5 | 1 kilometer |

Dark Peak

ELEVATION: 8504' (2592 m)

CLIMBING ROUTE: Dark Glacier

DISTANCE: 29 miles

ELEVATION GAIN: 6800'

DAYS: 3–4

MAPS: USGS McGregor Mountain, Mt. Lyall, Agnes Mountain; Green Trails McGregor Mountain No. 81

RATING: E4T3

LOCATION: Lake Chelan National Recreation Area administered by North Cascades National Park, Stehekin Ranger Station; Glacier Peak Wilderness administered by Wenatchee National Forest, Chelan Ranger District

PERMITS: Visitors are asked to sign in at the trailhead register.

SUMMARY AND HIGHLIGHTS: Dark Peak is a good example of the drudgery involved in climbing some of Washington's highest peaks. Just getting within striking distance of the summit requires perseverance: you must take the boat up Lake Chelan, ride the shuttle bus, then hike for miles. After that, depending on the season, you must navigate through a long stretch of either leg-wrenching snow or cursed slide alder to get to the pocket glacier, which still has dangerous ice patches and crevasses. So why climb Dark Peak? Many climbers choose to forgo the headache. But the remote and wild location ensures crowds found on better-known mountains won't plague you here. It is likely you will be completely alone after leaving the valley floor. Also, this peak is spectacular in its own right, and it offers a stirring view of neighboring Bonanza Peak. Although this trip requires focus and energy, in return you'll get the unmitigated feeling of exploration and adventure, as if you were the first person on earth to be here.

HOW TO GET THERE: Drive to north Wenatchee either from the west on Highway 2, or from the south using Interstate 90 and then Highway 97 over Blewett Pass. From north Wenatchee drive north on Alternate

Highway 97 on the west side of the Columbia River. At 9 miles past the town of Entiat go north on Navarre Coulee Road (State Route 971) at the sign for Fields Point Landing. Continue to Lake Chelan State Park, situated on the southern shore of Lake Chelan. Go left (north) on South Lakeshore Road for 8 miles along the shore of Lake Chelan until you reach Fields Point Landing. Here find a huge space for parking and the ticket station for the *Lady of the Lake*. Be sure to get here early enough to catch the daily boat that leaves at 9:45 A.M. You can also pay more money and catch a faster boat that leaves a half hour earlier.

TRIP DESCRIPTION: Take either boat to Stehekin at the headwaters of Lake Chelan. From Stehekin take the Lower Valley bus to the last stop at High Bridge Camp (1700'). Hike on the Pacific Crest National Scenic Trail (Crest Trail No.2000) along the south shore of Agnes Creek. Do not confuse this trail with the Agnes Gorge Trail on the north shore of Agnes Creek. In 8.6 miles (2800'), take the left junction onto Swamp Creek Trail No. 1242 on the south side of the creek. This trail is not maintained, and many blowdowns and patches of slide alder obscure the route. In 1.5 miles at 3800 feet, the trail crosses to the northeast side of Swamp Creek. Continue hiking until the end of the footpath (4000'). Try to keep going up the valley rather than camp here, so that the next day the summit push will be shorter. At 4400 feet enter the lower basin of Swamp Creek and make camp where there are many flat spots and plenty of water. Your camp will be close to a waterfall that flows from the upper basin.

The next day, angle up and east from the head of the basin along the base of the cliff, scrambling up 200 vertical feet on game trails. Find a cleft in the cliff and ascend into a small box canyon. Scramble up roots and rock on the right side of the canyon and then through timber to the upper basin (class 4). At 5000 feet enter the nearly flat upper basin. Continue cross-country to the Dark Glacier (6700'). Although the Dark Glacier is relatively small, it still harbors significant crevasses and icy cliffs in summer. Rope up and ascend rightward on the western lobe of the glacier to its southern terminus. Trend left (east) underneath the cliffs toward the saddle. Attain the west-ridge saddle at 8300 feet. The remainder of the crest is moderately exposed but blocky (class 3). Go left (northeast) to gain the summit.

HAZARDS AND TIPS: Glacier gear is required on Dark Glacier. You can avoid most of the bushwhacking through slide alder if you can find the abandoned trail on the east side of Swamp Creek before the lower basin. The best plan is to pay more money, take the fast boat up Lake Chelan, and attempt to reach the camp in the lower basin before night-

Keith Wilson

Dark Peak and Dark Glacier

fall — a feat that most parties will find exhausting. Nevertheless, this makes reaching the summit of Dark Peak the next day more likely, for if the snow is deep you might be turned back for lack of time. Plan your return trip well, so at noon you can catch the bus at High Bridge Camp that will arrive in Stehekin in time to catch the 2 P.M. boat back down the lake. You may want to pay more money and take the fast boat that departs from Stehekin at 4:15 P.M. Otherwise, be prepared to camp another night and catch the boat the next day.

GPS WAYPOINT ROUTE:

1. 10U 660063, 5360556, 1700': Crest Trailhead
2. 10U 654343, 5352457, 8.6 miles, 2800': Swamp Creek Trail
3. 10U 656933, 5349036, 3.6 miles, 4400': lower basin
4. 10U 657002, 5348494, 0.5 mile, 5000': upper basin
5. 10U 656848, 5347175, 0.8 mile, 6700': Dark Glacier
6. 10U 657176, 5346494, 0.7 mile, 8300': saddle
7. 10U 657346, 5346576, 0.5 mile, 8504': Dark Peak summit

TRIP TIMES:

Crest Trailhead to lower basin camp: 12.2 miles, 2700', 8 hours
Lower basin camp to Dark Peak summit: 2.5 miles, 4100', 6 hours

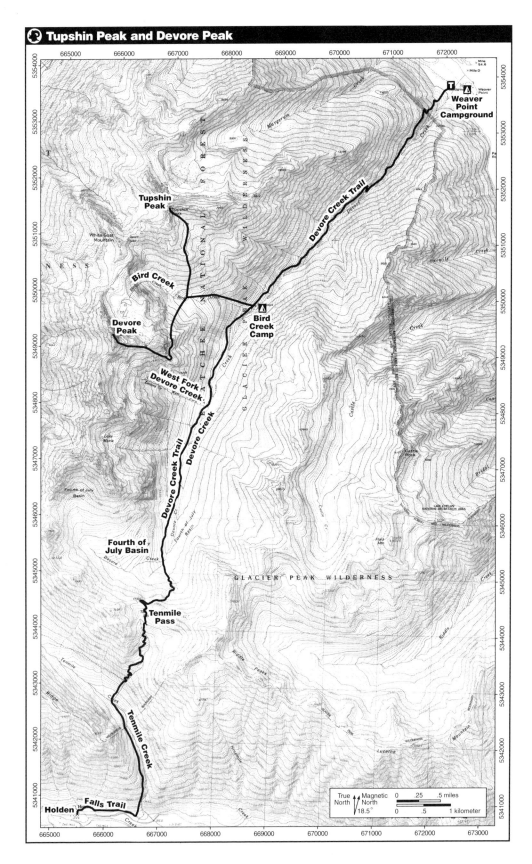

ROUTE 24

Tupshin Peak and Devore Peak

ELEVATIONS: 8320+', 8360+' (2536+ m, 2548+ m)

CLIMBING ROUTES: Tupshin: Southeast Face; Devore: Southeast Ridge

DISTANCE: 16 miles round trip to Weaver Point; 22 miles one way from Weaver Point to Holden

ELEVATION GAIN: 10,200' round trip to Weaver Point; 12,500' one way from Weaver Point to Holden

DAYS: 4–5

MAPS: USGS Stehekin, Mt. Lyall, Pinnacle Mountain, Holden; Green Trails Stehekin No. 82, McGregor Mountain No. 81, Lucerne No. 114, Holden No. 113

RATING: E4T5

LOCATION: Lake Chelan National Recreation Area administered by North Cascades National Park, Stehekin Ranger Station; Glacier Peak Wilderness administered by Wenatchee National Forest, Chelan Ranger District

PERMITS: Visitors are asked to sign in at the trailhead register.

SUMMARY AND HIGHLIGHTS: Tupshin and Devore Peaks are an eye-catching twosome along the Devore Creek Trail, which winds its way up from Lake Chelan toward the Cascade Crest. Because the two mountains are situated along the same stream, this trip is best done as a one-way journey from Stehekin to Holden. The trip through these villages makes for a charming blend of backwoods human contact and lonesome high alpine climbing. While Tupshin is ragged and spiked, Devore is blocky and bulky. Meaning "needle" in the Chinook language, Tupshin requires technical skills (class 5) to reach the top. In contrast, many parties do not use a rope on Devore. The final leg of the trip from Tenmile Pass requires some backcountry navigation along a short "missing link" that crosses a creek and connects with a newly maintained trail to complete this unofficial overland route from Stehekin to Holden.

Steve Fry

Northeast face of Devore Peak

HOW TO GET THERE: Drive to north Wenatchee either from the west on Highway 2, or from the south using Interstate 90 and then Highway 97 over Blewett Pass. From north Wenatchee drive north on Alternate Highway 97 on the west side of the Columbia River. At 9 miles past the town of Entiat, go north on Navarre Coulee Road (State Route 971) at the sign for Fields Point Landing. Continue to Lake Chelan State Park, situated on the southern shore of Lake Chelan. Go left (north) on South Lakeshore Road, and continue for 8 miles along the shore of Lake Chelan until you reach Fields Point Landing. Here find a huge space for parking and the ticket station for the *Lady of the Lake*. Be sure to get here early enough to catch the daily boat that leaves at 9:45 A.M. You can also pay more money and catch a faster boat that leaves a half hour earlier.

TRIP DESCRIPTION: Take either boat to Stehekin at the headwaters of Lake Chelan. Walk north on the road to Purple Point Campground on the east shore of Lake Chelan and try to hitch a ride on a powerboat across the lake about 1 mile to Weaver Point Campground. Otherwise you will have to take the bus or walk north past Rainbow Falls to the bridge across the Stehekin River and then walk south to Weaver Point, adding from 4 to 9 miles to the trip, depending on whether you can take the Lower Valley bus for part of the way.

Just west of Weaver Point Campground find the start of Devore Creek Trail No. 1244 (1200'). Hike along Devore Creek for 4.0 miles until you reach Bird Creek Camp at 4200 feet. Although you can find a reasonable camp here, you will be better situated to approach both Tupshin and Devore if you leave the trail and ascend the slopes along the north side of Bird Creek and camp in a basin at 5400 feet below White Goat Mountain.

Tupshin Peak

The next day bring only a daypack with climbing gear. Leave camp and ascend slightly northeast, then northwest, on wooded slopes into the high basin (7100') southeast of Tupshin. Climb northwest up talus and approach the southeast face at about 7600 feet. Climb rightward on ramps, then along ledges and up a chimney almost to the top of the east ridge (class 4). The final push to the summit involves routefinding and rock protection. Cross to the small basin beneath the summit rocks on broken ledges (class 5). Scramble easy rock to the summit. Outside the gullies the rock is reasonably sound. Rappel and downclimb from the summit and return to camp.

Devore Peak

For Devore, bring a rope and runners, with only a small rack for rock protection. From camp ascend the steep, brushy slopes briefly along Bird Creek. Then go cross-country southwest toward the east shoulder of Devore Peak. Skirt around Point 7657 by traversing at about 7000 feet onto the south slopes of Devore Peak in the West Fork Devore Creek drainage. Gain the southeast ridge of Devore at a saddle at 7500 feet. Climb the left side of the southeast ridge, which requires one large rock step (class 4). Either go up and over the step, or go around it to the left (easy but airy). The final summit block is attained via a dirty gully system (class 3). Return to camp using short rappels as needed.

To Get to Holden

From the camp in Bird Creek Basin, go down the hill to Bird Creek Camp on the Devore Creek Trail. Continue southwest up the trail through the Fourth of July Basin to Tenmile Pass (6500'). You can find a good camp near the pass. Continue down the trail toward the Tenmile Creek drainage. In two miles, at a sharp bend, the trail turns right (west) and becomes Company Creek Trail No. 1243. Do not follow the trail. Instead continue off-trail down the slope about a hundred feet and cross Tenmile Creek (4700'). Just after the creek crossing go off-trail in timber, descending along the west bank of the creek. At about 4500 feet you should intersect the Falls Trail, which will take you to the road to Holden. Camp at the Holden Campground, or if you are in time to catch the bus ($5 cash per person, one-way; small bills only) and the boat to Lucerne, begin your journey back down Lake Chelan.

HAZARDS AND TIPS: The most interesting way to do this trip is a one-way journey, beginning at Stehekin and ending at Holden. For those with less time, a trip back to Stehekin for the return is feasible. The time-saving trick is finding someone with a boat who is willing to take you from Stehekin to Weaver Point. Plan accordingly to catch the daily boat back down the lake from either Holden or Stehekin. Tupshin is a class 5 climb requiring a rope and rack for rock protection. Helmets are strongly advised, and two ropes are quicker for rappels on Tupshin, but one rope will work. Be aware of loose rock, both large and small, while climbing and rappelling. Devore also can be approached from the trail by going up the West Fork Devore Creek drainage into the basin southeast of the peak.

GPS WAYPOINT ROUTE:

1. 10U 672097, 5353838, 1200': Devore Creek Trailhead
2. 10U 668528, 5349836, 4.0 miles, 4200': Bird Creek
3. 10U 667340, 5349975, 1.0 mile, 5400': Bird Creek basin
4. 10U 667249, 5351254, 1.0 mile, 7100': Tupshin basin
5. 10U 666915, 5351538, 0.4 mile, 8320+': Tupshin summit
6. 10U 667017, 5349173, 2.4 miles, 7000': Devore east shoulder
7. 10U 666509, 5349071, 0.5 mile, 7500': saddle
8. 10U 665919, 5349227, 0.4 mile, 8360+': Devore summit
9. 10U 666688, 5344264, 7.4 miles, 6500': Tenmile Pass
10. 10U 666093, 5342677, 2.0 miles, 4700': Tenmile Creek
11. 10U 665504, 5340677, 2.4 miles, 3200': Holden

TRIP TIME:

Bird Creek Basin to Tupshin summit: 1.4 miles, 2900', 6 hours
Bird Creek Basin to Devore summit: 1.9 miles, 3000', 5 hours

Mountain goats are most often seen in meadows, dustbaths, and on bare rock benches in the Cascades

Bonanza Peak and Martin Peak

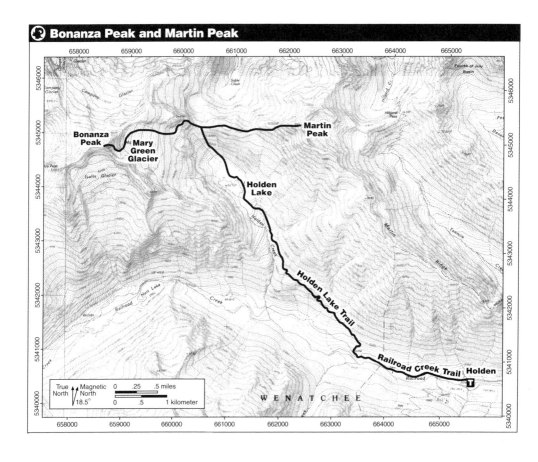

Bonanza Peak · Mary Green Glacier · Martin Peak · Holden Lake · Holden Lake Trail · Railroad Creek Trail · Holden · WENATCHEE

True North · Magnetic North 18.5°

0 .25 .5 miles

0 .5 1 kilometer

Bonanza Peak and Martin Peak

ELEVATIONS: 9511', 8511' (2899 m, 2594 m)

CLIMBING ROUTES: Bonanza: Mary Green Glacier; Martin: West Ridge

DISTANCE: 21 miles

ELEVATION GAIN: 8400'

DAYS: 4

MAPS: USGS Holden; Green Trails Holden No. 113

RATING: E4T4

LOCATION: Glacier Peak Wilderness administered by Wenatchee National Forest, Chelan Ranger District

PERMITS: Visitors are asked to sign in at the trailhead register.

SUMMARY AND HIGHLIGHTS: Bonanza Peak is the king of the realm. Being the highest nonvolcanic peak in Washington, it dominates the entire western Chelan sector. It is even a smidgen higher than mighty Mt. Stuart (Trip 34), another favorite of mountaineers. But unlike Mt. Stuart, which sits in a much drier location east of the Cascade Crest, Bonanza is in the middle of a weather convergence zone. It accumulates huge amounts of winter snow and is one of the most heavily glaciated peaks of the region.

The greater Bonanza massif resembles a giant octopus with seven glaciers and 10 intersecting ridges that radiate from principal and satellite peaks. There are two prominent southern ribs and a complex series of high points at the summit block. Most approaches require glacier travel. The Mary Green Glacier route is the easiest and certainly one of the most scenic. It requires traversing toward a chaotic icefall on waterfall-polished granite slabs that make up the sloping terrace of the broad cirque above Holden Lake. Martin Peak, an impressive sidekick, is situated just east of Bonanza Peak and connected to it by a sparsely timbered ridge. Here you can conveniently camp to attain both summits. The approach to camp is along a well-traveled trail to lovely Holden Lake from the village of Holden. If you plan your trip well, you can enjoy a hearty, home-cooked meal in Holden at the beginning or ending of your journey—or both.

HOW TO GET THERE: Drive to north Wenatchee either from the west on Highway 2, or from the south using Interstate 90 and then Highway 97 over Blewett Pass. From north Wenatchee drive north on Alternate Highway 97 on the west side of the Columbia River. At 9 miles past the town of Entiat, go north on Navarre Coulee Road (State Route 971) at the sign for Fields Point Landing. Continue to Lake Chelan State Park, situated on the southern shore of Lake Chelan. Go left (north) on South Lakeshore Road for 8 miles along the shore of Lake Chelan until you reach Fields Point Landing. Here find a huge space for parking and the ticket station for the *Lady of the Lake*. Be sure to get here early enough to catch the daily boat that leaves at 9:45 A.M.

TRIP DESCRIPTION: Take the boat up Lake Chelan to Lucerne. Then take the school bus ($5 cash per person, one-way; small bills only) that drives up the switchbacks for 2000 feet to the village of Holden. Walk on the road from Holden to Railroad Creek Trail No. 1256 trailhead (3300') just past the campground a mile outside the village. After hiking on the trail 0.9 mile, take the right junction (Holden Lake Trail No. 1251). In 4.0 miles, arrive at Holden Lake (5300'). At the outlet, follow a foot tread around the east side of the lake. The climber's trail is easy to find, but marshy in spots. Begin the ascent up the lightly wooded talus slope trending northwest toward the low spot in the ridge called Holden Pass. Again the trail is easy to follow although it has been washed out in spots. Continue climbing along rock cliffs until you reach a junction in the tread in a meadow almost at the crest of the ridge. The left fork heads toward Bonanza Peak, but take the right fork up to timbered Holden Pass. Find a camp on the flat portion of the ridge just beyond the crest (6400').

Bonanza Peak

The next morning, pack a daypack for the climb of Bonanza. From Holden Pass ascend the westward path on the ridge, scrambling below the cliffs on your right. Gain a heather bench and then traverse on a talus field to the start of the slabs below the Mary Green Glacier. If the snow is gone, waterfalls coat the polished granite and create treacherously slick conditions. Try to go up the slabs on snow between the waterfalls. You can avoid the waterfalls if you climb 200 yards left of them, but beware of glacial seracs and crevasses there. Arrive at the eastern margin of the glacier at 7400 feet. Make a nearly level westward traverse at the north margin to attain the snow finger that abuts on the rock face. Be cautious as the glacier has significant crevasses. Continue to the southwest terminus of the glacier. In late summer a bergschrund on the snow

Steve Fry

Climbers near Holden Lake approaching Bonanza Peak

finger and a moat may present a problem, but in early summer you can cross the snow finger to the rock on snow bridges. Get onto the rock below the hanging snow patch. The path to the summit consists of a series of gullies separated by rocky ridges with downsloping horns (class 4). Most parties stay right of the first gully above the hanging snow on the face. Look carefully for solid anchors, as the rock in the gullies is loose. About four pitches of roped climbing are required but the climbing is easy enough that some parties use a running belay. Continue westward (trending left) in the series of gully systems, ascending toward the summit block. Reach the northeast summit ridge at a notch about 150 feet from the summit. Traverse on a series of blocky, sometimes loose boulders for about 50 feet to the last southern block at the summit. Rappel and downclimb to the glacier and return to camp at Holden Pass.

Martin Peak

The next morning, head east up the sparsely timbered ridge. Go southeast across scree to avoid a rocky bulge on the ridge between 6800 and 7000 feet. Avoid the first narrow gully and go up the wider ramp that trends left, through trees, until you reach Martin's west ridge. Stay near the crest on the south face. Some areas have exposed bowls of smooth rock slabs covered in small gravel debris that form a slippery surface (class 3). At the summit the rock is blocky and more reliable. A minor ledge-and-chimney system lead to a short, exposed rock scramble at the top (class 3). Some climbers will want a hand line, or will prefer short rappels or belays for the descent.

HAZARDS AND TIPS: Although the Mary Green Glacier can be reached from a camp at Holden Lake, a camp at Holden Pass on the ridge above the lake is desirable if both Bonanza and Martin are done in the same trip. Bonanza is best attempted early in summer (late May to mid July) when snow covers the slippery-when-wet slabs below the Mary Green Glacier. The bergschrund and moat that form on the snow finger to the rock can be impassable if you attempt the trip after the snow bridges have melted. The rock on Bonanza is loose but most parties find sound anchors if they search hard enough. Glacier gear, a minimal rock-protection rack, and helmets are needed on Bonanza. Martin has loose debris on downsloping rock. Helmets are advised. Some climbers will want a rope for exposed sections.

GPS WAYPOINT ROUTE:
1. 10U 665410, 5340650, 3200': Holden
2. 10U 663374, 5341112, 1.9 miles, 3600': Holden Lake Trail
3. 10U 661310, 5343775, 4.0 miles, 5300': Holden Lake
4. 10U 661282, 5345121, 1.0 mile, 6400': Holden Pass

5. 10U 659817, 5345047, 0.5 mile, 6900': slabs
6. 10U 659568, 5345035, 0.4 mile, 7400': Mary Green Glacier
7. 10U 658696, 5344760, 0.6 mile, 8600': snow finger
8. 10U 658533, 5344767, 0.3 mile, 9511': Bonanza summit
9. 10U 661877, 5345219, 2.9 miles, 7600': Martin west ridge
10. 10U 662267, 5345263, 0.6 mile, 8511': Martin summit

TRIP TIMES:

Holden to Holden Pass: 6.9 miles, 3200', 5 hours
Holden Pass to Bonanza summit: 1.8 miles, 3100', 6 hours
Holden Pass to Martin summit: 1.4 miles, 2100', 4 hours

Mt. Fernow and Copper Peak

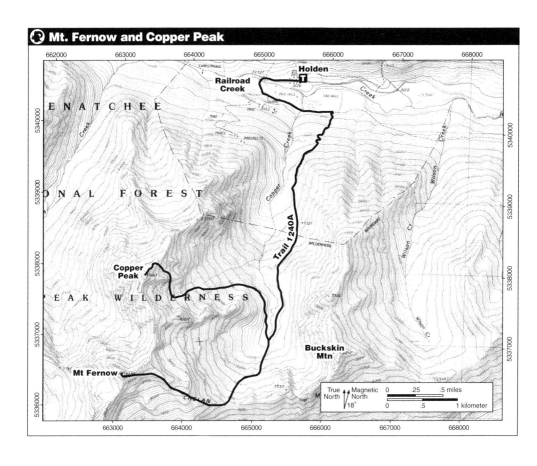

Mt. Fernow and Copper Peak

ELEVATIONS: 9249', 8964' (2819 m, 2732 m)

CLIMBING ROUTES: Fernow: Southeast Slope; Copper: East Face

DISTANCE: 17 miles

ELEVATION GAIN: 9400'

DAYS: 4

MAPS: USGS Holden; Green Trails Holden No. 113

RATING: E4T2

LOCATION: Glacier Peak Wilderness administered by Wenatchee National Forest, Chelan Ranger District

PERMITS: Visitors are asked to sign the trailhead register.

SUMMARY AND HIGHLIGHTS: Highest of the Entiat Mountains, Mt. Fernow rivals Bonanza Peak for the supreme summit west of Lake Chelan. Only a few hundred feet lower than Bonanza (Trip 25), Fernow is drier and less glaciated, and therefore more welcoming to entry-level mountaineers. Copper Peak is the imposing, pyramidal mass to the north on the rough rocky ridge that connects to Mt. Fernow. Both can be reached from a camp in Copper Basin high above the town of Holden. Luxuriant meadows open at the higher levels of the subalpine forest in a succession of comfortable basins. But then shorter trees surround wide-spread loose talus and scree, and south-facing slopes become sharply folded into gullies with corrugated rock-strewn ribs. Although the lower valley slopes are densely forested, the blocky crests lose their snow cover by June and then stand nearly barren.

Appreciably more arid than the Stehekin group (Trip 22) farther north along the lake, this sector can be blisteringly hot and parched in summer. The best time to do this trip is in late spring or early summer. June is the best month. Go too early and you will find avalanches that threaten your progress; go too late and the mosquitoes at camp in Copper Basin will eat you alive. The trip could also be attempted in fall after the mosquitoes have quit, but you must be prepared to carry enough water for each day trip.

Mt. Fernow and Copper Peak reflected in Holden Lake

HOW TO GET THERE: Drive to north Wenatchee either from the west on Highway 2 or from the south using Interstate 90 and then Highway 97 over Blewett Pass. From north Wenatchee drive north on Alternate Highway 97 on the west side of the Columbia River. At 9 miles past the town of Entiat, go north on Navarre Coulee Road (State Route 971) at the sign for Fields Point Landing. Continue to Lake Chelan State Park, situated on the southern shore of Lake Chelan. Go left (north) on South Lakeshore Road for 8 miles along the shore of Lake Chelan until you reach Fields Point Landing. Here find a huge space for parking and the ticket station for the *Lady of the Lake*. Be sure to get here early enough to catch the daily boat that leaves at 9:45 A.M.

TRIP DESCRIPTION: Take the boat up Lake Chelan to Lucerne. Then take the schoolbus shuttle ($5 cash per person, one-way; small bills only) that drives up the switchbacks for 2000 feet to Holden. Cross Railroad Creek on the bridge and walk past the old mining buildings. Turn left and cross Copper Creek on a small bridge. Just past Copper Creek, find the start of the trail that leads upward to Copper Basin. Go south along Copper Creek, gaining 2300 feet in 3 miles to reach upper Copper Basin (5600'). The basin has ample flat spots for camping. In summer the ground is marshy, creating a fertile breeding ground for hordes of mosquitoes.

Mt. Fernow

The next morning from camp, follow the open terrain, going cross-country southwest to the saddle between Buckskin Mountain and Mt.

Fernow. Use a steep gully to get through the cliff band. Pass south over the saddle (7200'). Turn west and ascend along the southeast ridge of Fernow, keeping on the south face to bypass obstacles. At about 8900 feet, begin a westward traverse on ledges to attain the southwest ridge 50 feet from the summit. Several variations will work. The final summit portion is not difficult but much of the rock on the face and in the gullies (class 3) is loose. Return to camp.

Copper Peak

From camp the next morning, cross Copper Creek and trend northwest cross-country to round the buttress of the southeast flank of Copper, traversing through alder patches and brush at about 5600 feet. Ascend the basin southeast of Copper. Go north on an easy crossing of the east ridge at about 7700 feet. Scramble up and across the east face on ledges, bypassing obstacles as you work up onto the northeast ridge (class 3). The small glacier, little more than a snowfield, can be avoided by keeping to the north. The slope to the summit is relatively solid with sparse ground cover. The final push to the summit is along the northeast ridge.

HAZARDS AND TIPS: On Fernow the rock is loose and helmets are recommended. A hand line may be useful in some exposed places, but it might cause increased danger from rockfall if used for long belays. Fernow can be approached easily from Leroy Creek Basin from the southwest or from Entiat Meadows from the southeast. But to combine Fernow with Copper, using the multi-day camp in Copper Basin, is the best plan. Copper Peak presents moderate routefinding difficulties, particularly at the base and near the summit block. Usually a ledge system can be found to traverse around obstacles such as small cliff bands and steep, icy snow patches.

GPS WAYPOINT ROUTE:

1. 10U 665517, 5340658, 3200': Holden
2. 10U 666022, 5340237, 1.0 mile, 3300': trail to Copper Basin
3. 10U 665311, 5337191, 3.0 miles, 5600': Copper Basin
4. 10U 664646, 5336107, 1.3 miles, 7200': saddle
5. 10U 663333, 5336451, 1.2 miles, 8900': traverse
6. 10U 663144, 5336488, 0.4 mile, 9249': Fernow summit
7. 10U 663836, 5337856, 4.1 miles, 7700': Copper east ridge
8. 10U 663393, 5337875, 0.7 mile, 8964': Copper summit

TRIP TIMES:

Holden to Copper Basin: 4.0 miles, 2400', 4 hours
Copper Basin to Fernow summit: 2.9 miles, 3600', 6 hours
Copper Basin to Copper summit: 1.6 miles, 3400', 6 hours

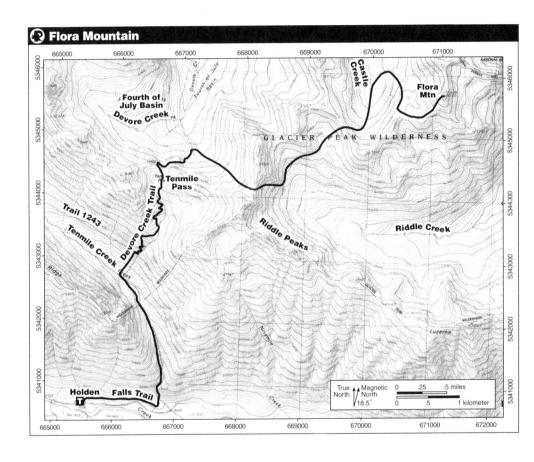

Flora Mountain

ROUTE 27

Flora Mountain

ELEVATION: 8320' (2536 m)

CLIMBING ROUTE: Southwest Slope

DISTANCE: 21 miles

ELEVATION GAIN: 9,700'

DAYS: 3

MAPS: USGS Holden, Pinnacle Mountain; Green Trails Holden No. 113, Lucerne No. 114

RATING: E3T1

LOCATION: Glacier Peak Wilderness administered by Wenatchee National Forest, Chelan Ranger District

PERMITS: Visitors are asked to sign the trailhead register.

SUMMARY AND HIGHLIGHTS: Set apart from the main mountains that line the western shores of Lake Chelan, Flora is a hulking mass—a huge blob—between the town of Holden and the lake. Flora's profile is mostly above timberline, and desolate and barren. Yet the mount does have some complexity at the top. The south point of the massif is the highest. In contrast to its stark appearance on the approach, the route up Flora is surprisingly verdant, undulating up several forested ridges and down deeply vegetated basins before ascending the final slog to the summit.

Flora is a long way from anywhere. The sharp pinnacles of nearby Riddle Peaks form an encircling barrier to Flora's south and west. The nearest trails are drainages away, requiring a cross-country odyssey. Consequently, Flora is little known and seldom attempted, yet it is the epitome of a tucked-away spot whose open country gives you the exhilaration of supremely lonesome high-country roaming.

HOW TO GET THERE: Drive to north Wenatchee either from the west on Highway 2 or from the south using Interstate 90 and then Highway 97 over Blewett Pass. From north Wenatchee drive north on Alternate Highway 97 on the west side of the Columbia River. At 9 miles past the town of Entiat, go north on Navarre Coulee Road (State Route 971) at the sign for Fields Point Landing. Continue to Lake Chelan State Park,

Keith Wilson

Lake Chelan and Domke Lake from Flora Mountain

situated on the southern shore of Lake Chelan. Go left (north) on South Lakeshore Road for 8 miles along the shore of Lake Chelan until you reach Fields Point Landing. Here find a huge space for parking and the ticket station for the *Lady of the Lake*. Be sure to get here early enough to catch the daily boat that leaves at 9:45 A.M. (the earlier boat will not take you to Lucerne).

TRIP DESCRIPTION: Take the boat up Lake Chelan to Lucerne. Then take the schoolbus shuttle ($5 cash per person, one-way; small bills only) that drives up the switchbacks for 2000 feet to Holden. Get off the bus and walk east down the road. Find the Falls Trailhead and ascend the wooded slope. This trail has been greatly improved in recent years and continues to about 4000 feet. From there continue hiking on a faint boot tread on the west side of Tenmile Creek to 4700 feet. Cross Tenmile Creek and ascend on the west side of the tributary that drains from Tenmile Pass above. Climb for about a quarter mile from 4700 to 5200 feet to connect with Company Creek Trail No. 1243; take a short right hike on the trail and find the terminus of Devore Creek Trail No. 1244. Ascend the unmaintained Devore Creek Trail to Tenmile Pass (6500'). Find a good camp away from the trail. (You can also reach Tenmile Pass on the Devore Creek Trail starting from Stehekin.)

The next day, go down the Devore Creek Trail for 0.9 mile. Leave the trail at 6000 feet and head southeast, traveling toward Riddle Peaks. Go to an opening in the crest of the ridge north of Riddle Peaks. Go through the pass (7800') between Fourth of July Basin and Riddle Creek. Descend the steep east face of the ridge coming north from Riddle Peaks (class 3–4). Reach the headwaters of Riddle Creek at about 6400 feet and start an ascent northeast toward Castle Creek basin. Thinking linearly, you may be able to pick your way through the steep terrain and contour at an elevation of about 6800 feet (as shown on map). But the climbing here is more difficult than descending to easier ground, although it means a heartbreaking loss of altitude. Continue to the saddle of Castle Creek basin at 7400 feet. Pass north into the drainage and then drop—up to about 800 feet for the most direct crossing—into the Castle Creek basin to cross over to the ridge point on the other side at 7300 feet. Finally you are on a broad plateau at the southwest foot of Flora. Cross benches to the east and northeast to the open slope. Scramble up loose scree and talus to a short rocky stretch at the very top (class 3).

HAZARDS AND TIPS: To coordinate with the boat on Lake Chelan, you must plan for enough time to finish the trip. Most parties can complete the itinerary in three days, but you may want to plan a fourth just to be safe. Instead of going through basins and losing elevation, you may choose to traverse around basins near their crests. But although you add elevation loss and gain to the trip, descending may be easier, particularly when you need to get water from the snow or creek in a basin floor. Because this trip can be hot, dry, and very buggy, it is best done before all the snow melts in July.

GPS WAYPOINT ROUTE:
1. 10U 665517, 5340658, 3200': Holden
2. 10U 666712, 5340899, 1.0 mile, 3500': Falls Trail
3. 10U 666093, 5342677, 1.3 miles, 4700': cross Tenmile Creek
4. 10U 666294, 5343087, 0.2 mile, 5200': Devore Creek Trail
5. 10U 666688, 5344264, 1.5 miles, 6500': Tenmile Pass
6. 10U 667162, 5344738, 0.9 mile, 6000': leave trail
7. 10U 668191, 5344128, 1.1 miles, 7800': Riddle Creek pass
8. 10U 669573, 5345152, 1.4 miles, 7400': Castle Creek pass
9. 10U 670438, 5345471, 1.6 miles, 7300': southwest slope
10. 10U 671181, 5345683, 0.8 mile, 8320': Flora summit

TRIP TIMES:
Holden to Tenmile Pass camp: 4.0 miles, 3300', 7 hours
Tenmile Pass camp to Flora summit: 5.8 miles, 6100', 8 hours

CHAPTER 7
Glacier Peak Wilderness

The Glacier Peak Wilderness contains 576,900 protected acres in an area 35 miles long and 20 miles wide in Washington's central Cascades. The Wilderness extends north from Stevens Pass to Cascade Pass, and east to Lake Chelan, and is dominated by Glacier Peak, a huge volcano and the fifth-highest mountain in the state. It is an area of extremely diverse terrain marked by parallel, roughly north-south sub-ranges east of the Cascade Crest between the Wenatchee River and Chiwawa River valleys. These sub-ranges are characterized by modest aspects to the south, but grow to increasing height and complexity to the north. Angular rock ribs surround cirques and glaciated valleys, and abundant talus accumulates at the base of steep slopes. In many places the terrain slopes downward into alluvial fans. Many of the peaks above 8300 feet in this region can be scrambled, including Fortress, Chiwawa, and Buck mountains, Mt. Maude, and Seven Fingered Jack. Others are more complicated and require basic-level climbing skills (see definition on page 3).

There is a marked difference in vegetation between the west and east sides of the Wilderness. While dense rainforest and verdant undergrowth swath the pumice-rich upper Suiattle River Valley on the west slope, the floors of the White and Little Wenatchee rivers on the east slope are notably arid, the Chiwawa River even more so. Summer temperatures here soar, while annual precipitation remains low. At medium altitudes, ground flora thins, favoring grass cover and meadows between clumps of subalpine fir, mountain hemlock, and Englemann spruce. At higher levels, broad benches give way to heather-covered parkland. Here the subalpine fir and whitebark pine provide a sparse yet tough cover. Lyall's larch grows upright at higher elevations more than any other tree species in the Cascades. Many stands can be found above 5500 feet, in particular near Lyman Lake and on high ridges along Buck Creek and the Napeequa and Chiwawa rivers. Ethereal and light bluish-green in springtime, Lyall's larch turns bright orange-gold in autumn and is a favorite sight for climbers in Washington. Flowers flourish in the alpine zone and reach particular brilliance in famed Meander Meadow and White Pass and Buck Creek Pass, where blue lupine, red columbine, and paintbrush abound.

The mountain crests of the region are snow-clad through June. At high altitudes, glaciers cover gentle summit slopes or rest above cirque floors in sheltered recesses beneath steep, north- or east-facing walls. The highlands east of the Cascade divide lack the grandeur of the massive ice fields on nearby Glacier Peak. Nevertheless, more than 25 glaciers cluster here in a distinct east-west orientation along the range crest between White and Suiattle passes.

Native Americans were the first humans to roam the valleys. Many of today's place names, applied by the Forest Service, were derived from the Chinook dialect, which is incongruous here since the Chinook is a coastal tribe. Other names originated from shepherds, prospectors, and surveyors. In the early 1900s, Albert H. Sylvester, a forest supervisor and surveyor, applied many fanciful names during his mapping of the region: Mt. Maude; Fortress, Cardinal, and Pinnacle mountains; and Lightning and Thunder creeks.

The Glacier Peak Wilderness was established on September 6, 1960. Four years later, Congress designated it as part of the National Wilderness Preservation system. The wilderness was enlarged in 1968 by the North Cascades Act, and is managed today by the Mt. Baker-Snoqualmie and Wenatchee National Forests. No motorized travel is allowed. Yet a good trail network—reaching virtually all the mountain uplands—facilitates travel to this secluded locale. The untamed and fascinating features of the Glacier Peak Wilderness attract hikers and climbers alike, resulting in a recent sizeable increase in the number of visitors. Therefore you are obliged to practice minimum impact travel. With care, this out-of-the-way wild area will be preserved for all to enjoy.

Steve Fry

Walrus Glacier on Clark Mountain, 1930s USFS photograph

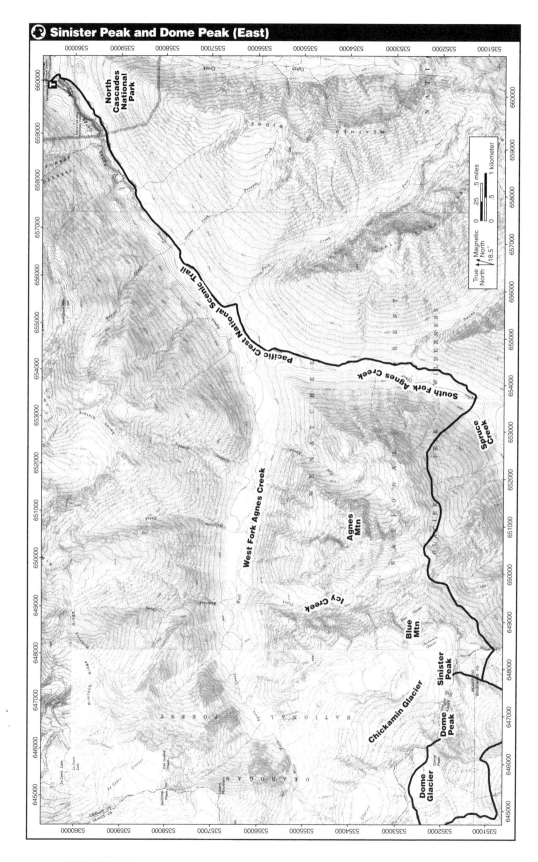

North Cascades National Park

WEATHER RIDGE

Pacific Crest National Scenic Trail

South Fork Agnes Creek

West Fork Agnes Creek

Spruce Creek

Agnes Mtn

Icy Creek

Blue Mtn

Chickamin Glacier

Sinister Peak

Dome Peak

Dome Glacier

WENATCHEE NATIONAL FOREST

OKANOGAN NATIONAL FOREST

True North
Magnetic North
18.5°

0 .25 .5 miles
0 .5 1 kilometer

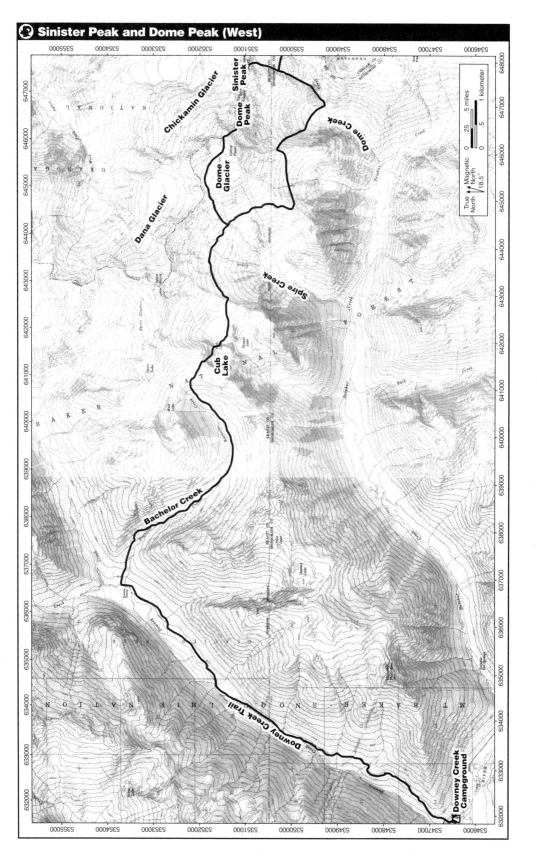

ROUTE 28

Sinister Peak and Dome Peak

ELEVATIONS: 8440+ ft, 8920+ ft (2573+ m, 2719+ m)

CLIMBING ROUTES: Sinister: East Ridge; Dome: Dome Glacier

DISTANCE: 40 miles

ELEVATION GAIN: 13,000'

DAYS: At least 6

MAPS: USGS McGregor Mountain, Mt. Lyall, Agnes Mountain, Dome Peak, Downey Mountain; Green Trails McGregor Mountain No. 81, Cascade Pass No. 80

RATING: E5T4

LOCATION: Lake Chelan National Recreation Area administered by North Cascades National Park, Stehekin Ranger Station; Glacier Peak Wilderness administered by Wenatchee National Forest, Chelan Ranger District; Mt. Baker-Snoqualmie National Forest, Darrington Ranger District

PERMITS: Visitors are asked to sign the trailhead register.

SUMMARY AND HIGHLIGHTS: Dome Peak is best known as the southern end of the world-famous Ptarmigan Traverse, a fine alpine trek along glaciers and high passes beginning at Cascade Pass. Nearly engulfing Dome Peak, the Dana, Chickamin, and Dome glaciers make up a massive ice form that is a showpiece of the region. If you do not access Dome Peak via the Ptarmigan Traverse, you must travel a long way through the Glacier Peak Wilderness before reaching a route to the summit. In the past, the usual approach from the Suiattle River along Downey Creek to Bachelor Creek, and then onto Itswoot Ridge, has been washed out along the river bottoms requiring a notoriously heartbreaking bushwhack through dense devils club and slide alder along the stream beds. But recently the trudge of many climbers, most of whom are exiting the Ptarmigan Traverse, has redefined the trail along Bachelor Creek and slide alder branches have been removed to the point that using the path is no longer an odious task, but a mild nuisance.

Sinister Peak is less than a mile east of Dome Peak on a connecting ridge. Although smaller than Dome Peak, Sinister's striking asymmetrical top, with its steep northern ice slopes, is as visible from many high points in the Cascades as its larger neighbor. There is no easy way to get to either peak, but Sinister Peak is especially secluded and sees little traffic. Although some climbers reach Sinister Peak directly from Dome Peak, the col is steep and dangerous and the south face is relatively small but abrupt. Although getting to Sinister Peak from the Chickamin Glacier is easy for some advanced climbers with ice-climbing skills, less-skilled climbers may be deterred when this area is highly crevassed, demanding complex routefinding plagued by a moat or bergschrund problem when transitioning from snow onto rock. Several other variations can be attempted, including a traverse across the Hanging Gardens from Dome Creek basin up moraine slopes to the notch below the summit. But this way, too, is fraught with steep, unsavory terrain. Consequently the easiest way to the top of Sinister Peak is on the east ridge, and the most direct line of approach is from Agnes and Spruce creeks from the east.

One way to tackle the easiest climbs on both mountains is from a grand traverse along the core of the mountain range from east to west, from Lake Chelan to the Suiattle River. This is an extraordinarily strenuous backcountry venture meant only for the most enthusiastic backwoods explorer. The cross-country portion covers steep, complex, and treacherous terrain, demanding great energy, fortitude, and judgment. There are brutal losses and gains in elevation. But the reward for your sweat is an archetypal North Cascades expedition through old-growth forests and flowery parklands, along an isolated mountain massif, over ridgecrests near great, beckoning glaciers. If you crave alpine quests, you will find this awesome and lonesome trek an irresistible objective.

HOW TO GET THERE: Arrange to leave a car at the Downey Creek Trailhead for the end of the trip. Drive north on Interstate 5 past the exit for Highway 2. Continue and take the exit for State Route 530 to Darrington. Drive north from Darrington for 7 miles on State Route 530. Just after you cross the Sauk River, turn right on the Suiattle River Road (FS Road 26). Continue for 20 miles to the Downey Creek Trail No. 768 trailhead (1400') and park the car.

In another vehicle, drive to north Wenatchee either from the west on Highway 2 or from the south using Interstate 90 and then Highway 97 over Blewett Pass. From north Wenatchee drive north on Alternate Highway 97 on the west side of the Columbia River. At 9 miles past the town of Entiat, go north on Navarre Coulee Road (State Route 971) at the sign for Fields Point Landing. Continue to Lake Chelan State Park, situated on the southern shore of Lake Chelan. Go left (north) on South Lakeshore Road for 8 miles along the shore of Lake Chelan until you reach Fields Point Landing. Here find a huge space for parking and the ticket station for the boat service on Lake Chelan. Plan to arrive in time to take the faster boat, the *Lady Express*, which departs at 9:20 A.M. You may chose to pay less money and take the slower *Lady of the Lake* (departs at 9:45 A.M.) for a more leisurely day, but this adds another day to your itinerary.

TRIP DESCRIPTION: Take the boat to Stehekin at the headwaters of Lake Chelan. From there, ride on the Lower Valley bus to the last stop of the lower valley service at High Bridge Campground. Private concessionaires operate the bus service in the lower Stehekin River valley to the High Bridge Campground. Schedules and busses vary depending on the time of the year. Reservations are not needed on the Lower Valley bus. The fare is $4 per person each way.

Start hiking along Agnes Creek on the Pacific Crest National Scenic Trail (Crest Trail No. 2000). At 8.6 miles, cross Swamp Creek (2800'). Continue on the trail for about a mile. Just before the intersection of Spruce Creek and the South Fork of Agnes Creek, find two huge trees that have blown down that completely span Agnes Creek. Cross the creek easily on a tree (3 feet wide) and exit onto sand bars. In late season you should get water here, as the slog up the slope is nearly dry. Begin the bushwhack to the northwest through slide alder and devils club along the creek. Aim toward the wooded slopes, using small, dry creek beds when possible to avoid most of the brush. Push your way through the undergrowth for 1000 feet, to where the timber begins to thin out. Continue up broken buttresses and on patches of ground cover. Make a camp on the steep slope along a stream bed where it flows with water at about 5000 feet.

The next day, begin a long ascending traverse going west through sparse forest and meadows. Agnes Mountain is on your right. Go northwest through the saddle at 6800 feet into the Icy Creek drainage. Make an abrupt turn left (west) and make your way on steep, rocky terrain (you may need to descend into the cirque) to the opening in the jagged ridge above the large lake (Blue Lake). Descend on heather and grass through the notch (6700') to the lake. You may find a faint boot tread here. At 6500 feet continue traversing southwest, roughly maintaining this elevation. You will have to negotiate the crossings of streams that have deeply eroded the talus and heather, heading either up or down to avoid obstacles. Parallel the base of Gunsight Peak (called Blue Mountain on the USGS map) and go past the Chickamin Glacier. At 7200 feet cross Sinister's southeast ridge—the relatively flat ridge that connects to Bannock Mountain via Ross Pass to the south. Continue traversing west at about 7000 feet of elevation into the basin below Sinister

Dave LeBlanc

Approaching the east ridge of Sinister Peak

Peak. Cross the basin on ice or snow above the snout of the small Garden Glacier on the south slope whose runoff creates Dome Creek. Make a camp on snow or on flat ledges on the other side of the glacier in the middle of the basin (7000').

Sinister Peak

The next morning prepare a daypack with glacier gear and a small rock rack for the climb of Sinister Peak. Ascend back to reach the Garden Glacier. Rope up and travel on easy slopes to the distinctively smooth gray slabs on the south face. On the right edge of the slabs locate a steep, 300-foot gully that slants rightward. The transition from snow to rock may be complicated by a small bergschrund on the snow finger and a moat along the rock rib at the mouth of the gully. Continue to belay the leader until the transition is made onto the rock. The gully is dirty and loose with several short chimney sections (class 4). The angle of the gully lessens near the notch it makes in Sinister's east ridge. In early season, climb on the snow on the north face along the ridge (you may need protection for steep snow and a possibly dangerous cornice on the north face); in later season you may be able to climb in the moat between the east ridge and the Chickamin Glacier. The rock here presents two short pitches of climbing on boulder slabs (class 5). Attain the east ridge and scramble on easy terrain (class 2) to the summit.

Use short rappels as needed to descend the ridge and gully and regain the glacier. Return to camp. Pack up and descend into Dome Creek basin. This descent is very tricky. Avoid the creek drainage that is directly below the precipitous, rocky southern ridge of Sinister Peak, as it is so sheer that it requires rappels to descend. Take the second small creek drainage east of the ridge. Make your way along alarmingly steep and wooded slopes as they summarily drop down into Dome Creek basin, staying on the easiest terrain that you can find. Descend until you finally reach a break in the rib before the slide alder gets thick (4700') where you can begin the traverse west through timber into the basin. Find a spot for your camp nearly in the center of the rocky basin along the creek (5000').

Dome Peak

The next day, begin the long ascent northward following the western cirque wall of Dome Creek basin. This rib is just as precipitous and intimidating as the matching configuration on the other side. Work your way up heather meadows along streams and through small cliffs until you finally find a small break in the rock at 6800 feet. Sneak through a small weakness in the rib on a steep heather ramp and cross over into the basin below Dome Peak. (This is the basin west of Dome Creek basin, which seems poorly named because Dome Creek originates from the Garden Glacier under Sinister Peak.) Traverse over talus, heather, and scree, again avoiding chasms created by erosion of glacier-fed streams. Cross the southwest ridge of Dome Peak at 6200 feet. Continue traversing at about 6200 feet above the eroded chasms of the creeks off

Keith Wilson

Dome Peak summit

the Dome Glacier. Make your way past and below the huge icefall at the snout of the Dome Glacier to a secondary stream that exits from the western part of the glacier and feeds Spire Creek. Work your way down slabs to a camp at 6000 feet on a flat gravel bed below a triangular tower that rises west of the icefall.

The next morning scramble up slabs, talus, and scree along the eastern side of the pyramid tower through a saddle to reach the Dome Glacier near its intersection with the Dana Glacier at 7400 feet. Traverse east on the flat bench of the Dome Glacier along its northern border. Aim toward the third snow finger, which leads to the farthest, highest col. Crevasses may be open where the slope steepens. Gain the summit ridge col on snow or sand (8600'). Go east along the ridge, climbing the arête (class 4), or cross over the col and go up the snow slope for 300 feet. Then continue on the rock ridge to the summit (class 3–4). Because the rock ridge is exposed, some parties prefer to protect the climb with rock gear or a hand line. The last portion of the ridge is on sandy benches, but the final push is an airy cross over a few blocky boulders to the summit.

Return to camp. If time permits, pack up camp that day and continue west, finally picking up the climber's trail as it traverses from Itswoot Ridge. Here the going is finally easy. Follow the tread to the crest of Itswoot Ridge at 6200 feet where many climbers camp on their way to attain Dome Peak. At this point you may see climbers exiting from the Ptarmigan Traverse or on their way to Dome Peak from Downey Creek. Continue on the tread, taking the left fork along the steep slope that forms the southern margin of the cirque east of Cub Lake. Find an established campsite at the lake (5300').

To the Car Shuttle

The next day, go right (north) along Cub Lake and ascend the steep northern cirque walls on the switchbacks of the climber's trail through the woods to Cub Lake Pass above Bachelor Creek (5900'). The tread becomes obvious as you go through open parkland. Reach Bachelor Creek at about 5600 feet. Even when the boot tread nears the creek and your view is obscured by leafy plants, the path is clearly defined. If the brush is wet, you will be soaked. Only occasionally must you push aside the trunks of slide alder to make your way. This part of the trail is not maintained and you must climb over many trees that have blown down on the trail and slog through some sections that are muddy. Continue along Bachelor Creek for 4 miles to the intersection with the Downey Creek Trail. Turn left (south), cross Bachelor Creek, and hike on the Downey Creek Trail for 6.6 miles to the trailhead.

Dome Peak from White Rock Lakes, North Cascades, Glacier Peak Wilderness

HAZARDS AND TIPS: Glacier gear is required. Most parties will need some slings and cams for rock protection. Sinister Peak can be climbed from all directions, but the car shuttle allows you to experience the entire sector south of Sinister Peak, one of the most remote destinations in the Cascades. This one-way trip is strenuous, and requires extensive cross-country travel over rough terrain with extensive elevation gains and losses. You must also plan adequate time to leave a car at the Downey Creek Trailhead for the car shuttle.

GPS WAYPOINT ROUTE:

1. 10U 660101, 5360526, 1700': Crest Trailhead
2. 10U 653695, 5351029, 9.6 miles, 2800': cross creek
3. 10U 652589, 5352026, 1.3 miles, 5000': camp
4. 10U 650472, 5352078, 1.5 miles, 6800': Icy Creek saddle
5. 10U 649840, 5351969, 0.5 mile, 6700': Blue Lake notch
6. 10U 648354, 5350496, 1.7 miles, 7200': Sinister southeast ridge
7. 10U 647844, 5351330, 1.3 miles, 8100': Sinister east ridge
8. 10U 647697, 5351354, 0.2 mile, 8440+': Sinister summit
9. 10U 646713, 5350188, 1.5 miles, 5000': Dome Creek basin
10. 10U 646016, 5350713, 1.2 miles, 6800': Dome basin west wall
11. 10U 644363, 5351719, 2.5 miles, 6000': Dome Glacier camp
12. 10U 646241, 5351892, 1.6 miles, 8600': snow finger col
13. 10U 646427, 5351587, 0.4 mile, 8920+': Dome summit
14. 10U 642779, 5351701, 2.9 miles, 6200': Itswoot ridge
15. 10U 641799, 5351872, 0.8 mile, 5300': Cub Lake
16. 10U 641222, 5352378, 0.7 mile, 5600': Bachelor Creek
17. 10U 636702, 5353848, 4.0 miles, 2400': Downey Creek Trail
18. 10U 631891, 5346464, 6.6 miles, 1400': Downey Creek Trailhead

TRIP TIMES:

Garden Glacier camp to Sinister summit: 1.0 mile, 1400', 4 hours
Dome Glacier camp to Dome summit: 2.0 miles, 2900', 5 hours

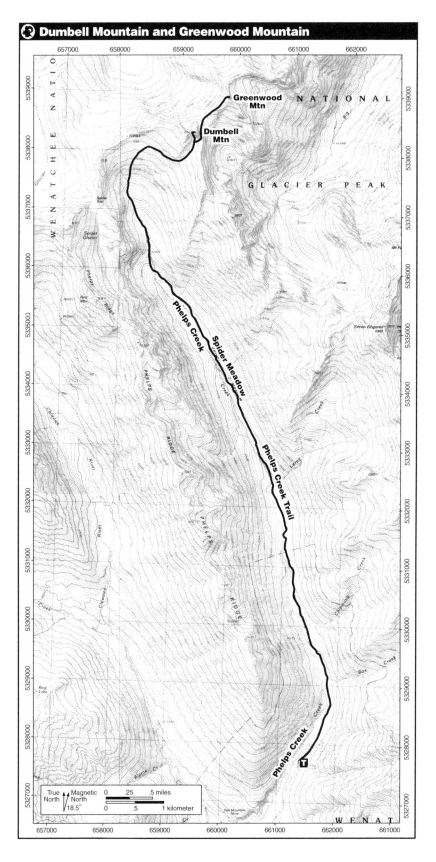

Greenwood
Mtn

Dumbell
Mtn

N A T I O N A L

G L A C I E R   P E A K

Phelps Creek

Spider Meadow

Phelps Creek Trail

Phelps Creek

True
North

Magnetic
North

18.5°

0   .25   .5 miles

0   .5   1 kilometer

Dumbell Mountain and Greenwood Mountain (NE Dumbell Mountain)

ELEVATIONS: 8421', 8415' (2567 m, 2564 m)

CLIMBING ROUTES: Dumbell: South Face; Greenwood: Southwest Ridge

DISTANCE: 22 miles

ELEVATION GAIN: 5700'

DAYS: 2

MAPS: USGS Trinity, Holden; Green Trails Holden No. 113

RATING: E2T2

LOCATION: Glacier Peak Wilderness administered by Wenatchee National Forest, Lake Wenatchee Ranger District

PERMITS: Visitors are asked to sign the trailhead register.

SUMMARY AND HIGHLIGHTS: Dumbell Mountain is a dominant peak southeast of Lyman Lake at the northern end of the Entiat Mountains. The origin of its name is unclear, but from the north the top appears to have two equal segments. Looking from the south, the highest point is on the right, with a permanent snow patch beneath. Although in the past Greenwood Mountain was thought to be merely the northeast peak of Dumbell Mountain, it is now considered its own separate mass. It is also the higher and bulkier of the two.

To reach Dumbell and Greenwood mountains you will hike along the Phelps Creek floor through Spider Meadow. This famous landmark is known for its striking setting in a rift between jagged red peaks with crashing waterfalls and luxuriant green fields. Spider Meadow begins the high route to Spider Gap, a rocky scramble that connects north to Lyman Lake and then to Lake Chelan. This high route is popular among hikers who desire a one-way trip from the Chiwawa River Basin to the ferry boat on Lake Chelan. The alpine climb of Dumbell and Greenwood is even more handsome in October when the larch is at its finest. But at almost any time of year the terrain is forgiving enough that you can reach both summits in a leisurely weekend.

HOW TO GET THERE: At Coles Corner, located 20 miles east of Stevens Pass on Highway 2, turn north on Lake Wenatchee Road (State Route 207) to Lake Wenatchee. Follow the signs to Chiwawa River Road. At 3.8 miles from Highway 2, take the right fork and drive east along the south shore of Fish Lake on Chiwawa River Road 62 (becomes FS Road 6200). Continue north for 22 miles. Just before the end of the road at Trinity, take the right fork at Phelps Creek Road No. 6211 for 2.5 miles to a gate. Find parking for the Phelps Creek Trail No.1511 trailhead (3500').

TRIP DESCRIPTION: Hike on the Phelps Creek Trail, at first along an abandoned road but then on a good, level trail, through dense Douglas fir forest. At 2.5 miles you enter the Glacier Peak Wilderness. In a half mile unmaintained Leroy Creek-Carne Mountain Trail No. 1512 exits just beyond the crossing of Leroy Creek at 4100 feet. Continue hiking north on the Phelps Creek Trail to Spider Meadow (2.0 miles from Leroy Creek). At the northern end of Spider Meadow at a trail junction, the left fork leads to Spider Pass. Instead, continue straight ahead along Phelps Creek into a basin. The established trail ends at about 5600 feet. Follow a foot tread farther into the basin until you reach a lingering snowfield. Make your camp here (6000').

Dumbell Mountain

The next morning, trek off-trail and contour northeast over rocky, sparsely timbered slopes into a high basin below the western false summit visible from the snowfield. At 7200 feet traverse southeast around the south shoulder of the false summit. Ascend farther north into a talus field south of Dumbell's higher east summit. Climb up the snowfield that is present until late summer. At the left of the base of the south face, scramble up a gully system (class 3). Eventually the broken rock gives way to a modest angle near the summit. The final push is on the west ridge to the top.

Greenwood Mountain

Descend from the top of Dumbell Mountain to the base of the summit pyramid. Traverse east and then north under the south face to the east shoulder of Dumbell. Climb a dirty gully about 100 feet to reach a notch in the ridge (7900'). Traverse to the left around an airy corner on a narrow ledge to reach the east face (class 4). Find a ramp that arcs counterclockwise around the southeast flank of Dumbell. The ramp is exposed below, but wide enough to walk on. Aim toward the saddle between Dumbell and Greenwood Mountain (sometimes referred to as the northeast summit of Dumbell). Bypass a small permanent snowfield. After the broad saddle at 7700 feet, ascend blocky talus and scree to the top of Greenwood. The way from the saddle is easy (class 2).

Dumbell Mountain from 7-Fingered Jack

HAZARDS AND TIPS: The most exposed portion of the climb is rounding the shoulder of Dumbell. Some parties may want a hand line or a short rope. Helmets are recommended for the gully portions of the route if the party is large (more than three people).

GPS WAYPOINT ROUTE:

1. 10U 661371, 5327613, 3500': Phelps Creek Trailhead
2. 10U 659613, 5334738, 5.5 miles, 4700': Spider Meadow
3. 10U 658169, 5337213, 2.0 miles, 6000': leave trail
4. 10U.658932, 5337820, 1.3 miles, 7200': south shoulder
5. 10U 659269, 5338335, 1.0 mile, 8421': Dumbell summit
6. 10U 659410, 5338230, 0.4 mile, 7900': Dumbell east shoulder
7. 10U 659421, 5338600, 0.4 mile, 7700': saddle
8. 10U 659847, 5338932, 0.5 mile, 8415': Greenwood summit

TRIP TIMES:

Phelps Creek Trailhead to camp: 7.5 miles, 2500', 5 hours
Camp to Dumbell summit: 2.3 miles, 2500', 4 hours
Dumbell summit to Greenwood summit: 1.3 miles, 700', 2 hours

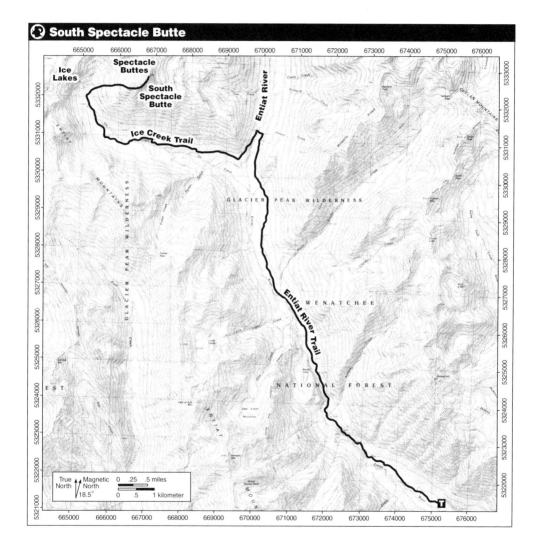

South Spectacle Butte

ROUTE 30

South Spectacle Butte

ELEVATION: 8392' (2558 m)

CLIMBING ROUTE: Southwest Ridge

DISTANCE: 27 miles

ELEVATION GAIN: 5300'

DAYS: 2–3

MAPS: USGS Saska Peak, Trinity, Holden; Green Trails Lucerne No. 114, Holden No. 113

RATING: E2T2

LOCATION: Glacier Peak Wilderness administered by Wenatchee National Forest, Entiat Ranger District

PERMITS: Visitors are asked to sign the trailhead register.

SUMMARY AND HIGHLIGHTS: The Spectacle Buttes are two rocky outcrops east of Mt. Maude in the Glacier Peak Wilderness. They lie in a pocket between the Entiat and Chelan mountains, framed on the north by the broad curve of the Entiat River, and on the south by the lesser curve of Ice Creek. A saddle separates two distinct high points. South Spectacle Butte, the true summit, resembles a pyramid with a large talus basin on the western side.

South Spectacle Butte can be approached from Ice Lakes, two alpine ponds that are at such a high elevation they thaw only in late August or early September. When they are free of snow they are renowned for their exquisite beauty. Ice Lakes can be reached via a cross-country path from upper Leroy Creek Basin. But they also can be attained nearly as quickly from the Entiat River by a longer route that is all on good trail. The trip to South Spectacle Butte is made more attractive by the dark face of the empress—mighty Mt. Maude in the foreground—and the king—Bonanza Peak in the background—with an entourage of tall courtiers in between.

HOW TO GET THERE: Drive to north Wenatchee either from the west on Highway 2, or from the south using Interstate 90 and then Highway 97 over Blewett Pass. From north Wenatchee drive north on Alternate

Highway 97 on the west side of the Columbia River. At 15 miles, just before the town of Entiat, go left on Entiat River County Road 371. When the road enters the National Forest, it becomes FS Road 51. Continue to the road's end at Cottonwood Campground (38 miles from Alternate Highway 97). Just beyond is the parking for the Entiat River Trail No. 1400 trailhead (3100').

TRIP DESCRIPTION: Hike in light forest on Entiat River Trail No. 1400 for 8.0 miles to a junction just before the trail crosses Aurora Creek. Take the left fork, cross the Entiat River, and in 0.2 mile go left at another junction onto Ice Creek Trail No. 1405 (4300'). Hike west along Ice Creek for 3 miles to a basin at 5300 feet. You may choose to camp here. But if you have the time, continuing to Ice Lakes is worth the effort. From the basin the boot tread continues north above timberline and climbs steadily to lower Ice Lakes (6800'). Find a suitable established camp site. Parties with more energy may continue to upper Ice Lakes and camp at 7200 feet.

The next day, from the camp in the Ice Creek basin at 5300 feet, hike northeast and up onto the open slope. Scramble up onto the southeast face of the southwest shoulder of South Spectacle Butte (7300'). Stay on the southeast side, near the top of the ridge, all the way to the summit (class 3). Alternatively, from lower Ice Lakes, trek cross-country trending east toward the broad col between North and South Spectacle buttes (North Spectacle Butte is the high point directly east of Ice Lakes on the connecting ridge). Traverse around the south shoulder of the north butte. You may have to descend to 6800 feet to complete the corner. Continue scrambling upward toward the saddle between North and South Spectacle buttes. At 7200 feet, trend southeast, using ledges and steps to progress across and up the west face (class 3). While you are traversing, some rock moves are needed to get over small ribs and around exposed corners (class 4). Trend upward to attain the summit on relatively solid rock, but with some downsloping slabs that have slippery debris.

HAZARDS AND TIPS: You may choose to shorten the trip and forgo the Ice Lakes camp. The approach to Ice Lakes overland from Leroy Creek Basin is much shorter and more direct. However, it requires off-trail travel with an overnight pack. Therefore some parties may find it just as fast to go the longer route along good trail the entire distance to Ice Lakes. Some of the ascent — crossing the gully system on South Spectacle Butte — is exposed; some parties may want to use a hand line or a short rope for limited sections.

GPS WAYPOINT ROUTE:

1. 10U 675263, 5321498, 3100': Entiat River Trailhead
2. 10U 670011, 5331144, 8.2 miles, 4300': Ice Creek Trail
3. 10U 665117, 5332062, 3.2 miles, 5300': Ice Creek basin
4. 10U 666233, 5332264, 1.3 miles, 7300': Southwest shoulder
5. 10U 666812, 5332584, 0.7 mile, 8392': South Spectacle Butte summit

TRIP TIMES:

Entiat River Trailhead to Ice Creek basin camp: 11.4 miles, 2200', 8 hours

Ice Creek basin to Ice Lakes: 2.5 miles, 1700', 2 hours

Ice Creek basin camp to South Spectacle Butte summit: 2.0 miles, 3100', 5 hours

Spectacle Buttes: South Spectacle Butte is the 4-sided pyramid

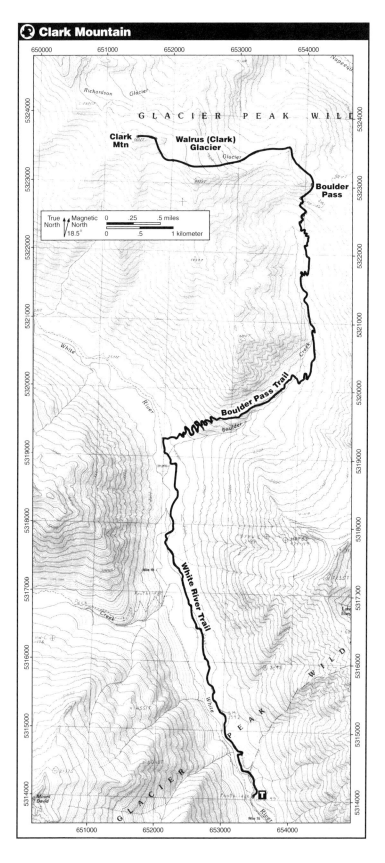

Clark Mountain

ELEVATION: 8602' (2622 m)

CLIMBING ROUTE: Walrus Glacier

DISTANCE: 26 miles

ELEVATION GAIN: 6300'

DAYS: 2

MAPS: USGS Mt. David, Clark Mountain; Green Trails Wenatchee Lake No. 145, Holden No. 113

RATING: E2T3

LOCATION: Glacier Peak Wilderness administered by Wenatchee National Forest, Lake Wenatchee Ranger District

PERMITS: Visitors are asked to sign the trailhead register.

SUMMARY AND HIGHLIGHTS: The term *DaKobed*—meaning "Great Parent"—is the Native American name for Glacier Peak. It is also the name of the compact, 11-mile sub-range anchored to Glacier Peak that forms a topographic crescent from the White Chuck and Suiattle glaciers on the west to the Napeequa River on the east, and from the Suiattle River on the north to the White River on the south. This dramatic crest meets the definition of a small sub-range by its compactness and continuity of summit terrain, for it is continuously high with no pass lower than 7000 feet. The DaKobed forms a deviation of the Cascade Crest from its general north-south axis to an eastward trend. But as in most other parts of the sector, due to intense alpine glaciations the entire sub-range is precipitous on the north and east while sloping and moderate on the south.

Clark Mountain rises at the eastern terminus, the highest and bulkiest mass of the DaKobed. Situated just 8 miles southeast of Glacier Peak, Clark has a distinctively carved rock summit tilted to the sky. The Napeequa side of Clark is clad with glaciers nearly 2 miles wide. The Richardson Glacier to the far west is the most heavily crevassed. The Walrus Glacier (named Clark Glacier on the USGS map) east of the summit is easier to travel. The glittering glacial terrain here contrasts with lowland meadows and intermittent parkland.

Keith Wilson

Clark Mountain from Luahna Peak

Clark is known for its relatively lengthy approach along river bottoms plagued for most of the summer by irritating biting black flies. Although you can find a scramble route on the south slope, many climbers prefer the climb up the Walrus Glacier, one of the more dramatic glaciers of the region. This approach yields an unusual view of Glacier Peak as the Cool and Chocolate glaciers come into view. Across the Napeequa River, Buck Mountain towers on Chiwawa Ridge, while in a huge cleft the White River thunders thousands of feet below.

HOW TO GET THERE: At Coles Corner, located 20 miles east of Stevens Pass on Highway 2, turn north onto Lake Wenatchee Road (State Route 207) to Lake Wenatchee. After crossing the Wenatchee River, drive along the north shore of Lake Wenatchee past the ranger station at the end of the lake. At 1.5 miles past the ranger station, take the right fork on White River Road (becomes FS Road 6400). Continue for 11 miles just past the White River Falls Campground to the end of the road where you'll find the White River Trail No.1507 trailhead (2300').

TRIP DESCRIPTION: Hike on the White River Trail for 4.1 miles. At the junction (2500'), leave the White River and go right (east) on Boulder Pass Trail No.1562. Ascend switchbacks in forest along the west side of Boulder Creek. At 4100 feet cross over Boulder Creek and continue on the trail, which is now east of the creek. At 6.5 miles from White River and just before Boulder Pass, leave the trail and go left (west) to camp at established sites (6000'). Alternative campsites for slower groups can be found at 4900 feet in a large basin along Boulder Creek.

The next day, ascend off-trail to the north and west of Boulder Pass. Trend northwest and traverse around the end of the ridge. At about 6300 feet, round the shoulder of the subsidiary peaks east of Clark Mountain and scramble west up talus to the eastern margin of the Walrus (Clark) Glacier (6900'). Rope up and go along the left (south) side while aiming toward the middle of the glacier. At 7200 feet the slope gets steeper and large crevasses must be avoided by traveling to the left. Climb to a flat bench on the glacier at 7600 feet. Reach a broad saddle (8200') on the ridge connecting the north and south high points. Cross south over the saddle onto the southeast face. Climb a gully system for 100 vertical feet to reach the east summit ridge between the true and false summits. From here the route west to the summit of Clark is easy (class 2).

HAZARDS AND TIPS: You can find a scramble route on the south slopes of Clark, but the path on the Walrus Glacier yields a more striking view and requires about the same effort. Boulder Pass can also be reached from the Chiwawa River on Little Giant Pass Trail No. 1518. But you must ford the Chiwawa River, and this route is therefore not recommended. You will need glacier gear on the Walrus Glacier, whose significant crevasses must be negotiated, particularly after the glacier breaks up by late July. The lowlands in this sector are notorious for annoying biting flies and mosquitoes. Bring along your favorite repellent—you will need it.

GPS WAYPOINT ROUTE:
1. 10U 653505, 5314034, 2300': White River Trailhead
2. 10U 651984, 5319229, 4.1 miles, 2500': Boulder Pass Trail
3. 10U 653946, 5322816, 6.5 miles, 6000': Boulder Pass camp
4. 10U 653777, 5323599, 0.7 mile, 6900': Walrus Glacier
5. 10U 651978, 5323378, 1.3 miles, 8200': saddle
6. 10U 651754, 5323621, 0.3 mile, 8300': east summit ridge
7. 10U 651481, 5323658, 0.2 mile, 8602': Clark summit

TRIP TIMES:
White River Trailhead to Boulder Pass camp: 10.6 miles, 3700', 7 hours

Boulder Pass camp to Clark summit: 2.5 miles, 2600', 5 hours

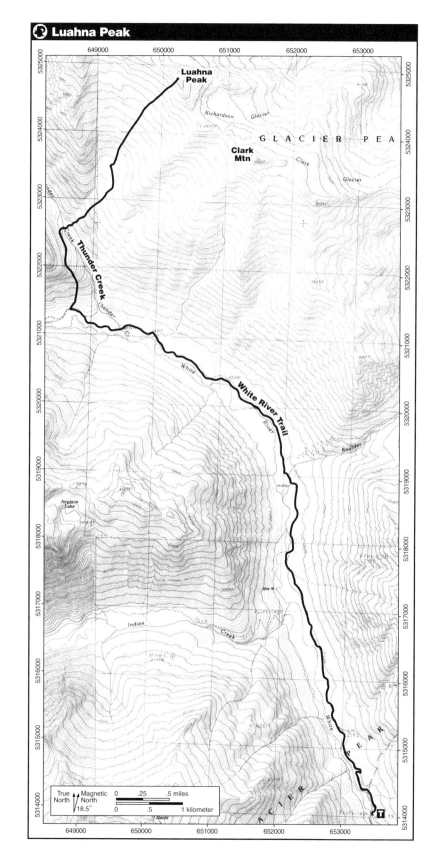

Luahna
Peak

Richardson   Glacier

G L A C I E R   P E A

Clark
Mtn   Clark

Glacier

Thunder Creek

White River Trail

White

River

Boulder

Airplane
Lake

Indian

Creek

P   E   A   K

White

True   Magnetic   0   .25   .5 miles
North   North
          18.5°   0   .5   1 kilometer

David   T

Luahna Peak

ELEVATION: 8400+ ft (2560+ m)

CLIMBING ROUTE: Southwest Face

DISTANCE: 20 miles

ELEVATION GAIN: 6100'

DAYS: 2

MAPS: USGS Mt. David, Glacier Peak East, Clark Mountain; Green Trails Lake Wenatchee No. 145, Holden No. 113, Glacier Peak No. 112

RATING: E2T1

LOCATION: Glacier Peak Wilderness administered by Wenatchee National Forest, Lake Wenatchee Ranger District

PERMITS: Visitors are asked to sign the trailhead register.

SUMMARY AND HIGHLIGHTS: Luahna Peak is one of the mountains of the DaKobed sub-range without an official USGS name. It is the high point northwest of Clark Mountain and also next highest in elevation. Luahna has a pyramidal shape with a long rock spur extending down to the east. On the north side, sloping toward the Napeequa River, the Pilz Glacier heads between Luahna and Chalangin Peak, the next in line.

Luahna is best approached from Thunder Creek Basin, a favorite spot of hunters. After ascending the wooded, southern slope of Tenpeak Mountain, you must ford Thunder Creek, no mean feat in early season when the meltwater from snow is high. Later in the summer, as the water volume decreases, clay benches and thick slide alder make the crossing easier. You may think that the next part of the journey is merely a bush-whack up the slope. But in the highest reaches of the basin, below the summit block, you will reach a pretty alpine cirque, covered by snow until late in the summer. From here the path is open and visible from your camp. The way up is pleasant and straightforward, with a short push on rock at the very top.

HOW TO GET THERE: At Coles Corner, located 20 miles east of Stevens Pass on Highway 2, turn north onto Lake Wenatchee Road (State Route 207) to Lake Wenatchee. After crossing the Wenatchee River,

Keith Wilson

On the summit of Luahna Peak with Napeequa Valley and the High Pass in the background

drive along the north shore of Lake Wenatchee past the ranger station at the end of the lake. At 1.5 miles past the ranger station, take the right fork on White River Road (becomes FS Road 6400). Continue for 11 miles just past the White River Falls Campground to the end of the road. Find the White River Trail No. 1507 trailhead (2300').

TRIP DESCRIPTION: Hike on the White River Trail in deep forest. At 4.1 miles the Boulder Pass Trail exits to the right. Continue on the White River Trail for another 2.3 miles. Cross a large stream whose headwaters originate on Clark Mountain to the east. Continue hiking on the trail a few hundred yards and cross Thunder Creek. About 0.2 mile beyond the creek, the trail makes a loop to the north. At the northernmost point in the trail is a marked tree (2800'). At the tree go north off the trail and in about 150 feet find an abandoned foot tread into Thunder Basin. This old shepherd trail has a sketchy start but is sometimes clearer farther along. At about 3600 feet the foot tread breaks out of forest into meadows. Turn right at a junction and ascend along Thunder Creek to about 3750 feet. Find a suitable place to cross Thunder Creek (it can be difficult when the water is running high). Continue steeply up the slope east of Thunder Creek, at first through dense brush then in thick forest. Go left (north) at 5100 feet to enter a huge, flat basin that is snow-covered until midsummer. Make a camp on the snow or on the flat meadow benches.

The next day, trend northeast to the Luahna summit. While you are scrambling upward, several false peaks may confuse you. Aim toward the middle high point, the true summit of Luahna, which is evident between the estimated 8350-foot point to the west (unofficially called Chalangin Peak) and Point 7970 to the east. The slope is moderate, open, and all above timberline. At the very top, gullies connect to the summit through small rocky slabs (class 3).

HAZARDS AND TIPS: The Thunder Creek crossing is difficult to find in patches of slide alder, and during high runoff the creek can be a torrential flow. Try to find a log crossing or make partial crossings on the braided, wider part of the creek. Thunder Creek Basin is popular with hunters. Even though a good time to do this trip is in fall, you must be prepared to deal with the sound of gunshots, particularly at dawn and dusk. Nevertheless, hunters rarely travel above timberline and most of this trip is therefore relatively safe and secluded.

GPS WAYPOINT ROUTE:
1. 10U 653505, 5314034, 2300': White River Trailhead
2. 10U 648746, 5321356, 6.9 miles, 2800': leave trail
3. 10U 648550, 5322638, 1.2 miles, 3800': Thunder Creek crossing
4. 10U 649224, 5323470, 0.8 mile, 5100': basin
5. 10U 650233, 5324800, 1.3 miles, 8400+': Luahna summit

TRIP TIMES:
White River Trailhead to basin: 8.9 miles, 2800', 8 hours
Basin to Luahna summit: 1.3 miles, 3300', 4 hours

Alpine Lakes Wilderness

C reated by Congress in 1964 by the Wilderness Act, the Alpine Lakes Wilderness encompasses approximately 394,000 acres and is accessed by 47 trailheads and 615 miles of trails. The Pacific Crest National Scenic Trail transects the rough country from Snoqualmie Pass to Stevens Pass. Named for the nearly 700 small mountain tarns set like jewels among high, rocky pinnacles, the remarkable beauty of the Wilderness as well as its proximity to the Seattle metropolitan area renders it one of the most popular natural resources of the Pacific Northwest.

The Wenatchee Mountains of the Alpine Lakes Wilderness are known for their diversity of landscape: deep U-shaped valleys, steep-walled cirques, small glaciers, rock-basin lakes, open meadows. All culminate in a sparse tree cover of alpine larch under picturesque rock towers of massive peaks. Much of the high country is barren, with perennial snow banks. In the Stuart Range, the mountain crests are deeply carved into sharp spires and crags. Steep slopes lead into rocky amphitheatres where remnants of glaciers persist. The most impressive

Cannon Mountain summit boulder

point is the monarch Mt. Stuart, the second-highest nonvolcanic peak in the state of Washington. One of the most striking features of it and the entire Stuart Range is the abundant fingerlike avalanche chutes that head chaotically from timberline down to elevations as low as 4500 feet. At the lower altitudes these deep ruts are often brush-filled. But at higher elevations, piles of dirty snow and freshly broken trees serve as evidence that avalanches hurtle down these slopes nearly every year.

Light-hued granite gives the rock a white color when seen from a distance and is particularly notable on the jagged group of mountains called the Cashmere Crags. This serrated crest overlooks polished granite, brilliantly clear lakes, and gnarled trees that decorate the isolated upland now popularly known as the "Lost World Plateau." This flat highland comprises the Enchantment Lakes Basin, a renowned group of rock tarns that is one of the most celebrated spots in the Cascade Range.

Although the Stuart Range was once extensively glaciated, it now maintains only remnants. Snow Creek Glacier has melted into five separate patches of ice in the Enchantment Lakes Basin from 7700 to 8600 feet—the highest mean altitude of a glacier not on a volcano in the Cascade Range. The largest rock glacier of the sector (a small glacier in a protected cirque) lies high on the northwest flank of Mt. Stuart and terminates in an elongated tongue of coarse rubble nearly 300 feet long.

More than half of the population of Washington state lives within a one-hour drive of the Alpine Lakes Wilderness, contributing to the overcrowding and overuse of this enormously popular area. With nearly 150,000 visitors each year, the region is far from wild or lonely. In order to preserve the integrity of the Wilderness, regulations are imposed in many areas. The Wenatchee and Mt. Baker-Snoqualmie national forests jointly administer the Alpine Lakes Wilderness. An overnight reservation permit is required from June 15 to October 15 for entry to the unique Enchantments Area. The mail-in permit applications for an overnight stay are available from the Leavenworth Ranger Station by calling (509) 548-6977 or can be printed from the Forest Service website (see Appendix A: Contact Information). Dogs are not allowed within any of the permit areas. Permits for dayhiking within the reservation area, as well as day use and overnight trips in other areas of the Alpine Lakes Wilderness, are available on a self-issue basis at the Leavenworth Ranger Station and at trailheads. Despite the logistics involved in visiting the Alpine Lakes Wilderness, the region is so special and inviting that if you plan in advance, you can have a superb outing in this otherworldly realm.

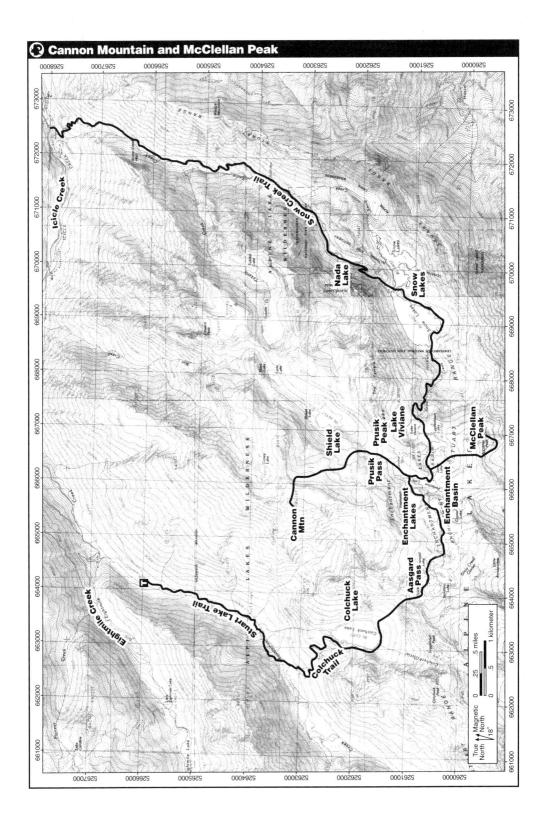

Cannon Mountain and McClellan Peak

ROUTE 33

Cannon Mountain
and McClellan Peak

ELEVATIONS: 8638', 8364' (2633 m, 2549 m)

CLIMBING ROUTES: Cannon: East Slope; McClellan: South Face

DISTANCE: 26 miles

ELEVATION GAIN: 7200'

DAYS: 3–4

MAPS: USGS Cashmere Mountain, Enchantment Lakes, Blewett, Leavenworth; Green Trails The Enchantments No. 209S

RATING: E3T2

LOCATION: Alpine Lakes Wilderness administered by Wenatchee National Forest, Leavenworth Ranger District

PERMITS: The Forest Service requires permits and fees for camping within the Enchantments. Before you visit the Enchantments area check with officials on what regulations may apply, and visit the Alpine Lakes Web site (see Appendix A: Contact Information).

SUMMARY AND HIGHLIGHTS: While working as a topographer for the USGS, A. H. Sylvester named the group of rock-basin lakes nestled in the Cashmere Crags of the Stuart Range "Enchantment" to express his reaction—and this reaction has been shared by all who have followed into this magical realm. Dazzling ponds and gnarled and twisted trees contrast with slabs of ice-polished stone. The granite blazes pink in the intensity of a setting summer sun. Fuzzy larch needles stand out boldly on the ridgecrests above the Snow Lakes. This is a land of extremes— from warm, luxuriant beauty to stunning, austere grandeur. The "Lost Plateau" of the Enchantments, with its wryly imaginative place names, has become a haven for the hiker, backpacker, scrambler, and rock climber. Cross-county travel is marvelously unconstrained in the up-lands. Many of the highest points are scrambles: Little Annapurna, Colchuck, Dragontail, and Enchantment peaks make up this group. But two other high mountains are more complicated alpine climbs. Cannon Mountain is the massive point with a boulder-strewn top that is easily reached via the long bedrock between Rat and Mountaineer creeks. McClellan Peak is yet more complex; its craggy and many-towered and needled face outlines the western end of Upper Snow Lake.

The Enchantment Lakes Area is one of the most overused spots in the Cascades. To protect the environment from damage, the Forest Service requires permits for camping within the permit zone and the surrounding wilderness area from June 15 to October 15, as well as day-use permits for some trails. Campsites within the Enchantments are so much in demand that permits are often gone by the spring for summer months. If you plan to camp in the Enchantment Lakes area, plan ahead by visiting or calling the Leavenworth Ranger District or the Wenatchee National Forest, or by checking the Alpine Lakes Wilderness Web site (see Appendix A: Contact Information). Apply for permits months in advance or take your chances with the daily permit "lottery"—a drawing held each summer morning to determine the few lucky campers to receive on-the-spot-permits. Enchantments overnight mail-in permit applications are available from the Leavenworth Ranger Station by calling (509) 548-6977, or can be printed from the Forest Service website. Permits are processed beginning March 1 and a fee is charged for each person for each day. Individuals who purchase an overnight Alpine Lakes Wilderness permit do not need a Northwest Forest Park permit to park at trailheads for the dates that they are visiting the Wilderness.

Despite the remote locale, this is not a trip for hermits. The Forest Service limits entry permits; hence the area is no longer overrun but is always busy. Be prepared to obey a strict Leave No Trace travel ethic. No fires or dogs are allowed. Camp only on bare ground at established sites, use toilets where provided, and walk on rock or snow, not on fragile vegetation. Limit your party size. If you can't agree to all that, then do without this trip. Despite the rules and difficulty in obtaining a permit, the journey is well worth the effort. This is a picturesque and radiant land any time of year, a high, lost upland sheltered from the world below, resplendent with transcendent towers and endless heavenly wandering.

HOW TO GET THERE: This trip is described as a car shuttle, going into the Enchantments from the west over Aasgard Pass and leaving via the Snow Creek Trail to the east. This way, you will continually encounter new terrain. If a car shuttle is inconvenient, you can retrace your steps over either approach and still enjoy a substantial variety of the alpine environment.

Drive to Leavenworth either on Highway 2 from the north, or via Interstate 90 and then Highway 97 over Blewett Pass from the south. Stop at the Leavenworth Ranger Station to register for the climb and to confirm your pre-made reservation, or to take your chances with the lot-

Climbers on Cannon Mountain summit

tery. Reserved passes will be left in a box in the evening before your permit begins. On the west side of Leavenworth turn west on Icicle Road No. 76. At 4.2 miles leave a car for the end of the trip at the large parking lot for the Snow Creek Trailhead. Continue driving on the Icicle Road. At 8.6 miles, go left on Eightmile Creek Road No. 7601. Drive past the parking for the Eightmile Lake Trail No. 1552. At 3.5 miles stop at the parking area for the Stuart Lake Trail No. 1599 trailhead (3400').

TRIP DESCRIPTION: Hike on the Stuart Lake Trail for 2.5 miles to a junction. Take the left (south) fork and continue on Colchuck Trail No. 1599A. Ascend switchbacks for 1.6 miles to reach Colchuck Lake (5600'). Continue on the marked trail around the west side of the lake. Parts of the route are a little sketchy as the trail hops over large boulders and rockslides. At the southeast lip begin up the talus and lightly wooded slope toward Aasgard Pass. (Aasgard Pass is labeled Colchuck Pass on the USGS Enchantment Lakes map.) This path sometimes changes due to avalanches that destroy the tread. Continue upward near the crest where the path turns directly south and then tops out at Aasgard Pass (7800'). Continue onto the Lost Plateau of the Enchantment Lakes Basin and camp at an established site. A camp near Perfection Lake is a central spot for both peaks.

Lake Viviane, Enchantment Lakes Basin with McClellan Peak in background

Cannon Mountain

Travel northeast to Prusik Pass (7400'). Prusik Peak is on your right as you go through the saddle. Trek cross-country to the northwest above treeline on the broad, nearly flat open slope west of Shield Lake. Cross over a moderately steep rim of the basin northwest of Shield Lake at 8200 feet to a flat, boulder-strewn bench. The summit of Cannon Mountain is the high point on the broad hill. Walk west across the bench to the summit rocks. The last 20 feet involves exposed climbing (class 3). The southeast edge of the summit block is easier than the northeast edge. The last boulder at the top may require some modest climbing (a couple of class 4 moves). Return by retracing your steps over Prusik Pass to Perfection Lake.

McClellan Peak

The next morning head south on the slope between Sprite Lake and Leprechaun Lake. Stay west of The Prong, a prominent north-tilting needle on the spur of the west ridge of McClellan. The gully next to The

Prong can be exited to the left half-way-up for safe, easy scrambling. Then pass through the notch on the west ridge (8000'). Continue on a traversing ascent onto the south face. Climb up gully systems to gain the ridge east of the summit (class 3). Finally scramble west on the crest to the top. Return to camp. From your camp in the Enchantment Lakes, find the boot tread going east past Leprechaun Lake and Lake Viviane. The trail is well established around the south shore of Upper Snow Lake. Cross over the dam between Upper and Lower Snow lakes; a tunnel allows a spectacular gush of water to come flying out of the cliffs below Snow lakes. The Snow Creek Trail then follows the north shore of Nada Lake. Continue hiking to the trailhead at Icicle Creek Road (10 miles from Perfection Lake).

HAZARDS AND TIPS: The gully system on McClellan is moderately exposed and loose. Cannon and McClellan can be combined on a single day, although you may have to spend some time working your way up the proper gully systems on McClellan Peak. You may want to plan an extra day or two to enjoy wandering around the Enchantment Basin or completing other climbs in the area.

GPS WAYPOINT ROUTE:
1. 10U 664148, 5265913, 3400': Stuart Lake Trailhead
2. 10U 663212, 5262504, 4.1 miles, 5600': Colchuck Lake
3. 10U 663501, 5261491, 1.0 mile, 5700': boot trail to Aasgard Pass
4. 10U 664220, 5260642, 1.0 mile, 7800': Aasgard Pass
5. 10U 666030, 5260986, 1.7 miles, 7100': Perfection Lake
6. 10U 666482, 5261521, 0.7 mile, 7400': Prusik Pass
7. 10U 665593, 5263179, 1.5 miles, 8638': Cannon summit
8. 10U 666615, 5259711, 3.5 miles, 8000': McClellan west ridge
9. 10U 666956, 5259579, 0.6 mile, 8364': McClellan summit
10. 10U 667372, 5260981, 3.2 miles, 6800': Snow Creek Trail
11. 10U 672437, 5267901, 8.6 miles, 1300': Snow Creek Trailhead

TRIP TIMES:
Stuart Lake Trailhead to Perfection Lake: 7.8 miles, 4400', 9 hours
Perfection Lake to Cannon summit: 2.2 miles, 1500', 2 hours
Cannon summit to McClellan summit: 4.1 miles, 1300', 5 hours

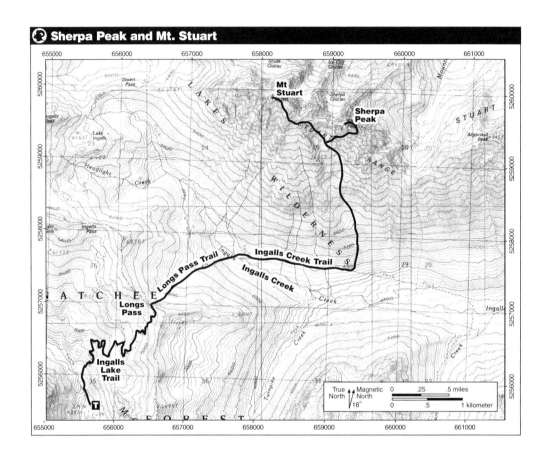

Sherpa Peak and Mt. Stuart

Sherpa Peak and Mt. Stuart

ELEVATIONS: 8605', 9415' (2623 m, 2870 m)

CLIMBING ROUTES: Sherpa: East Ridge; Stuart: Cascadian Couloir Variation

DISTANCE: 17 miles

ELEVATION GAIN: 9700'

DAYS: 3–4

MAPS: USGS Mt. Stuart, Green Trails Mt. Stuart 209

RATING: E4T4

LOCATION: Alpine Lakes Wilderness administered by Wenatchee National Forest, Cle Elum and Leavenworth Ranger districts

PERMITS: In this area of the Alpine Lakes Wilderness, day-use and overnight trip permits are available on a self-issue basis at the Leavenworth Ranger Station and at trailheads. Before you visit the Alpine Lakes Wilderness check with officials on what regulations may apply, and visit the Alpine Lakes Web site (see Appendix A: Contact Information).

SUMMARY AND HIGHLIGHTS: Mt. Stuart is the king of the Enchantments, mighty and mean, the second-highest nonvolcanic summit in the Cascade Range and possibly the largest single granitic mountain in the United States. This massive hulk features some of the most diverse climbing terrain for a single mountain. Its sheer immensity and variety have made it a popular objective for Northwest climbers.

In contrast, Sherpa, just down the crest from Mt. Stuart, is less famous. It therefore makes for an interesting alternative to some of the busier peaks in the area. Both Stuart and Sherpa can be reached from a camp near the col that connects the two. This twosome makes for an extended outing in the Stuart Range but with the added advantage of being just outside the region that requires the complicated process of obtaining an overnight permit.

HOW TO GET THERE: Drive on Interstate 90 to South Cle Elum. Take exit 85 and drive east on State Route 970. At 6.6 miles from the inter-

Climber on Mt. Stuart

state turn left on the Teanaway River Road. Follow North Fork Teanaway Road (FS Road 9737) for 23 miles until it ends. Find parking for Ingalls Way Trail No. 1390 (4200').

TRIP DESCRIPTION: Hike on Ingalls Way Trail No. 1390 along the North Fork Teanaway River. At 0.4 mile Esmeralda Basin Trail No. 1394 exits to the left. Continue on the Ingalls Lake Trail, ascending switchbacks through the forest onto the open slope. In 2 miles find a junction. Take the right fork on Longs Pass Trail No. 1229. Top out at Longs Pass (6300'), then descend on a foot tread into Ingalls Creek valley. Continue into the valley and cross Ingalls Creek on a log at about 4800 feet. Connect with Ingalls Creek Trail No. 1215 shortly after. Turn right (east) and walk for a half mile down the trail to the junction on the right with Beverly-Turnpike Trail No. 1391. Continue past the junction for an additional half mile. Here at about 4700 feet scramble off-trail up the grassy

Keith Wilson

Climber on the summit of Sherpa with the balanced rock in the background

slope, aiming at the col between Stuart and Sherpa. Ascend talus around minor cliffs to a basin at 7500 feet. Make a camp on a flat bench, where snow or water is usually present until mid-August.

Sherpa Peak

To climb Sherpa the next day, scramble east into the basin just south-east of the summit block. Climb a broad gully to a notch several hundred feet east of the balanced rock, an easily recognized formation on the summit ridge. Go up the ridge to just below the balanced rock and cross to the north side of Sherpa. From here, traverse west on an exposed slab

High on Mt. Stuart

for about 30 feet (class 5). Rock protection and handholds are available in the crack at the top of the slab. Go west past the balanced rock to a short chimney system and climb to the summit (class 4). Belay or use a hand line to descend the route back to the balanced rock. Retrace your steps and return to camp.

Mt. Stuart

From camp make an ascending traverse northwest to intersect the Cascadian Couloir route. The route steepens at 7800 feet. Climb up gully systems filled with snow or scree to 8200 feet, aiming toward the upper snowfield of the false summit. At 8500 feet you can go up the snowfield or bypass it to the left on steep rock (class 4). From the false summit (9100') scramble west along the ridge, bypassing obstacles by dropping onto the south face. Climb through broken rock and on some blocks to the summit (class 3). The route is marked with cairns at the highest levels.

HAZARDS AND TIPS: On Sherpa, at least a hand line is necessary for safety over the exposed slab and other exposed portions of the climb. For Stuart, a hand line or a short belay may be desirable around portions of the false summit if snow does not cover the steep gully system back to the Cascadian Couloir.

GPS WAYPOINT ROUTE:

1. 10U 655668, 5255583, 4200': Ingalls Way Trailhead
2. 10U 656490, 5256973, 3.0 miles, 6300': Longs Pass
3. 10U 657710, 5257679, 1.0 mile, 4800': Ingalls Creek
4. 10U 659617, 5257502, 1.0 mile, 4700': leave trail
5. 10U 658928, 5259254, 1.2 miles, 7500': high camp
6. 10U 659302, 5259492, 0.6 mile, 8200': balanced rock
7. 10U 659182, 5259579, 0.4 mile, 8605': Sherpa summit
8. 10U 658475, 5259535, 1.5 miles, 8500': Cascadian Couloir
9. 10U 658404, 5259739, 0.3 mile, 9100': false summit
10. 10U 658150, 5259909, 0.3 mile, 9415': Stuart summit

TRIP TIMES:

Ingalls Way Trailhead to high camp: 6.2 miles, 4900', 8 hours
High camp to Sherpa summit: 1.0 mile, 1100', 4 hours
High camp to Stuart summit: 1.1 miles, 1900', 5 hours

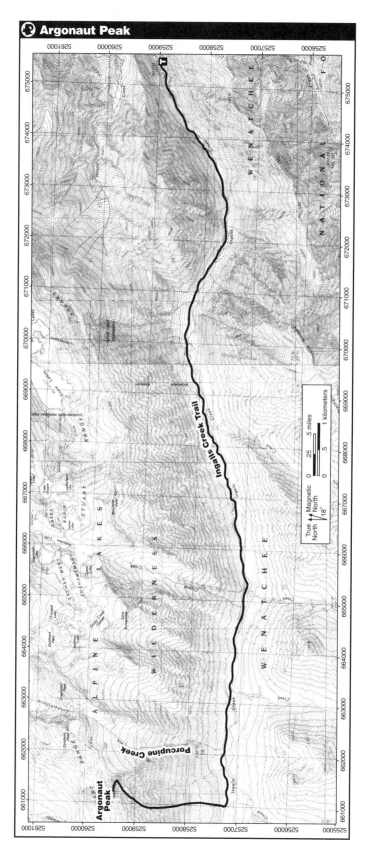

Argonaut Peak

ELEVATION: 8453' (2577 m)

CLIMBING ROUTE: South Route

DISTANCE: 25 miles

ELEVATION GAIN: 6500'

DAYS: 2–3

MAPS: USGS Blewett, Enchantment Lakes; Green Trails Liberty No. 210, Mt. Stuart No. 209

RATING: E2T3

LOCATION: Alpine Lakes Wilderness administered by Wenatchee National Forest, Leavenworth Ranger District

PERMITS: Permits are required for camping and for day use in the Alpine Lakes Wilderness. Self-issue permits at the trailheads are available for approaches from Blewett Pass via the Ingalls Creek Trail and from Teanaway River Road.

SUMMARY AND HIGHLIGHTS: Argonaut appears as one of the orderly lines of high priests lined up behind the monarch, Mt. Stuart. Despite its somewhat dwarfed appearance, it is still a prominent feature in the Stuart Range. Argonaut's southeast and west high points are of almost equal elevation, but the west peak is the true summit. Because it is beside Colchuck Peak, one is tempted to approach Argonaut from Colchuck Col, a relatively straightforward entry into the high "Lost Plateau" of the Enchantments. But there the class 5 climbing is more complicated. Instead, the southern route is more moderate as Ingalls Creek is located at the base of the long southern slope. Although it seems much longer, this easier route probably requires no more energy to reach the top.

HOW TO GET THERE: On Interstate 90 take Exit 85 (Cle Elum) and follow State Highway No. 970, which becomes U.S. Highway No. 97. Drive north on the highway for 38.9 miles to Ingalls Creek junction. Here take the left fork over a bridge across Peshastin Creek, and drive south for 1.3 miles to the Ingalls Creek Trail No. 1215 trailhead (2000').

Keith Wilson

Argonaut Peak from Colchuck Peak

TRIP DESCRIPTION: Hike on Ingalls Creek Trail No. 1215 for 10.3 miles to the Fourth Creek Trail junction. (This is a long approach. If you do not want to hike this far along Ingalls Creek, you can reach the Fourth Creek junction from the west via Longs Pass in 6 miles, but with 2000 feet of additional elevation gain. Follow the driving instructions for Sherpa Peak and Mt. Stuart (Trip 34), then hike over Longs Pass, cross Ingalls Creek to get on the Ingalls Creek Trail going east, and continue to the junction of Fourth Creek, which exits to your right.) Make a camp at 4300 feet along Ingalls Creek.

The next morning leave the trail and go north straight up Argonaut's fall line while paying attention to stay in the big timber and out of the brush. Ascend the slope to the upper basin at 6500 feet and then contour east until reaching the main drainage below the summit. Climb up the drainage until a rightward gully emerges at 7200 feet. Follow this gully up and right (class 4), topping out on the east ridge at 8200 feet. Follow the ridge to the summit (class 3).

An alternative route from camp that is equivalent but that some climbers prefer is to leave the trail about a quarter mile west of Porcupine Creek (about a mile east of the Fourth Creek Trail intersection with the Ingalls Creek Trail). This way you can avoid most of the worst slide alder along the creek. Continue up the ridge that parallels the west side of Porcupine Creek. Go up through heavy timber that thins out with patches of chaparral and mountain ash at about 5500-feet. Then make a rising traverse west, staying below 6100 feet to avoid the black rib that comes down just east of the summit access gully. The correct gully has huge, white granite blocks in it between 6300 and 6600 feet. From the ridge on the west side of this gully, at 6600 feet, you can see the wide, reddish-colored summit formation with the access gully starting up to the left of the summit and then swinging to the right to end just south of the summit. At the apex of the gully, climb a crack on the left to get onto the east ridge (class 4). Then scramble west to the summit, skirting around to the south side of the summit blocks on a wide ledge. Finally climb a 12-foot wall with good holds to the final summit area (class 3).

HAZARDS AND TIPS: Helmets are recommended as the summit gully on Argonaut has loose rock. The trail along Ingalls Creek is easy but long. Approaches over Longs Pass or via Beverly Creek are good alternatives. If you use Longs Pass, you will have more elevation gain and loss. If you use Beverly Creek you will have to find a way to cross Ingalls Creek (bring wading shoes).

GPS WAYPOINT ROUTE:
1. 10U 675479, 5259038, 2000': Ingalls Creek Trailhead
2. 10U 661012, 5257200, 10.3 miles, 4300': Fourth Creek camp
3. 10U 660912, 5258663, 1.3 miles, 6500': upper basin
4. 10U 661442, 5259373, 0.6 mile, 8200': east ridge
5. 10U 661239, 5259430, 0.3 mile, 8453': Argonaut summit

TRIP TIMES:
Ingalls Creek Trailhead to Fourth Creek Camp: 10.3 miles, 2300', 8 hours

Fourth Creek Camp to Argonaut summit: 2.2 miles, 4200', 7 hours

APPENDIX A

Contact Information

(Note: Phone numbers and addresses subject to change)

NATIONAL PARK SERVICE

Pacific Northwest Regional Office
83 South King St., Suite 212
Seattle, WA 98104
(206) 553-5622
(206) 553-0171 (recreation information)

MOUNT RAINIER NATIONAL PARK

Park Headquarters Communications
Center
Tahoma Woods, Star Rte.
Ashford, WA 98304
(360) 569-2211
www.nps.gov/mora/

NORTH CASCADES NATIONAL PARK SERVICE COMPLEX

Park Headquarters
810 SR 20
Sedro-Woolley, WA 98284
(Corner of Hwy 9 and SR 20)
(360) 856-5700
www.nps.gov/noca/

Wilderness Information Center
7280 Ranger Station Rd.
Marblemount, WA 98267
(360) 873-4500 ext 39

Golden West Visitor Center
Stehekin, WA 98852
(360) 856-5703, ext. 340 + 14

Lake Chelan National Recreation Area
Chelan Ranger Station
PO Box 549
Chelan, WA 98816
(509) 682-2549

U.S. FOREST SERVICE

MT. BAKER-SNOQUALMIE NATIONAL FOREST

Forest Headquarters
21905 64thth Ave. W
Mountlake Terrace, WA 98043-2278
(425) 775-9702
(800) 627-0062
www.fs.fed.us/r6/mbs/

Mt. Baker Ranger District
810 SR 20
Sedro-Woolley, WA 98284
(Corner of Hwy. 9 and SR 20)
(360) 856-5700

Glacier Public Service Center
1094 Mt. Baker Hwy.
Glacier, WA 98244
(360) 599-2714

Darrington Ranger District
1405 Emmens St.
Darrington, WA 98241
(360) 436-1155

Skykomish Ranger District
74920 NE Stevens Pass Hwy.
P.O. Box 305
Skykomish, WA 98288
(360) 677-2414

Snoqualmie Ranger District:

North Bend Office
42404 SE North Bend Way
North Bend, WA 98405
(425) 888-1421

Snoqualmie Pass Visitor Center
PO Box 17
Snoqualmie Pass, WA 98068
(425) 434-6111

Enumclaw Office
450 Roosevelt Ave. E
Enumclaw, WA 98022
(360) 825-6585

Outdoor Recreation Information
Center:

Seattle REI Building
222 Yale Ave. North
Seattle, WA 98109-5429
(206) 470-4060

OKANOGAN AND WENATCHEE NATIONAL FORESTS

Forest Supervisor,
Okanogan and Wenatchee National
Forests
215 Melody Lane
Wenatchee, WA 98801-5933
(509) 662-4396

Okanogan National Forest:

Okanogan Valley Office,
Okanogan and Wenatchee
National Forests
1240 2nd Ave. S
Okanogan, WA 98840-9723
(509) 826-3275
www.fs.fed.us/r6/oka/

Methow Valley Visitor Center
Building 49 Hwy. 20
24 West Chewuch Road
Winthrop, WA 98862
(509) 996-4000

Methow Valley Ranger District
24 West Chewuch Road
Wintrhop, WA 98862
(509) 996-4003

Tonasket Ranger District
1 West Winesap
Tonasket, WA 98855
(509) 486-2186

Wenatchee National Forest:

Forest Headquarters
215 Melody Ln.
Wenatchee, WA 98801-5933
(509) 662-4335
www.fs.fed.us/r6/wenatchee/

Chelan Ranger District
428 W. Woodin Ave.
Chelan, WA 98816-9724
(509) 682-2576

Cle Elum Ranger District
803 W 2nd St.
Cle Elum, WA 98922
(509) 674-4411

Entiat Ranger District
PO Box 476,
2108 Entiat Way
Entiat, WA 98822
(509) 784-1511

Lake Wenatchee Ranger District
22976 State Hwy. 207
Leavenworth, WA 98826
(509) 763-3103

Leavenworth Ranger District
600 Sherbourne St.
Leavenworth, WA 98826
(509) 548-6977
Alpine Lakes: www.fs.fed.us/r6/
wenatchee/recreate/wilderns.html

Naches Ranger District
10061 Hwy. 12
Naches, WA 98937
(509) 653-2205

ADDITIONAL CONTACT SOURCES

Northwest Weather and Avalanche Center	(206) 526-6677
National Weather Service Forecast	(206) 526-6087
Road Information	(206) 455-7900
SnoPark Information	(206) 586-0185
Recreation Information Center	(206) 470-4060
Bureau of Land Management	(509) 536-1200
State Department of Wildlife	(360) 902-2200
State Department of Natural Resources	(360) 902-1650
State Parks and Recreation	(800) 233-0321
U.S. Geological Survey	(509) 353-2524

APPENDIX B

Trip Statistics

(Notes: The elevation listed is the highest peak of the trip. The USGS
map is of the climbing route; Green Trails map given in order)

ROUTE NO.	TRIP	ELEVATION	DISTANCE (MILES)	ELEV. GAIN (FT)	TRIP TIME (DAYS)	USGS MAP
1	Rainier	14,410 ft (4392 m)	15	10,500	2–3	Sunrise, Mt. Rainier East, Mt. Rainier West
2	Little Tahoma	11,138 ft (3395 m)	18	7300	2	Mt. Rainier East
3	Baker	10,781 ft (3287 m)	12	7100	2	Groat Mountain, Mt. Baker
4	Glacier	10,520+ ft (3207+ m)	22	8200	2–3	Glacier Peak West, Glacier Peak East
5	Shuksan	9131 ft (2784 m)	15	6700	2	Mt. Shuksan
6	Chilliwack Group	8979 ft (2738 m)	38	16,500	8–10	Mt. Redoubt, Mt. Spickard
7	Snowfield	8347 ft (2544 m)	15	7600	2	Ross Dam, Diablo Dam
8	Inspiration Glacier	8868 ft (2703 m)	23	11,600	6–9	Forbidden Peak, Eldorado Peak
9	Forbidden	8815 ft (2687 m)	10	5700	2–3	Cascade Pass, Forbidden Peak
10	Sahale and Boston	8894 ft (2711 m)	12	6200	2	Cascade Pass
11	Buckner and Horseshoe	9112+ ft (2778+ m)	20	9500	3	Cascade Pass, Goode Mountain
12	Formidable	8325 ft (2537 m)	20	7800	3	Cascade Pass
13	Ragged Ridge	8795 ft (2681m)	30	13,200	5–6	Mt. Logan, Mt. Arriva
14	Black	8970 ft (2734 m)	12	4700	1–2	Washington Pass, Mt. Arriva
15	Harts Pass	8444 ft (2574 m)	44	12,500	5–7	Washington Pass, Azurite Peak
16	Silver Star	8876 ft (2705 m)	7	5200	1–2	Silver Star Mountain
17	Big Snagtooth	8330+ ft (2539+ m)	7	4600	1	Silver Star Mountain
18	Reynolds	8512 ft (2594 m)	20	7300	2–3	Sun Mountain
19	Jack	9066 ft (2763 m)	21	9600	3	Crater Mountain, Jack Mountain
20	Cathedral and Amphitheater	8601 ft (2622 m)	49	6700	4–6	Remmel Mountain
21	Blackcap	8397 ft (2559 m)	38	12,700	3–4	Mt. Lago
22	Stehekin Group	9200+ ft (2804+ m)	31	13,900	5–6	Goode Mountain, Mt. Logan
23	Dark	8504 ft (2592 m)	29	6800	3–4	Agnes Mountain
24	Tupshin and Devore	8360+ ft (2548+ m)	22	12,500	4–5	Stehekin, Mt. Lyall
25	Bonanza and Martin	9511 ft (2899 m)	21	8400	4	Holden
26	Fernow and Copper	9249 ft (2819 m)	17	9400	4	Holden
27	Flora	8320 ft (2536 m)	21	9700	3	Holden, Pinnacle Mountain
28	Sinister and Dome	8920+ ft (2719+ m)	40	13,000	6–8	Agnes Mountain, Dome Peak
29	Dumbell and Greenwood	8421 ft (2567 m)	22	5700	2	Holden
30	South Spectacle Butte	8392 ft (2558 m)	27	5300	2–3	Trinity, Holden
31	Clark	8602 ft (2622 m)	26	6300	2	Clark Mountain
32	Luahna	8440+ ft (2560+ m)	20	6100	2	Glacier Peak East, Clark Mountain
33	Cannon and McClellan	8638 ft (2633 m)	26	7200	3–4	Enchantment Lakes, Cashmere Mountain
34	Sherpa and Stuart	9415 ft (2870 m)	17	9700	3–4	Mt. Stuart
35	Argonaut	8453 ft (2577 m)	25	6500	2–3	Enchantment Lakes

GREEN TRAILS MAP (NO.)	RATING	LOCATION	RANGER STATION	PERMITS	PARK* FEE	BUS/BOAT FEE
270, 269	E4T3	Mt. Rainier National Park	White River	Yes	Yes	No
270	E3T3	Mt. Rainier National Park	White River	Yes	Yes	No
13	E3T3	Mt. Baker Wilderness	Sedro-Woolley	No	No	No
111, 112	E3T3	Glacier Peak Wilderness	Darrington	No	No	No
14	E2T3	North Cascades National Park	Sedro-Woolley	Yes	No	No
15, 16	E5T5	North Cascades National Park	Sedro-Woolley	Yes	No	No
48	E3T3	North Cascades National Park	Marblemount	Yes	No	No
48, 80	E5T5	North Cascades National Park	Marblemount	Yes	No	No
80, 48	E2T5	North Cascades National Park	Marblemount	Yes	No	No
80	E2T4	North Cascades National Park	Marblemount	Yes	No	No
80, 81	E4T4	North Cascades National Park	Marblemount	Yes	No	No
80	E3T3	Mt. Baker-Snoqualmie Nat'l Forest	Marblemount	No	No	No
49	E5T3	North Cascades National Park	Marblemount	Yes	No	No
50, 49	E1T3	Mt. Baker-Snoqualmie Nat'l Forest	Marblemount	No	No	No
50, 49	E4T3	Okanogan National Forest	Methow Valley Visitor Ctr.	No	No	No
50	E1T3	Okanogan National Forest	Methow Valley Visitor Ctr.	No	No	No
50	E1T4	Okanogan National Forest	Methow Valley Visitor Ctr.	No	No	No
83, 82	E3T1	Lake Chelan-Sawtooth Wilderness	Methow Valley Visitor Ctr.	No	No	No
49, 17	E3T4	Pasayten Wilderness	Methow Valley Visitor Ctr.	No	No	No
20	E4T4	Pasayten Wilderness	Methow Valley Visitor Ctr.	No	No	No
50, 51, 19, 18	E4T1	Pasayten Wilderness	Methow Valley Visitor Ctr.	No	No	No
81, 49	E5T4	North Cascades National Park	Stehekin	Yes	No	Yes
81	E4T3	Glacier Peak Wilderness	Stehekin	No	No	Yes
82, 81, 114, 113	E4T5	Glacier Peak Wilderness	Stehekin	No	No	Yes
113	E4T4	Glacier Peak Wilderness	Chelan	No	No	Yes
113	E4T2	Glacier Peak Wilderness	Chelan	No	No	Yes
113, 114	E3T1	Glacier Peak Wilderness	Chelan	No	No	Yes
81, 80	E5T4	Glacier Peak Wilderness	Darrington	No	No	Yes
113	E2T2	Glacier Peak Wilderness	Lake Wenatchee	No	No	No
114, 113	E2T2	Glacier Peak Wilderness	Entiat	No	No	No
145, 113	E2T3	Glacier Peak Wilderness	Lake Wenatchee	No	No	No
145, 113, 112	E2T1	Glacier Peak Wilderness	Lake Wenatchee	No	No	No
209S	E3T2	Alpine Lakes Wilderness	Leavenworth	Yes	Yes	No
209	E4T4	Alpine Lakes Wilderness	Leavenworth	Yes	No	No
210, 209	E2T3	Alpine Lakes Wilderness	Leavenworth	Yes	No	No

*You must purchase a Northwest Forest Pass to park at most trailheads.

APPENDIX C
Bulger Top 100 List

(Note: Some elevations on the Bulger List are not the same
as noted on the USGS map.)

RANK	NAME	ELEVATION (FT)	RANK	NAME	ELEVATION (FT)
1	Mt. Rainier	14,410	27	Forbidden Peak	8815
2	Mt. Adams	12,276	28	Mesahchie Peak	8795
3	Little Tahoma	11,138	29	Oval Peak	8795
4	Mt. Baker	10,781	30	Fortress Mountain	8760+
5	Glacier Peak	10,520+	31	Mt. Lago	8745
6	Bonanza Peak	9511	32	Robinson Mountain	8726
7	Mt. Stuart	9415	33	Colchuck Peak	8705
8	Mt. Fernow	9249	34	Star Peak	8690
9	Mt. Goode	9200+	35	Remmel Mountain	8685
10	Mt. Shuksan	9131	36	Katsuk Peak	8680+
11	Buckner Mtn.	9112	37	Sahale Mountain	8680+
12	SevenFingered Jack	9100	38	Cannon Mountain	8638
13	Mt. Logan	9087	39	Mt. Custer*	8630
14	Jack Mountain	9066	40	Ptarmigan Peak	8614
15	Mt. Maude	9040+	41	Sherpa Peak	8605
16	Mt. Spickard	8979	42	Clark Mountain	8602
17	Black Peak	8970	43	Cathedral Peak	8601
18	Mt. Redoubt	8969	44	Kimtah (Gendarmes*) Peak	8600+
19	Copper Peak	8964			
20	North Gardner Mtn.	8956	45	Mt. Carru	8595
21	Dome Peak	8920+	46	Monument Peak	8592
22	Gardner Mountain	8898	47	Cardinal Peak	8590
23	Boston Peak	8894	48	Osceola Peak	8587
24	Silver Star Mountain	8876	49	Raven Ridge	8580
25	Eldorado Peak	8868	50	Buck Mountain	8528+
26	Dragontail Peak	8840+	51	Storm King	8520+

RANK	NAME	ELEVATION (FT)	RANK	NAME	ELEVATION (FT)
52	Enchantment Peak	8520	76	Saska Peak	8404
53	Reynolds Peak	8512	77	Azurite Peak	8400+
54	Primus Peak	8508	78	Luahna Peak*	8400+
55	Dark Peak	8504	79	Pinnacle Mountain	8400+
56	Mox Peaks		80	Blackcap Mountain	8397
	(SE Twin Spire*)	8504	81	Courtney Peak	8392
57	Cashmere Mtn.	8501	82	South Spectacle Butte	8392
58	Martin Peak	8500+	83	Martin Peak	8375
59	Klawatti Peak	8485	84	Lake Mountain	8371
60	Horseshoe Peak	8480+	85	Golden Horn	8366
61	Mt. Rahm	8480+	86	West Craggy Peak	8366
62	Big Craggy Peak	8470	87	Mt. Saint Helens	8365
63	Hoodoo Peak	8464	88	McClellan Peak	8364
64	Lost Peak	8464	89	Devore Peak	8360+
65	Chiwawa Peak	8459	90	Amphitheater Mtn.	8358
66	Argonaut Peak	8453	91	Snowfield Peak	8347
67	Tower Mountain	8444	92	Austera Peak	8334
68	Dorado Needle	8440+	93	Windy Peak	8333
69	Mt. Bigelow	8440+	94	Cosho Peak	8332
70	Little Annapurna	8440+	95	Big Snagtooth	8330+
71	Sinister Peak	8440+	96	Mt. Formidable	8325
72	Emerald Peak	8422	97	Abernathy Peak	8321
73	Dumbell Mountain	8421	98	Switchback	
74	NE Dumbell			(Cooney) Mountain*	8321
	(Greenwood*) Mtn.	8415	99	Tupshin Peak	8320+
75	Mox Peaks		100	Mt. Flora	8320
	(NW Twin Spire*)	8407			

*unofficial names not on USGS map

APPENDIX D

Difficulty Ratings

The Rating, included in the information block at the top of each trip, may be your best source for determining if a trip is right for you. It is a two-part number, devised by the author, that is based on the physical effort required for a trip and its technical difficulty. Each part is an overview of the trip as a whole in comparison to other trips in the book. Both parts represent increasing intensity as their scale progresses from 1 to 5.

The first part of the rating, Exertion ("E"), is a measure of the amount of physical effort that the trip requires. This measurement is based on a subjective and cumulative impression of the trip's total distance, off-trail terrain, ruggedness, elevation gain, and amount of bushwhacking. Due to the broad range of conditioning of climbers, a trip that is rated "E3" might be a stretch for a person who enters the mountains infrequently, whereas the same trip might be almost effortless for someone who climbs every weekend. An "E5" trip is strenuous for even the most aerobically fit climber and arduous for anyone not in the best physical condition.

The second part of the rating, Technical ("T"), represents a composite of the skills required for the technical aspects of the climb. This number also depends on several subjective and cumulative factors: degree of exposure, type of terrain, whether the rock is excessively loose requiring more than the ordinary amount of caution, and need for specialized equipment. A climb that has a glacier traverse is given at least a "T3" rating, and a climb that is class 5, requiring leading skill and placing rock protection, is given a "T5" rating.

The combined rating is meant to convey subjective but useful information so that with experience using the rating, the reader can choose the trip that most closely matches the skill and desire of his or her climbing party. The following is a detailed description of each "E" and "T" rating. Following that is a breakdown of the Yosemite Decimal System, also used in trip descriptions throughout this book.

DIFFICULTY RATINGS

Exertion (E)
E1 Easy; one day
E2 Comfortable, overnight trip; less than 7000 feet elevation gain
E3 Moderate, 2–3 day trip; more than 7000 feet gain
E4 Strenuous, 3–5 day trip; substantial on-trail portion, some off-trail
E5 Extremely difficult, 5+ day trip; heavy pack with climbing and glacier gear; substantial off-trail portions; more than 11,000 feet elevation gain

Technical (T)
T1 Several class 3 moves
T2 Stretches of sustained class 3 moves
T3 Glacier travel; some class 4 moves
T4 Sustained glacier travel; portions of class 4, some low class 5 moves
T5 Multiple class 5 pitches

YOSEMITE DECIMAL SYSTEM CLIMBING CLASSES

Class	Description	Comments
1	Hiking	Hands not needed
2	Scrambling	Hands helpful; rope not needed
3	Easy climbing	Hands needed for balance; rope desirable for an inexperienced climber
4	Climbing	Roped climbing; belaying using natural anchors or climbing hardware
5	Climbing	Roped climbing requiring protection such as chocks, stoppers and camming devices; basic-level up to 5.3–5.4

Index

A

Aasgard Pass 200, 202, 203, 205
ability xii
Adams, Mt. 3
advanced-level climber 3
Agnes Creek 135, 146, 148, 175, 176
Agnes Gorge Trail 148
Agnes Mtn. 172, 176
aid climbing 3
alpine climb xi, 2, 3, 4, 6, 115
Alpine Lakes Wilderness 8, 198-199, 201, 207, 213
Amphitheater Mtn. 118, 124, 126-129
Apex Pass 124, 127
Argonaut Peak 212, 213-215
Arriva, Mt. 92, 97
Arts Knoll 86
Aurora Creek 188
Austera Peak 54, 57, 60-61, 63
avalanche 20, 28, 41, 61, 63, 70, 88, 89, 163, 199, 203, 219
Azurite Peak 88, 100, 101,102-103, 104, 105
Azurite Pass 100, 101, 102, 103, 105
Azurite Pass Trail 102, 103, 105

B

Bachelor Creek 173, 174, 179
Baker, Mt. 2, 13, 26, 27-29
Baker Lake 40
Baker Lake-Grandy Lake Highway 40
balanced rock 209, 211
Banded Glacier 140
Bannock Mtn. 176
Barlow Pass 33
basic-level climber xi, 3, 4, 9, 225
Basin Creek 80, 83
Bastile Ridge 27
Beckey, Fred 6
belay 3
Bellingham 28, 44
Bellingham Bay 27
Beverly Creek 215
Beverly-Turnpike Trail 208
"Big Boys" 5

Big Snagtooth xi, 88, 110, 111-113
Bigelow, Mt. 115
Bird Creek 150, 153, 154
Bird Creek Camp 150, 152
Black Buttes 26, 28, 29
Black Peak 88, 96, 97-99
Black Tooth 142
Black Warrior Mine 65, 78, 80
Blackcap Mtn. 118, 130, 132-134
Blewett Pass 140, 147, 152, 158, 164, 167, 175, 187, 202, 213
Blue Lake 176, 181
Blue Mtn. (see Gunsight Peak)
Bonanza Peak 147, 156, 157-161, 163, 187
border crossing (see Canadian border)
Borealis Glacier 57, 60, 63
Boston Basin 65, 69, 70, 75, 76, 77
Boston Glacier 66, 74, 75, 77, 79
Boston Mine 65, 75
Boston Peak 10, 74, 75-77
Boulder Basin 33, 35, 73
Boulder Creek 192, 193
Boulder Pass 190, 192, 193
Boulder Pass Trail 190, 192, 193
Boulder Glacier 27
Boundary Trail 124, 127, 128
Brush Creek 103
Buck Creek 170
Buck Creek Pass 170
Buck Mtn. 170, 192
Buckner Glacier 80
Buckner Mtn. 54, 60, 65, 78, 79-83
Buckskin Mtn. 162, 164
Bulger Top 100 List xi, 1, 2, 5, 222-223
Bulgers ix, 1, 6
Burgundy Col 107, 108, 109
Burgundy Creek 107, 108, 112
Burgundy Spire 107, 108

C

Cache Col 67, 84, 86, 87
Cache Glacier 86
Camels Hump 117
Camp Muir 20
Camp Curtis 16, 18, 21
Camp Schurman 16, 17, 19-20, 21

Canadian border 27, 36, 43, 45, 51, 118
cannon hole 46-47
Cannon Mtn. 198, 200, 201-205
Canyon Creek Trail 122
Cardinal Mtn. 171
Carru, Mt. 118, 132, 133, 134
Cascade Crest 36, 54, 58, 59, 101, 126, 135, 139, 151, 157, 170, 191
Cascade Pass 65-67, 75, 78, 79, 80, 83, 84, 85, 86, 87, 170, 174
Cascade Pass Trail 65, 78, 80, 83, 84, 86, 87, 137
Cascade Range 5, 13, 23, 36, 39, 88, 97, 119, 121, 140, 199, 207
Cascade River 59, 66
Cascade River Road 60, 63, 65, 70, 76, 80, 86
Cascades, northern 36-37
Cascadian Couloir 210, 211
Cashmere Crags 199, 201
Castle Creek 166, 169
Cathedral Lakes 124, 126
Cathedral Pass 124, 126, 127, 128, 129
Cathedral Peak 118, 124, 126-129
Cedar Creek 112
Chalangin Peak 195, 197
Chelan 137
Chelan Mountains 187
Chelan Ranger District 147, 151, 157, 163, 167, 174, 217, 218
Chelan-Sawtooth Crest 115
cheval 59, 61
Chewack River (see Chewuch River)
Chewuch River 125, 127
Chewuch River Trail 124, 127, 128, 129
Chickamin Glacier 172, 173, 174, 175, 176, 177
Chilliwack Group 42, 43-51
Chilliwack River Road 44
Chiwawa Mtn. 170
Chiwawa Ridge 192
Chiwawa River 170, 183, 193
Chiwawa River Road 184
Chocolate Glacier 30, 192
Clark Glacier (see Walrus Glacier)
Clark Mtn. 171, 190, 191-193, 194, 195, 197
class, climbing (see Yosemite Decimal System)
Cle Elum 207, 213
Cle Elum Ranger District 207, 218

climbing register 10
Cloudcap Peak 39
Colchuck Col 213
Colchuck Lake 200, 203, 205
Colchuck Pass (see Aasgard Pass)
Colchuck Peak 201, 213
Colchuck Trail 200, 203
Coleman Glacier 27-29
Colfax Peak 26, 28
Colonial Creek Campground 60
Colonial Glacier 52, 55
Colonial Peak 54
Coles Corner 184, 192, 195
Columbia Crest 5, 16, 20, 148
Columbia River 140, 152, 158, 164, 167, 175, 188
Company Creek Trail 153, 166, 168
composting toilet 15
Contact Information 217-219
convergence zone 157
Cool Glacier 192
Copper Basin 163, 164, 165
Copper Creek 164, 165
Copper Peak 162, 163-165
Corridor, The 20
Corteo Peak 97, 98
Cosho Camp 92, 95
Cosho Peak 90, 92, 94, 95
Cottonwood Camp 65
Cottonwood Campground (Entiat) 188
Crater Creek 122
Crater Lake 122
Crater Mtn. 120, 122, 123
Crater Mountain Trail 120, 123
crevasse rescue 3, 14
Crystal Mtn. 18, 24
Cub Lake 173, 179, 181
Curtis Glacier 39, 41
Custer Ridge 43, 50
Custer, Mt. 42, 44, 50, 51
Cutthroat Creek Campground 102
Cutthroat Pass 100, 101, 102, 105
Cutthroat Pass Trail 100, 102, 105

D

DaKobed 13, 191, 195
Dana Glacier 173, 174, 179
danger (see safety)
Dark Glacier 146, 148, 149
Dark Peak 146, 147-149

Darrington 33, 175
Darrington Ranger District 31, 174, 217
Darrington Ranger Station (see Darrington
  Ranger District)
datum, map 9
Depot Creek 42, 44, 45, 46, 49, 51
Depot Creek Road 44
devils club 36, 174, 176
Devore Creek 150, 152, 166
Devore Creek Trail 150, 151, 152, 153,
  154, 166, 168, 169
Devore Peak 150, 151-154
Diablo Dam 98
Diablo Lake 54
Diamond Mine road 68, 70, 73, 74, 76,
  77
Difficulty Ratings 8, 224-225
Disappointment Cleaver 20
Distance (trip statistics) 220
Dome Creek 173, 175, 177, 178, 181
Dome Glacier 172, 173, 174, 179
Dome Peak 172, 173, 174-181, 85
Domke Lake 168
Dorado Needle 54, 57, 59, 61, 63
Doubtful Basin 65, 66
Douglas Glacier 140
Downey Creek 174, 179
Downey Creek Campground 173
Downey Creek Trail 173, 175, 179, 181
Dragontail Peak 201
driving 9
Dumbell Mtn. 182, 183-185

E

Early Winters Creek 107, 108, 109, 112
Easton Glacier 27
"Easy" Mox (see Northwest Twin Spire)
Easy Pass 90, 92, 94, 95
Easy Pass Trail 90, 92, 95
Eightmile Creek 200
Eightmile Creek Road 203
Eightmile Lake Trail 203
Eldorado Creek 57, 62
Eldorado Glacier 57, 59, 62, 79
Eldorado Peak 4, 6, 54, 57, 58, 59, 61,
  62, 63
Elevation (trip statistics) 220
Emmons Flat 17, 20-21
Emmons Glacier 12, 14, 15-21, 23
Enchantment Basin 200, 204, 205

Enchantment Lakes 8, 199, 200, 201-205,
  213
Enchantment Peak 201
Enchantments (see Enchantment Lakes)
Entiat 140, 148, 152, 158, 164, 167, 175, 188
Entiat Meadows 165
Entiat Mountains 163, 183, 187
Entiat Ranger District 187, 218
Entiat River 186, 187, 188
Entiat River Trail 186, 188, 189
Enumclaw 18, 24
Esmeralda Basin Trail 208
Eureka Creek 130, 131, 132
Everett 33

F

fee(s) 221
fee, climbing 15
Falls Trail 150, 153, 166, 168, 169
Fernow, Mt. 162, 163-165
Fields Point Landing 137, 140, 148, 152,
  158, 164, 168, 175, 176
Fish Lake 184
Fisher Camp 92
Fisher Creek 91, 92
Fisher Creek Trail 91, 92, 94
Fivemile Camp 140, 145
Flora Mtn. 166, 167-169
Forbidden Peak 7, 54, 60, 64, 65, 68, 69-
  73, 76, 79
Forbidden Glacier 68
Forest Service (see US Forest Service)
Formidable, Mt. 67, 84, 85-87
Fortress Mtn. 170, 171
Fourth Creek 214, 215
Fourth Creek Trail 214
Fourth of July Basin 150, 153, 166, 169
Fraser River 36
Fremont Glacier 138, 140, 144, 145
Fivemile Camp 140, 145
Fryingpan Creek 22, 24
Fryingpan Glacier 23, 24
Fuller, Fay 14
fumarole 27

G

GPS (see Global Positioning System)
GPS Waypoint Route, definition 9
Garden Glacier 177, 178

Gendarme 70
Glacier 28
glacier climb xi, 2, 3, 6, 17
glacier gear 9
Glacier Basin Trail 16, 18, 21
Glacier Pass 101, 103
Glacier Peak 13, 30, 31-35, 170, 171,
   191, 192
Glacier Peak Wilderness 31, 85, 136, 147,
   151, 157, 163, 167, 170-171, 174, 183,
   184, 187, 191, 195
Glacier Public Service Center 10, 27, 28, 217
Global Positioning System 9
Golden Horn 88, 89, 100, 101, 102, 104,
   105
Golden West Visitor Center 217
Goode Mtn. 60, 79, 136, 138, 139, 140,
   141-142, 144, 145
Goode-Storm King camp 145
Goode-Storm King col 140
Gorge Creek 36
Granite Creek 36, 98, 122, 123
Granite Pass 100, 101, 102
Grant Peak 26, 28
Grasshopper Pass 101
Green Trails map 7, 8, 221
Greenwater 18, 24
Greenwood Mtn. 182, 183-185
grid reader 9
Grotesque Gendarmes 92, 93
Gunsight Notch 67
Gunsight Peak 172, 176

H

Hanging Gardens 175
hanging glacier 36, 39, 44
Hannegan Pass 36
"Hard" Mox (see Southeast Twin Spire)
Harts Pass 89, 100, 101, 102, 103, 104,
   105, 118
Harts Pass (group) 100, 101-105
Harts Pass Road 102, 103, 133
Hazards and Tips, definition 9
Heather Pass 96, 98
Heliotrope Ridge 27, 28
Heliotrope Ridge Trail 26, 28, 29
Hells Highway 38, 41
High Bridge Camp 137, 139, 140, 148,
   149, 176
High Pass 196

Hogsback 28
Holden 136, 150, 151, 153, 154, 156,
   157, 158, 160, 162, 163, 164, 165, 166,
   167, 168, 169
Holden Campground 153, 158
Holden Lake 156, 157, 158, 159, 160
Holden Lake Trail 156, 158, 160
Holden Mine 135
Holden Pass 158, 160
Hoodoo Peak 115
Horse Heaven Camp 102
Horseman, The 55
Horseshoe Basin 65, 78, 79, 80, 81, 83
Horseshoe Peak 78, 79-83
Hourglass, The 38, 41
Hypothermia 14

I

ice ax self-arrest 3, 14
Ice Creek 187, 188, 189
Ice Creek Trail 186, 188, 189
Ice Lakes 186, 187, 188
Icicle Creek 200
Icicle Road 203
Icy Creek 172, 176, 181
Ingalls Creek 206, 208, 211, 213, 214,
   215
Ingalls Creek Trail 206, 208, 212, 213,
   214, 215
Ingalls Lake Trail 206, 208
Ingalls Way Trail 208, 211
Ingraham Glacier 23
Inspiration Glacier 4, 57, 58, 61
Inspiration Glacier Traverse 56-63
Inter Glacier 16, 18, 20, 21
Itswoot Ridge 174, 179, 181

J

Jack Mtn. 118, 120, 121-123
Jagged Ridge 39
Jerry Glacier 120, 122
Jerry Lakes 120, 122
Johannesburg Mtn. 65
jurisdiction 8, 221

K

Kangaroo Ridge 89, 111
Katsuk Glacier 91

Katsuk Peak 90, 91, 94, 95
Kennedy Hot Spring 30, 33, 35
Kennedy Ridge Trail 33
Kimtah Peak 90, 91, 92-93, 94, 95
Klawatti Col 61, 63
Klawatti Glacier 57, 58, 60, 61
Klawatti Peak 61, 57, 63
Koma Kulshan 13
Kool-Aid Lake 84, 85, 86, 87
Kulshan Cabin 28

L

Lady Express 176
Lady of the Lake 137, 140, 148, 152, 158,
    164, 168, 176
Lago, Mt. 118, 132, 133, 134
Lake Ann 96, 98
Lake Ann-Maple Pass Trail 96, 97, 98
Lake Chelan 65, 115, 135-137, 139, 140,
    147, 148, 151, 152, 153, 158, 163, 164,
    167, 168, 169, 170, 175, 176, 183
Lake Chelan National Recreation Area
    136, 147, 151, 174, 217
Lake Chelan State Park 140, 148, 152,
    158, 164, 167, 175
Lake Chelan-Sawtooth Wilderness 88,
    114, 115, 136
Lake Mtn. 118, 132
Lake Shannon 40
Lake Viviane 200, 204, 205
Lake Wenatchee 184, 192, 196
Lake Wenatchee Ranger District 183, 191,
    195, 218
Lake Wenatchee Ranger Station (see Lake
    Wenatchee Ranger District)
Lake Wenatchee Road 184, 192, 195
Le Conte Mtn. 85
Leave No Trace 9, 15
Leprechaun Lake 204, 205
Levenworth 202, 203
Leavenworth Ranger District 8, 199, 201,
    202, 207, 218
Leavenworth Ranger Station (see
    Leavenworth Ranger District)
lenticular cloud 14
Leroy Creek 184
Leroy Creek Basin 165, 187, 188
Leroy Creek-Carne Mountain Trail 184
Lewis Glacier 96, 98
Lewis Lake 96, 98

Liberty Bell 89
Liberty Cap 5
Lick of Flame 81
Lightning Creek 171
Little Annapurna 201
Little Giant Pass Trail 193
Little Tahoma Peak 5, 12, 14, 22, 23-25
Little Wenatchee River 170
Logan, Mt. 59, 60, 79, 92, 138, 139, 140,
    144-145
Longs Pass 206, 208, 211, 214, 215
Longs Pass Trail 206, 208
Lost Peak 118, 132
Lost Plateau 199, 201, 203, 213
Lost River 132, 133
Lost River-Monument Creek-Ptarmigan
    Creek Trail (see Monument Creek
    Trail)
Lost River Gorge 133
Lost River Road 102
Lost World Plateau (see Lost Plateau)
Lower Curtis Glacier 41
Lower Valley bus 137, 140, 145, 148,
    152, 176
Luahna Peak 194, 195-197
Lucerne 136, 137, 153, 158, 164, 168
Lucky Pass 60, 63
Lyman Lake 170, 183

M

Magic Mtn. 85
Mantle 61
maps 1, 8, 9
map datum (see datum, map)
Marblemount 65, 76, 80, 86, 92, 97, 107,
    112
Marblemount Ranger Station (see
    Wilderness Information Center) 10
Martin Peak 156, 157-161
Martin Peak (Lake-Chelan Sawtooth
    Wilderness) 115
Mary Green Glacier 156, 157, 158, 160
Maude, Mt. 170, 171, 187
Mazama 102, 132
McAllister Glacier 57, 58, 61
McAllister Camp 56, 60
McAllister Creek 56, 135
McClellan Peak 201-205, 200
McMillian Park-Jackita Ridge Trail 120,
    122

Meadow Mountain-Fire Mountain Trail 33
Meander Meadow 170
Meany Crest 22, 23, 24, 25
Meebee Pass 102
Mesahchie Glacier 91
Mesahchie Peak 90, 92, 93, 95
Methow Pass 100, 101, 102
Methow Mountains 115, 135
Methow River Valley (see Methow Valley)
Methow Valley 65, 89, 119, 131, 133
Methow Valley Ranger District 218
Methow Valley Visitor Center 101, 107, 111, 115, 121, 126, 132, 218
Middle Cascade Glacier 86, 87
Mix-up Arm 66
Mix-up Peak 84, 85, 86
Monument Creek 133, 134
Monument Creek Trail 130, 131, 132, 133, 134
Monument Peak 118, 132
Mount Vernon 60
Mt. Baker-Snoqualmie National Forest 31, 39, 40, 85, 91, 97, 121, 171, 174, 199, 217
Mt. Baker Club 37
Mt. Baker Highway 28
Mt. Baker Ranger District 10, 27, 37, 39, 43, 217
Mt. Baker Trail (see Heliotrope Ridge Trail)
Mt. Baker Wilderness 27, 28, 37
Mt. Rainier National Park 8, 17, 18, 23, 24, 217
Mountain Loop Highway 33
Mountaineer Creek 202
mountaineering x,-xii, 5, 14, 37
Mountaineers, The 37
Mox Peaks (see Twin Spires)

N

NAD 27 (see datum, map)
NPS (see National Park Service)
Naches Ranger District 218
Nada Lake 200, 205
Napeequa River 170, 191, 192, 195
Napeequa Valley 196
National Geographic Maps 9
National Park Service 217, 8, 10, 18, 136, 137, 139
National Wilderness Preservation 171

Navarre Coulee Road 140, 148, 152, 158, 164, 167, 175
navigation 3, 23
Neve Glacier 52, 53-55
Newhalem 54, 92, 122
Nohokomeen Glacier 121, 122
Nooksack Tower 39
North Cascades Act 171
North Cascades National Park ix, 8, 10, 37, 39, 43, 53, 58, 66, 69, 75, 79, 85, 88, 91, 92, 97, 118, 136, 137, 139, 147, 151, 174, 217
North Cascades Scenic Highway 11, 54, 60, 70, 76, 80, 86, 88, 89, 92, 96, 97, 106, 107, 108, 109, 110, 111, 112, 113, 120, 122, 127, 132
North Cascades Scenic Highway Corridor 97, 107, 111, 121
North Cascades Stehekin Lodge 140
North Fork Cascade River 57, 62, 69
North Fork Nooksack River 39
North Fork Teanaway River 208
North Fork Teanaway Road 208
North Klawatti Glacier 57, 60
North Spectacle Butte 188
northern Cascades (see Cascades, northern)
Northwest Forest Pass 8, 202, 221
Northwest Twin Spire 44, 48-49, 51
nunatak 59

O

obelisk 45
Ohanapecosh Glacier 23
Okanogan National Forest 88, 91, 97, 101, 107, 111, 114, 115, 117, 119, 121, 126, 127, 132, 218
Okanogan Range 118
Osceola, Mt. 118, 132, 134
Olympus, Mt. 3
Outdoor Recreation Information Center 218
Oval Peak 115

P

Pacific Crest National Scenic Trail 30, 33, 35, 100, 101, 102, 103, 146, 148, 149, 172, 176, 181, 198
Panther Creek 91
Paradise 17, 28

Park Creek 140
Park Creek Camp 140, 141, 145
Park Creek Pass 138, 139, 140, 144, 145
Park Creek Trail 138, 140, 141, 144, 145
Pasayten Wilderness 118-119, 121, 126,
    132
Paul Bunyan's Stump 54
Perfection Lake 203, 204, 205
permit(s) 8, 10, 221
permits, Enchantment Lakes 199, 201,
    202
permits, North Cascades National Park
    10, 37, 39, 43, 44, 53, 66, 69, 75, 79,
    80, 92, 139
permits, self-issue (see self-registration)
Peshastin Creek 213
Phelps Creek 182, 183, 184
Phelps Creek Road 184
Phelps Creek Trail 182, 184, 185
Phelps Creek Road 184
photographs 10
Picket Range 43, 121
Picture Lake 40
Pilz Glacier 195
Pinnacle Mtn. 171
Pinnacle Peak 52, 54
Pistol Pass 130, 132, 133, 134
pocket glacier 147
Porcupine Creek 212, 214
Price Glacier 39
Primus Peak 60, 57, 59, 63
profile 7
prominence, definition 1, 5
Prong, The 204-205
protection, rock 3, 4, 9, 225
Prusik 45
Prusik Pass 200, 204, 205
Prusik Peak 200, 204
Ptarmigan Climbing Club 85
Ptarmigan Creek 133
Ptarmigan Peak 118
Ptarmigan Traverse 60, 65, 85, 174, 179
Puget Sound 13, 17, 18, 27
Purple Point Campground 152
Pyramid Lake 55
Pyramid Lake Trail 52, 54, 55
Pyramid Peak 52, 54, 55

Q

Quien Sabe Glacier 74, 76, 77

R

Ragged End (see Cosho Peak)
Ragged Ridge 91-95, 88, 90
Rahm, Mt. 42, 44, 50, 51
Railroad Creek 135, 162, 164
Railroad Creek Trail 156, 158
Rainier, Mt. 5, 12, 15, 16, 17-21, 23, 27,
    60
Rainbow Falls 152
Rainy Pass 96, 98
Ranger Station (see jurisdiction) 221
rappel 3
Rat Creek 202
rating, definition 2, 221
Ratings, Difficulty (see Difficulty
    Ratings)
Raven Ridge 115
recreation areas (see Ross Lake and Lake
    Chelan National Recreation Areas)
Red Ledge 86, 87
Redoubt Glacier 42, 46, 47, 49, 51
Redoubt, Mt. 42, 44, 46-47, 51
register, climbing (see climbing register)
Remmel Creek 124, 128
Remmel Lake 124, 128
Remmel, Mt. 118
reservation (see permits, Enchantment
    Lakes)
Reynolds Creek 116, 117
Reynolds Creek Trail 117
Reynolds Peak 88, 114, 115-117
Richardson Glacier 191
Riddle Creek 166, 169
Riddle Peaks 166, 167, 168, 169
Ridge of Gendarmes 42, 47, 51
Ripsaw Ridge 79, 80, 82
River Bend Campground Road 103
Robinson Mtn. 118
rockfall x, 5, 13, 14
Roman Wall 26, 28, 29
Roosevelt Glacier 27
Ross Dam 36
Ross Lake 36, 119, 121, 123
Ross Lake Resort 123
Ross Lake National Recreation Area 53,
    58
Ross Pass 176
Roush Creek 57, 60, 62, 63
route, climbing (see climbing route)
routefinding 3

S

safety x, xii, 3, 9, 10, 14, 15
Sahale-Boston col 75, 76, 77
Sahale Arm 66, 75, 80
Sahale Mtn. 1, 2, 74, 75-77, 79
Sahale Glacier 74
Saint Helens, Mt. 3, 14, 28
Sardis 44
Sauk River 175
Sawtooth Ridge 115
Schoening, Pete 46
Scimitar Glacier 30, 33
scramble, definition 3, 225
Search and Rescue 10
Seattle City Light 36
Sedro-Woolley 40, 44
Sedro-Woolley Ranger Station (see Mt. Baker Ranger District)
Sedro-Woolley Ranger Station (North Cascades National Park) 139
self-issue permit (see self-registration)
self-registration 66, 199, 207, 213
Sentinel Peak 85
Seven Fingered Jack 170
Shannon Creek 41
Shannon Creek Campground 40
Shannon Ridge Trail 38, 41
Sharkfin Tower 76
Shasta, Mt. 17
Shellrock Pass 130, 134
Sherman Crater 27
Sherman Peak 27, 29
Sherpa Peak 206, 207-211
Shield Lake 200, 204
Shuksan, Mt. 39-41, 38, 43
Silver Lake 44, 49, 50
Silver Star Glacier 5, 108, 109
Silver Star Mtn. xi, 88, 89, 106, 107-109, 111, 112
Sinister Peak 3, 172, 173, 174-181
Sitkum Creek 33
Sitkum Glacier 30-35
Sitkum Spire 33
Skagit River 36, 139
Skagit Valley 36
Skykomish Ranger District 217
Slate Pass 134
Snagtooth Ridge 89, 110, 111, 112
Snoqualmie Pass 198
Snoqualmie Ranger District 217

Snow Creek Glacier 199
Snow Creek Trail 200, 202, 203, 205
Snow Lakes 200
snow travel 3
snowbridge 14, 160
Snowfield Peak 52, 53-55
Snowy Lakes 100, 101, 102, 105
Snowy Lakes Pass 100, 102
South Fork Agnes Creek 172, 176
South Lakeshore Road, 140, 148, 152, 158, 164, 168, 176
South Spectacle Butte 186, 187-189
Southeast Twin Spire 47-48, 51
Spectacle Buttes 186, 187
Spickard, Mt. 42, 44, 49, 51
Spickard, Warren 44
Spider-Formidable col 86, 87
Spider Gap 183
Spider Meadow 182, 183, 184, 185
Spider Mtn. 84, 85
Spider Pass (see Spider Gap)
Spire Creek 173, 179
Spire Point 85
Sprite Lake 204
Spruce Creek 172, 175, 176
Star Peak 115
statistics, trip (see trip statistics)
Steamboat Prow 16, 18
Stehekin 65, 135, 136, 137, 139, 140, 145, 148, 149, 151, 152, 154, 168, 176
Stehekin Group 138, 139-145, 163
Stehekin Ranger Station 139, 147, 151, 174
Stehekin River 135, 136, 152, 176
Stehekin Valley Road 137
Stevens Pass 170, 184, 192, 195, 198
Strait of Juan de Fuca 119
Storm King 138, 139, 142-144, 145
Stuart Lake Trail 200, 203, 205
Stuart Range 198, 199, 201, 207, 213
Stuart, Mt. 157, 199, 206, 207-211, 213
Summer Land 23, 24, 25
Suiattle Glacier 31, 191
Suiattle Pass 171
Suiattle River 36, 170, 174, 175, 191
Suiattle River Road 175
Sulfide Glacier 39-41
Sumas 44
Summary and Highlights, definition 9
Sunrise Road (see White River Road)
Sunset Highway (see Mt. Baker Highway)
Swamp Creek 148, 176

Swamp Creek Trail 146, 148, 149
Sylvester, Albert H. 171, 201

T

Tatie Peak 100, 103
Teanaway River Road 208, 213
Tenmile Creek 150, 153, 154, 166, 168, 169
Tenmile Pass 150, 151, 153, 154, 166, 168, 169
Tenpeak Mtn. 195
Tepeh Towers 57, 61
Thieves Peak 92
Thirtymile Campground 125, 127, 128
Thunder Basin 197
Thunder Creek 56, 58, 60, 135, 144, 171
Thunder Creek (Glacier Peak Wilderness) 194, 195, 197
Thunder Creek Basin 195
Thunder Creek Trail 56, 60, 63
Tonasket Ranger District 218
Tony Basin 117
Top 100 (see Bulger Top 100 List)
Tower Mtn. 88, 100, 101, 102, 104, 105
training xii
Tricouni Peak 57, 59, 60
Trinity 184
trip (statistics) 220-221
trip statistics 220-221
trip times, definition 9, 220
Tungsten Creek Trail 124, 127, 128, 129
Tupshin Peak 151-154, 150
Twin Spires: 42, 43, 44, 47-51
Twisp 117
Twisp River 117
Twomile Camp 140

U

US Forest Service 8, 36, 202, 217
US Geological Survey 1, 219
USFS (see US Forest Service)
USGS (see US Geological Survey)
USGS map 7, 8, 220
USGS name 195, 222-223
UTM (see Universal Transverse Mercator)
Universal Transverse Mercator 9
updates x
Upper Cathedral Lake 124, 127, 128, 129
Upper Snow Lake 202, 205
Upper White Chuck Trail 33

V

Van Trump, Philemon 14
Vancouver, Captain George 13
Vasiliki Ridge 106, 107
volcanoes 4, 5, 13-15

W

Walrus (Clark) Glacier 171, 190, 191, 192, 193
War Creek 117
War Creek Ridge 117
War Creek Trail 115
Washington Pass 11, 88-89, 107, 108, 111, 112, 115
weather x, xi, 14
Weaver Point 152, 154
Weaver Point Campground 150, 152
web sites (see Contact Information)
Wenatchee 140, 147, 152, 158, 164, 167, 175, 187
Wenatchee Mountains 198
Wenatchee National Forest 8, 136, 147, 151, 157, 163, 167, 171, 174, 183, 187, 191, 195, 199, 201, 202, 207, 218
Wenatchee River 170, 192, 196
West Chewack Road (see West Chewuch Road)
West Chewuch Road 127
West Fork Agnes Creek 172
West Fork Devore Creek 150, 153, 154
West Fork Methow River 100, 102
West Fork Methow Trail 103, 104
White Chuck Glacier 31, 191
White Chuck River Road 33
White Chuck River Trail 30, 33, 35
White Goat Mtn. 153
White Pass 170, 171
White River 170, 191, 192
White River Ranger Station 18, 23, 24
White River Falls Campground 192, 196
White River Road 18, 24, 192, 196
White River Trail 190, 192, 193, 194, 196, 197
Whitman Glacier 23, 24
wilderness, definition 8, 15, 31
Wilderness Act 31, 198
Wilderness Information Center 37, 43, 44, 53, 58, 60, 66, 69, 70, 75, 76, 79, 80, 85, 86, 91, 92, 97, 217

Williams Butte 114, 117
Williams Creek Trail 114, 115, 117
Williams Lake 114, 117
Willow Creek 110, 112, 113
wind cirque 143, 144
Windy Peak 118
Wine Spires 107, 108, 112
Wing Lake 96, 97, 98
Winthrop 127
Winthrop Glacier 13
women xii
Wonderland Trail 22, 24, 25
Wyeth Glacier 144

Yang Yang Lakes 87
Yosemite Decimal System 2, 225

About the Author

Peggy Goldman is an avid outdoorswoman and accomplished mountaineer who has years of experience backpacking, scrambling, rock climbing, and back-country skiing throughout Washington State. Since 1994 she has been a Scrambling Leader for The Mountaineers organization and is the author of *75 Scrambles in Washington: Classic Routes to the Summits*. In 2003 she became the twentieth person and the third and oldest woman to complete the Bulger Top 100 list (the 100 highest mountains in Washington). Goldman has extensive experience with map and compass and GPS use. For over twenty years she was a staff physician in the Department of Emergency Medical Services at Swedish Hospital and Medical Center in Seattle. She is presently a medical consultant and writer. She makes her home in the Puget Sound with her husband, Jim Quade, and four Siamese cats, Mickey, Rajah, Victor, and Princess Tatiana.